GOING WITH THE WIND

Carolina In My Mind

Photos by
Joe Randazzo

A Sprezzatura Book
from New Renaissance Press

Sprezzatura Books
New Renaissance Press
8 Woodside Drive
South Burlington, VT 05403

ISBN 978-0-9708279-9-9
Library of Congress Control Number 2009903885

Book design and author's photographs: Rita Randazzo

For Rita:

No photograph could ever...

Also by Joe Randazzo:

Coffee House
His/Hers: Mars and Venus Write Poetry
    (with Rita Randazzo)
Screen
van Eyck's Secret
See Dick Run: A Grownup's Picture Book

INTRODUCTION

Going With the Wind took five years to shoot, from summer 1969 to summer 1974. It took 40 years to become a book. Until recently the negatives had been lost, disappearing somewhere in the moving process from South Carolina to my new home in Vermont. When I rediscovered them and started making prints again, I was surprised and delighted by what I saw.

Anne Rivers Siddons, in her book *Downtown*, said it eloquently: "I think that sometimes the great changes in our lives, the ones that divide time, happen so deep down and silently that we don't even know when they occur."

When we live with a loved one for decades, the changes, the aging process, isn't obvious because it's so gradual. But when we view photos of him or her taken 40 years earlier, the changes are dramatic. So it is, and so it was with my Carolina experience. I compared the photos in this book to the sights I saw on a recent visit to South Carolina, and they seem like two different worlds. Many things worth losing have, thankfully, been lost. Many things worth keeping have, unfortunately, also been lost.

As a native New Yorker who saw the South with an outsider's eyes, I was amazed at the confluence of the old and the new living side by side. Companies like Michelin Tire were arriving from Europe and employing thousands of people who had previously worked at low-paying jobs. The modern world grabbed Aunt Pittypat by the arms and pulled her faster than she ever dreamed she could go. In the twenty-first century, she can now build and progress as well or better than people from any other part of the country.

To me, North and South Carolina were magic lands. I saw wraparound porches with families sitting on swings. I ate okra, scuppernong and muscadine grapes, hot sausage biscuits, and hush puppies. The dirt was red, and kudzu grew fast and wherever it wanted. I heard the words "yes ma'am," "yes sir," and "y'all come see us" from people who were honest and who meant what they said. I've been to general stores that had only a couple of rooms but carried everything that a family could possibly want. I've been on deer drives, seen plow mules, coon hunters, dirt racetracks, bootleggers, and banjo makers.

I worked as a surveyor and was a contributing editor to *South Carolina Magazine*, based in Columbia. I was blessed to be able to travel to places where time moved at a slower pace than in cities like Charlotte or Greenville.

The spirit of a land, for good and for ill, is passed from generation to generation. I had the unique opportunity to witness a true paradigm shift. I could sense that it was happening, as it was happening. I knew that many of the old ways and sights would be gone in a decade, so I set to work capturing what I could.

I had some trepidation about moving from New York City to a little town in North Carolina. I was told that I would not be accepted, and I was told that race relations were very bad. I found those warnings to be mostly a bunch of boloney. Sure, there were still some pockets of people with the old prejudices (witness the shocking Ku Klux Klan photos in section VII), but I've never been to *anyplace* in the country where people of all races and religions got along better in general. When the South Boston schools experienced racial discord in 1974, they sent a delegation to the Charlotte/Mecklenburg school system in North Carolina to learn how integration was supposed to work.

As I write this, the feelings that are pouring out are as clear as springwater. Time can do that for us, if we let it. My Carolina experience was wonderful. I learned *way* more than I taught. I learned that if you give respect, you'll get it back. I've never met a harder working people who got so little for their efforts. It's a good thing that companies like BMW have moved in; I'm certain that nobody wants to return to the era of poor-paying jobs. But with dramatic change, some valuable old ways have disappeared. It's hard to describe them, or even to define exactly what they are, but I'm painfully aware that some priceless qualities have been lost. Perhaps it's families going to church together, or attending annual reunions. Do people still fish with cane poles from the riverbanks? Now we all live in our private electronic worlds, and the social fabric of the South has forever changed, as it has in every other part of the country.

There is much that I miss. We lived first in Shelby and Asheville, North Carolina, and then in Greenville, South Carolina. On many a Sunday afternoon, we would all bring our guitars, fiddles, and banjos and jam on the front porch.

What else do I remember? Everyone loved to race. A senior citizen driving a

Buick would try to beat you when the stoplight turned green. We bought a Chevy with a 327 engine, but were no match for those guys driving their custom hotrods. I bet their grandchildren are now racing their hybrid-electric cars from the same stoplights. Some things never change; at least I hope not.

I thought I'd share some technical information about the photos. I couldn't afford a Nikon or a Hasselblad, but I did have a good Konica 35mm SLR. I used three lenses: a 57mm normal, a 35mm wide angle, and a 135mm telephoto. I didn't have a motor drive, because they didn't make one for that camera. I developed my own film, both Plus-X and Tri-X, and printed the negatives in my darkroom, which was in the bathroom.

This book was created with a digital-optical scanner that took the original negatives and put them right into the computer. Except for removing some blotches here and there, the negatives and prints have not been altered. How they survived undamaged for 35-plus years is beyond me.

It was quite moving to enter a negative into the system and watch it come to life on the screen as a positive image. Suddenly, as the James Taylor song says, I was gone to Carolina in my mind. I could almost feel the hot sun, and listen to the crickets. The people and the places are inseparable. The cotton field and the person doing the picking, the red dirt and the farmer doing the plowing, are what this book is about.

The great French photographer Henri Cartier-Bresson had a theory called The Decisive Moment. He believed that every photo strives for a precise split-second where the action is at its peak. For example, if a person is swinging an ax over his or her head, you aim to capture the exact moment when the ax is in the best position. This is what I tried to do in my photos. I also developed the ability to shoot from the hip. I was often able to photograph people who were not looking directly into the camera. I worked out many ways to blend into a scene and go largely unnoticed. When people accepted my presence and were at ease, I got my best photos. I was always honest with the people I photographed; I told them I was doing a photo book on the Carolinas. I had no idea then that it would take so long to be published.

I am forever grateful to my wife, Rita Randazzo, for her excellent book design. She recognized that the photos told a story when they were placed in sections, and had special meaning when they were paired with similar or contrasting photos on the same page. As she explains it, the entire book tells a story from first photograph to last, with ten separate plots, each in its own chapter. We spent many enjoyable hours (with only a few fights) laying out each section. I could not ask for a better partner.

Joe Randazzo
South Burlington, Vermont
May 2009

I

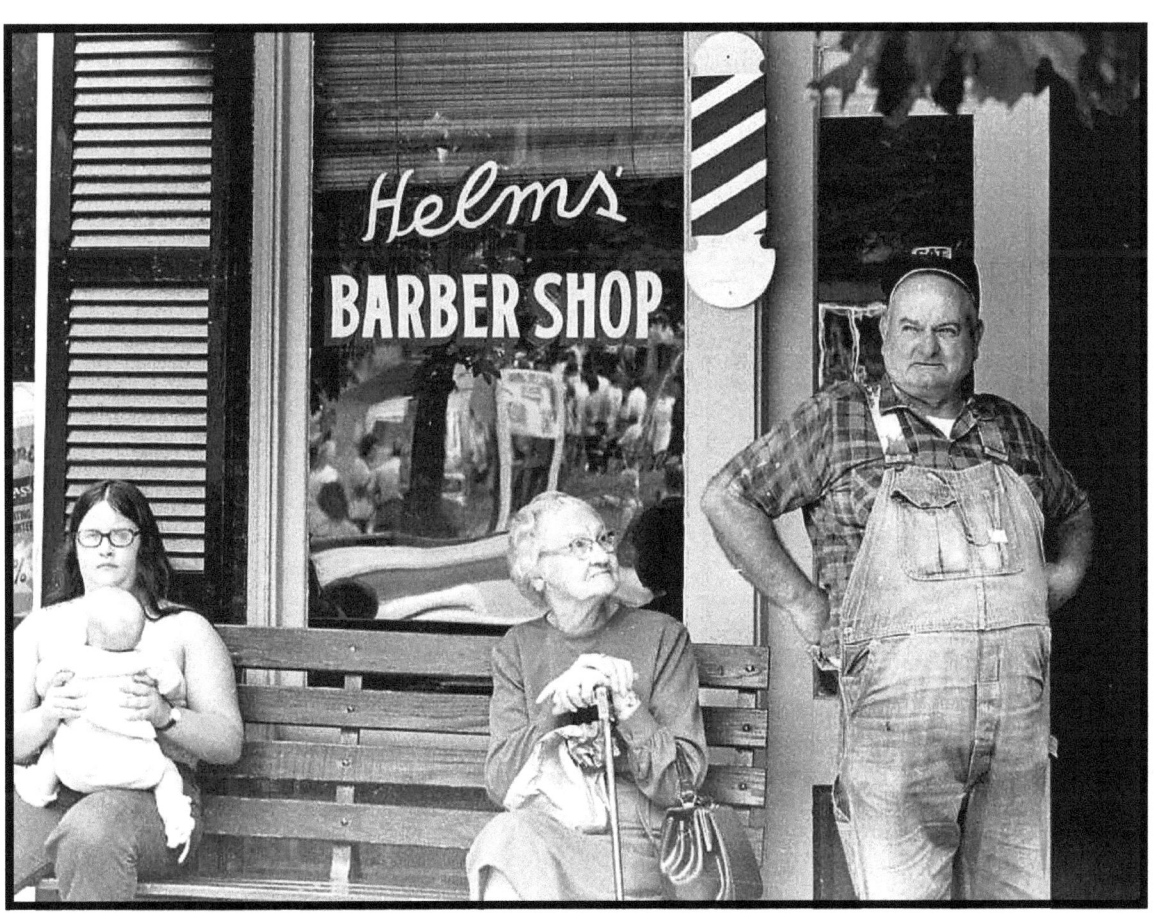

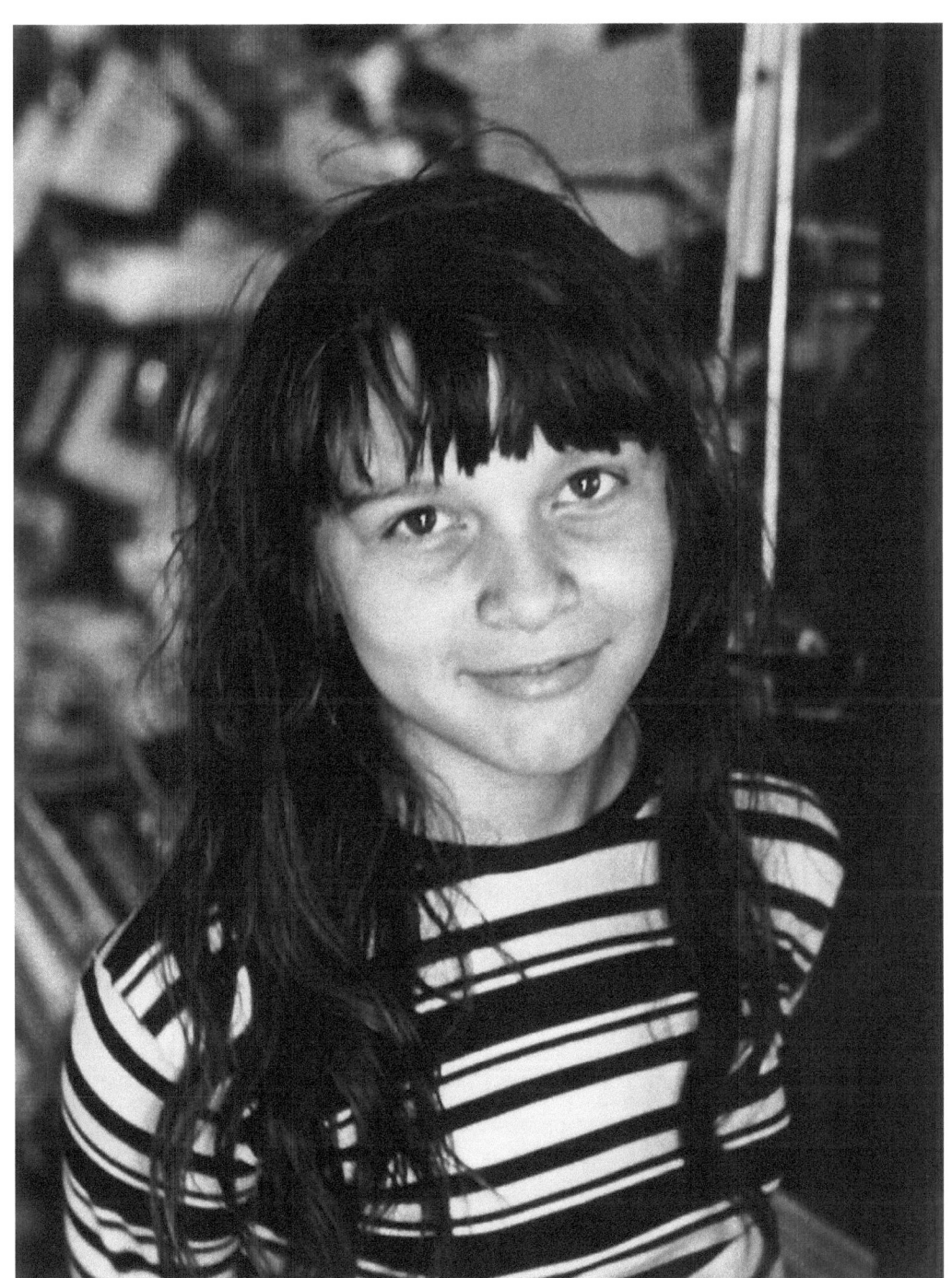

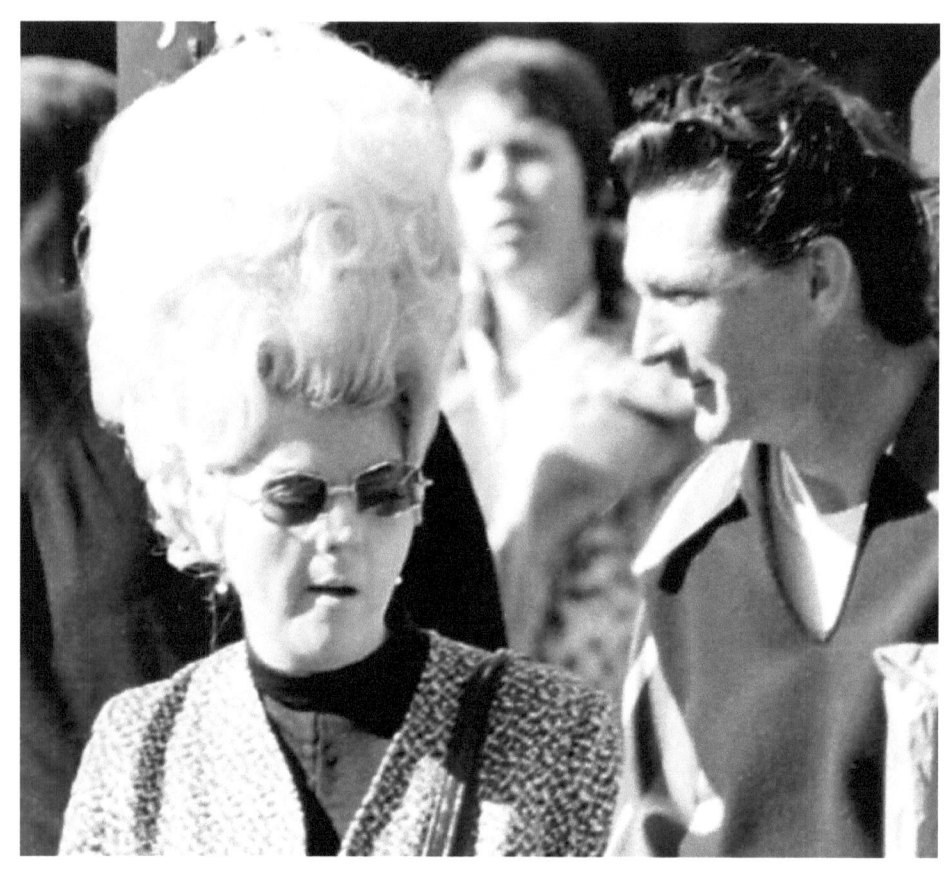

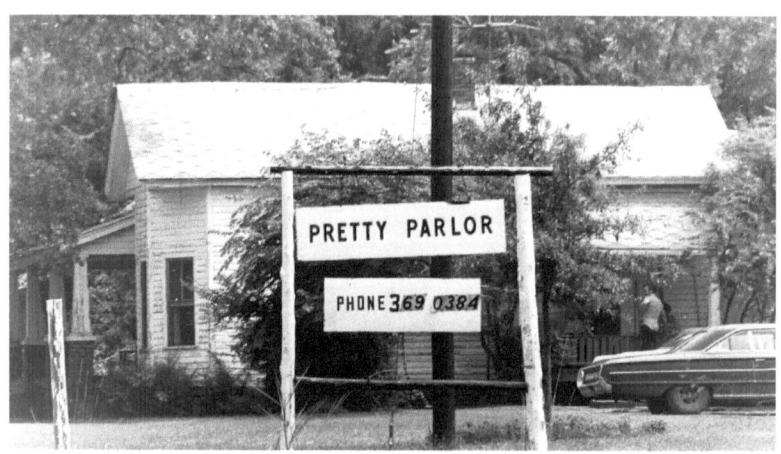

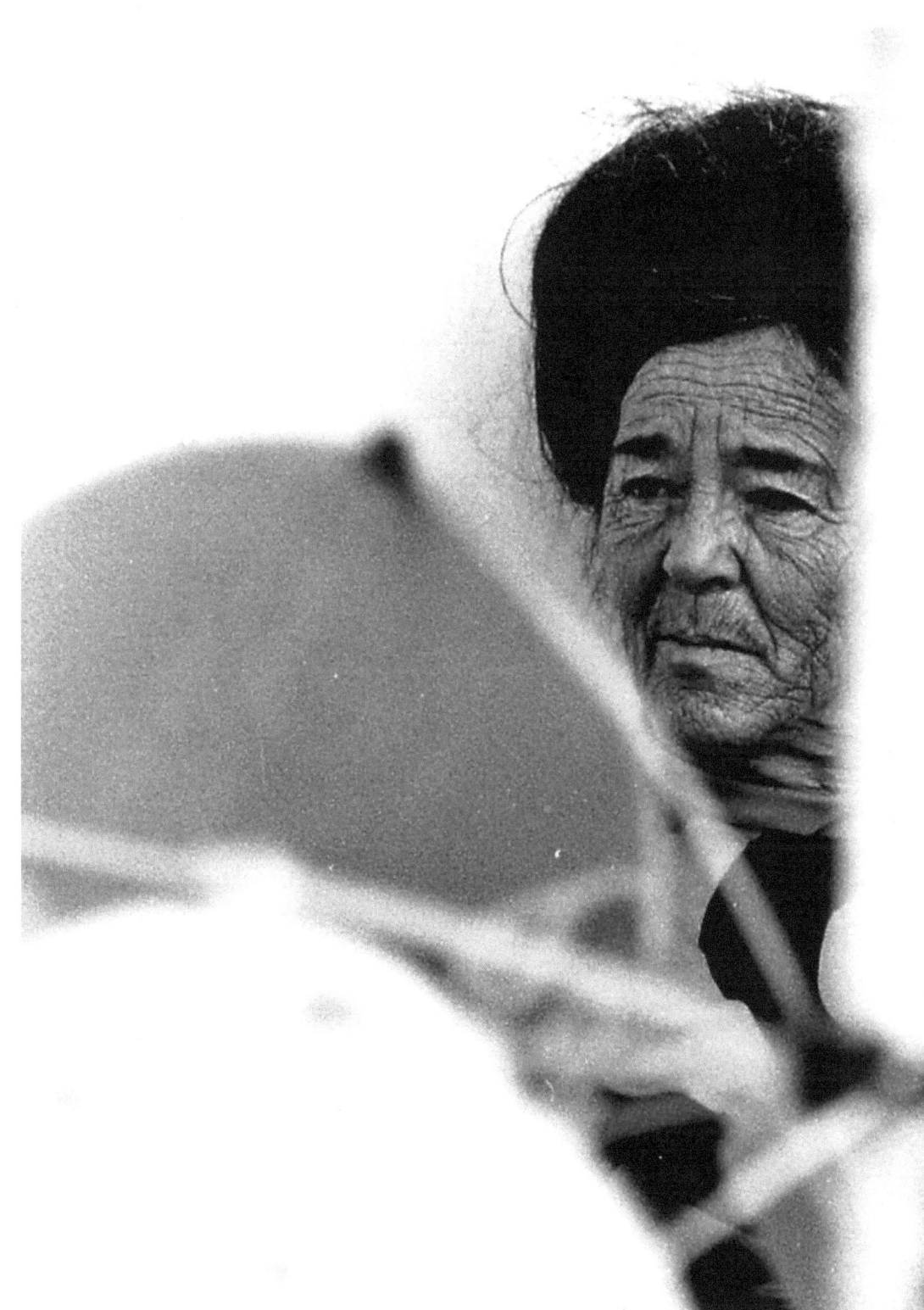

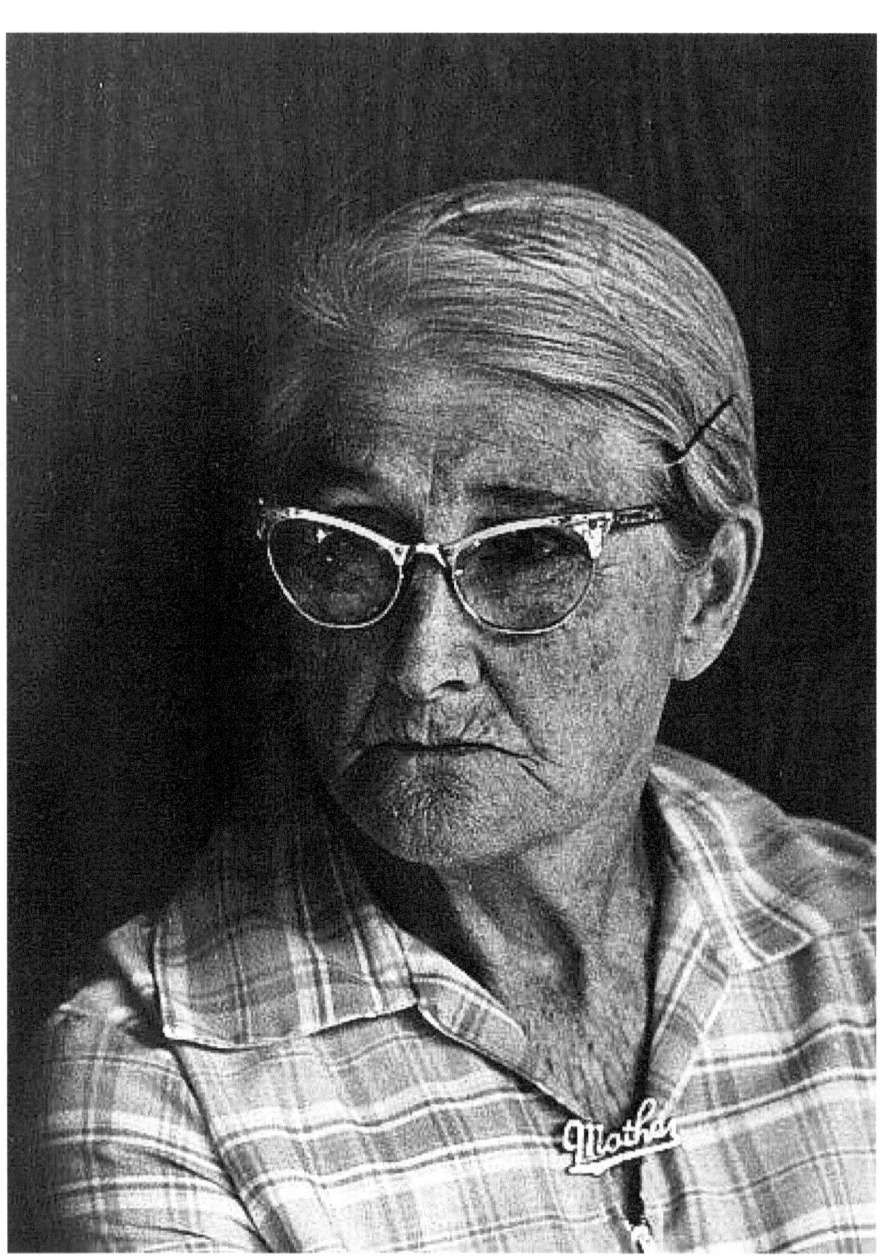

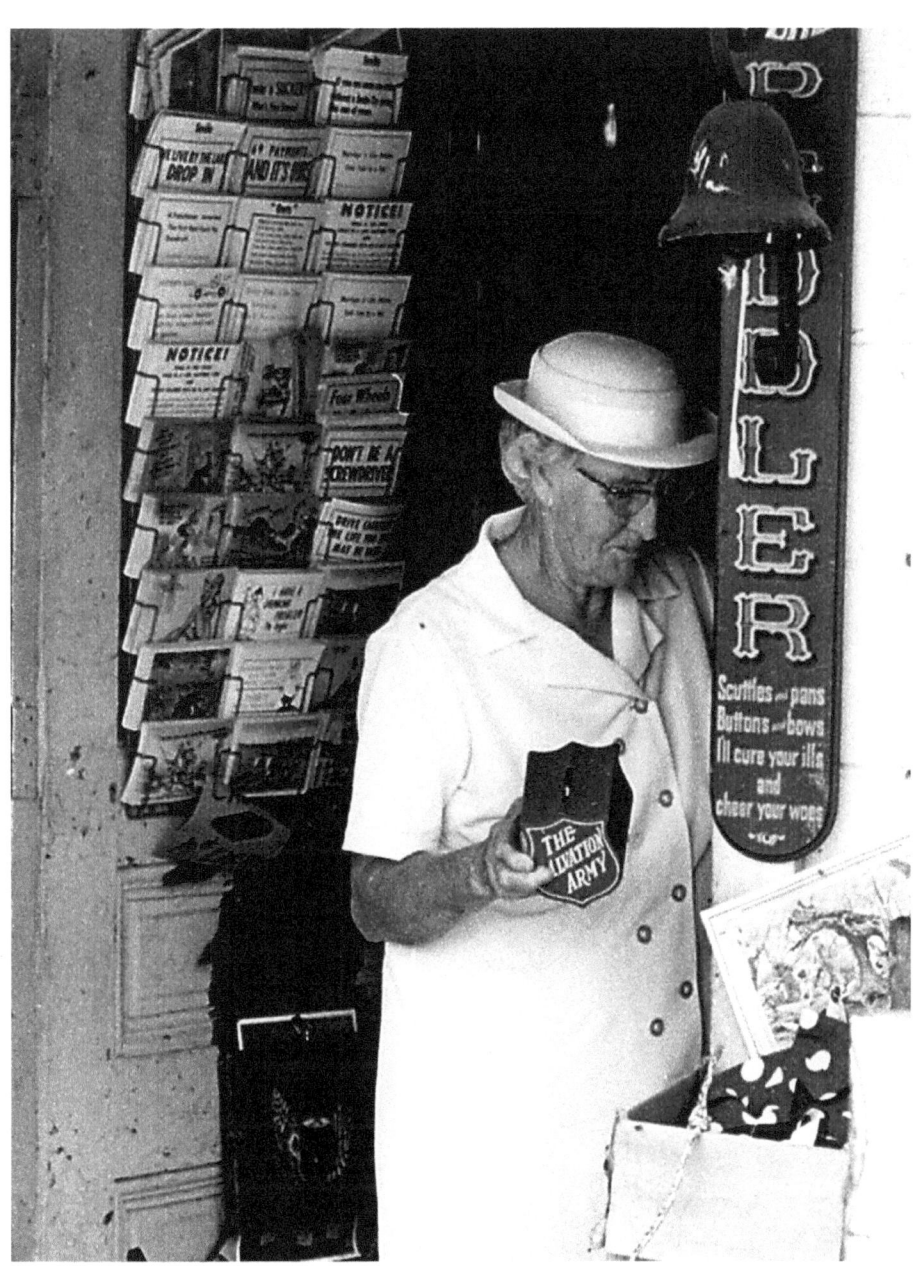

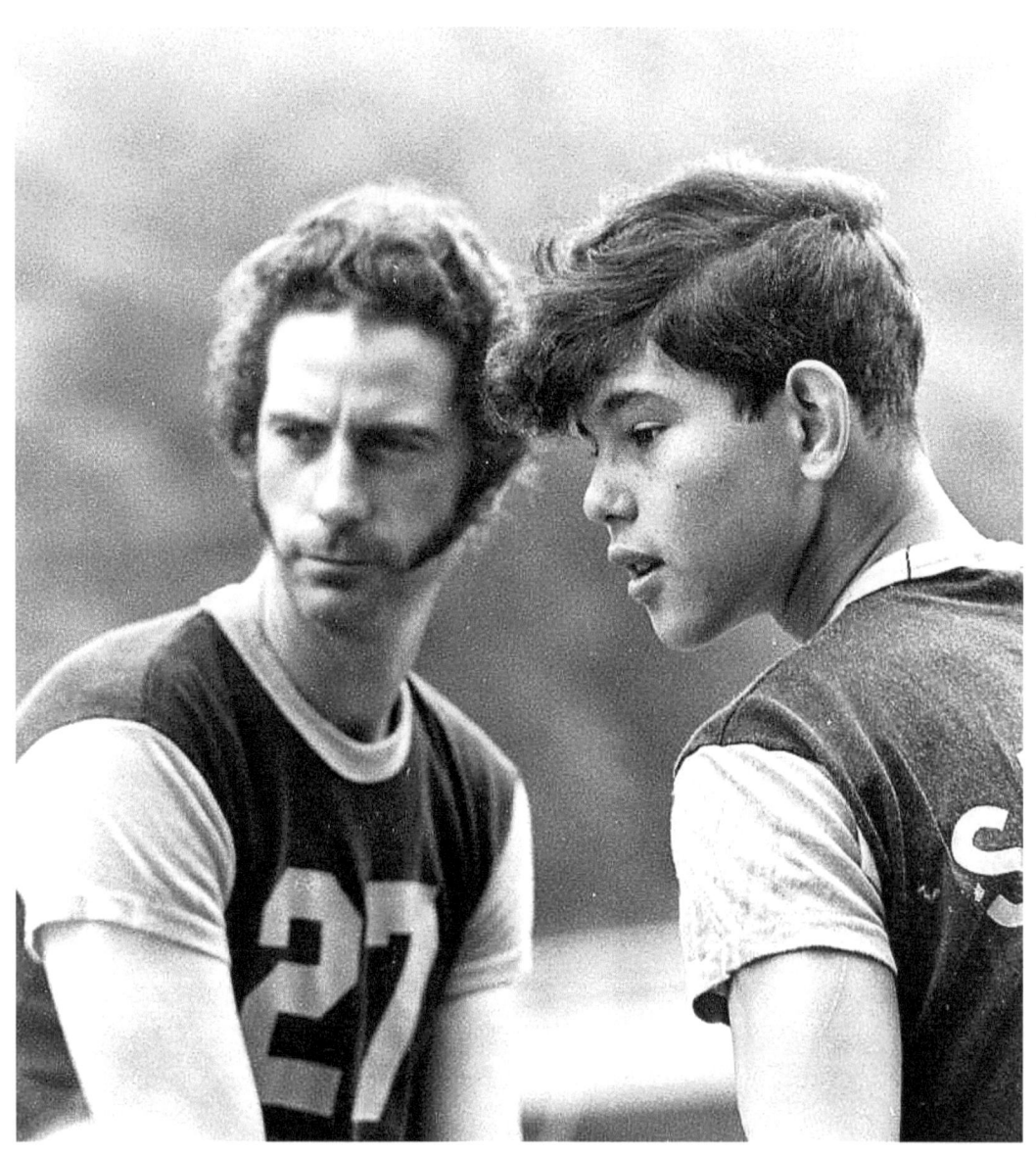

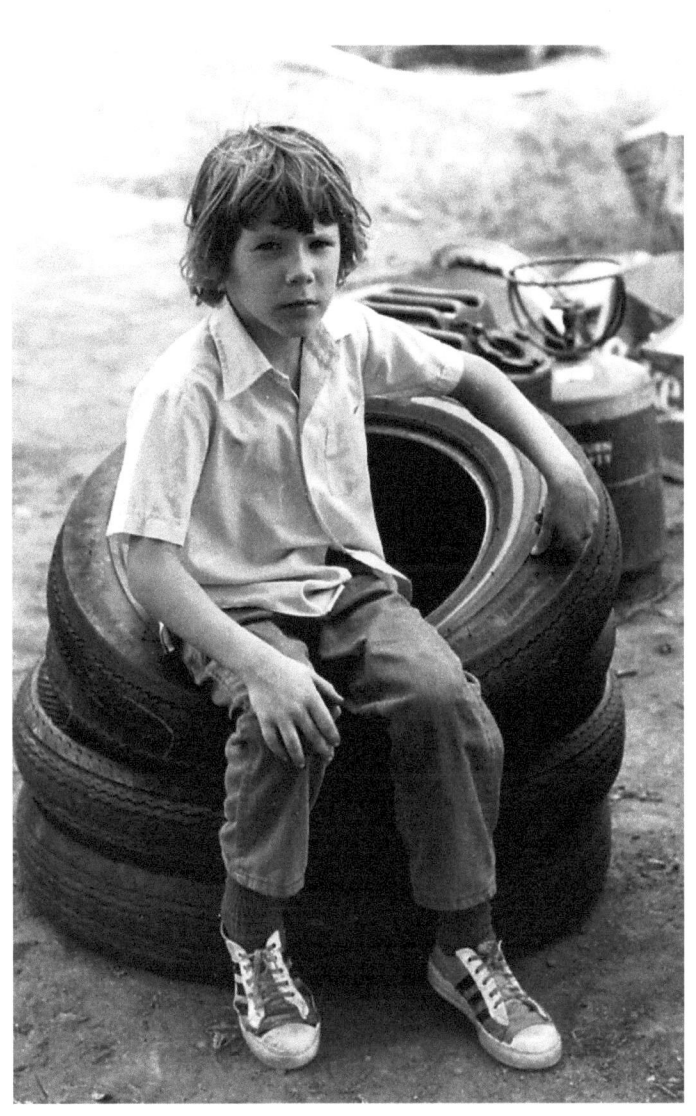

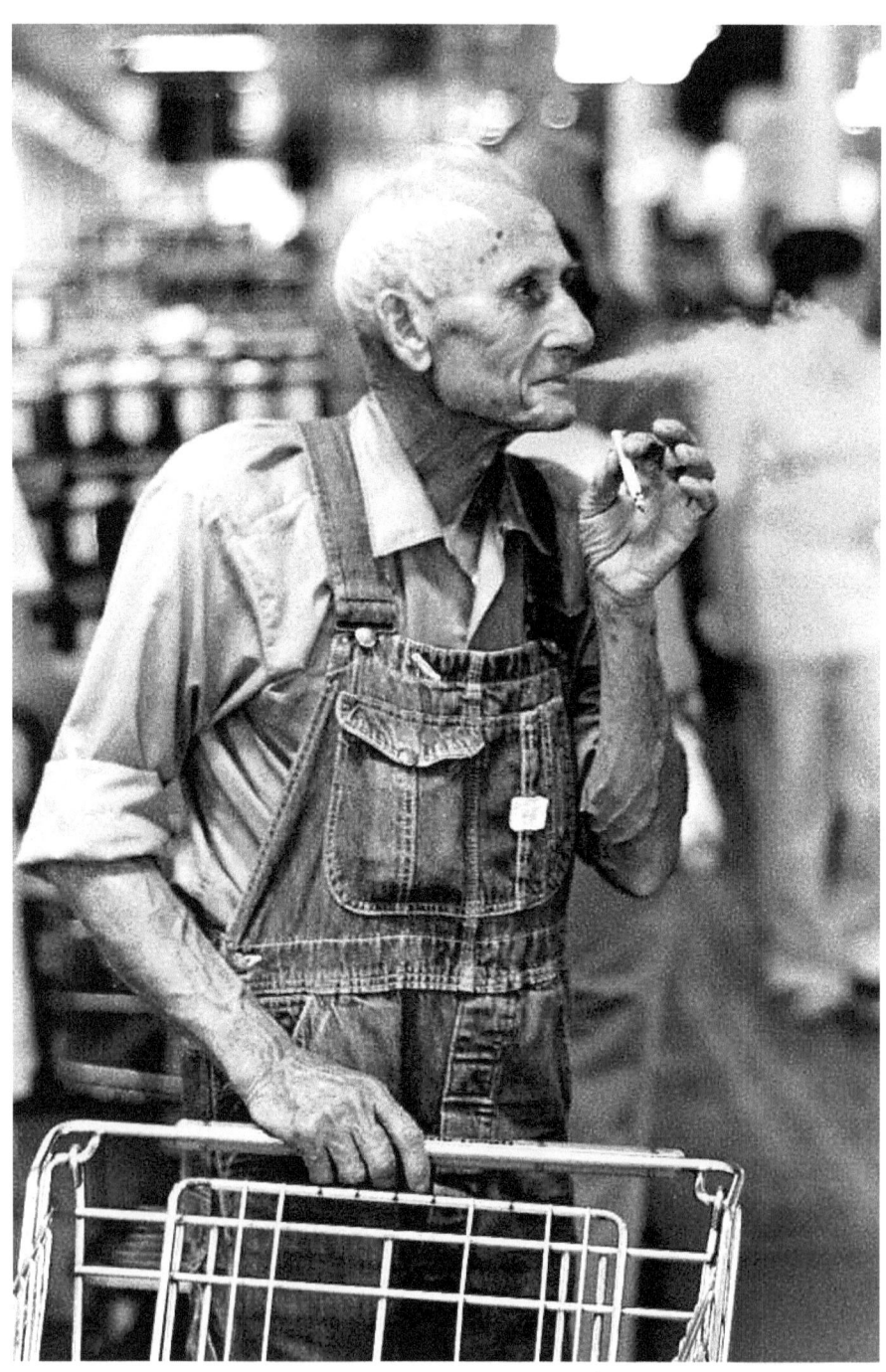

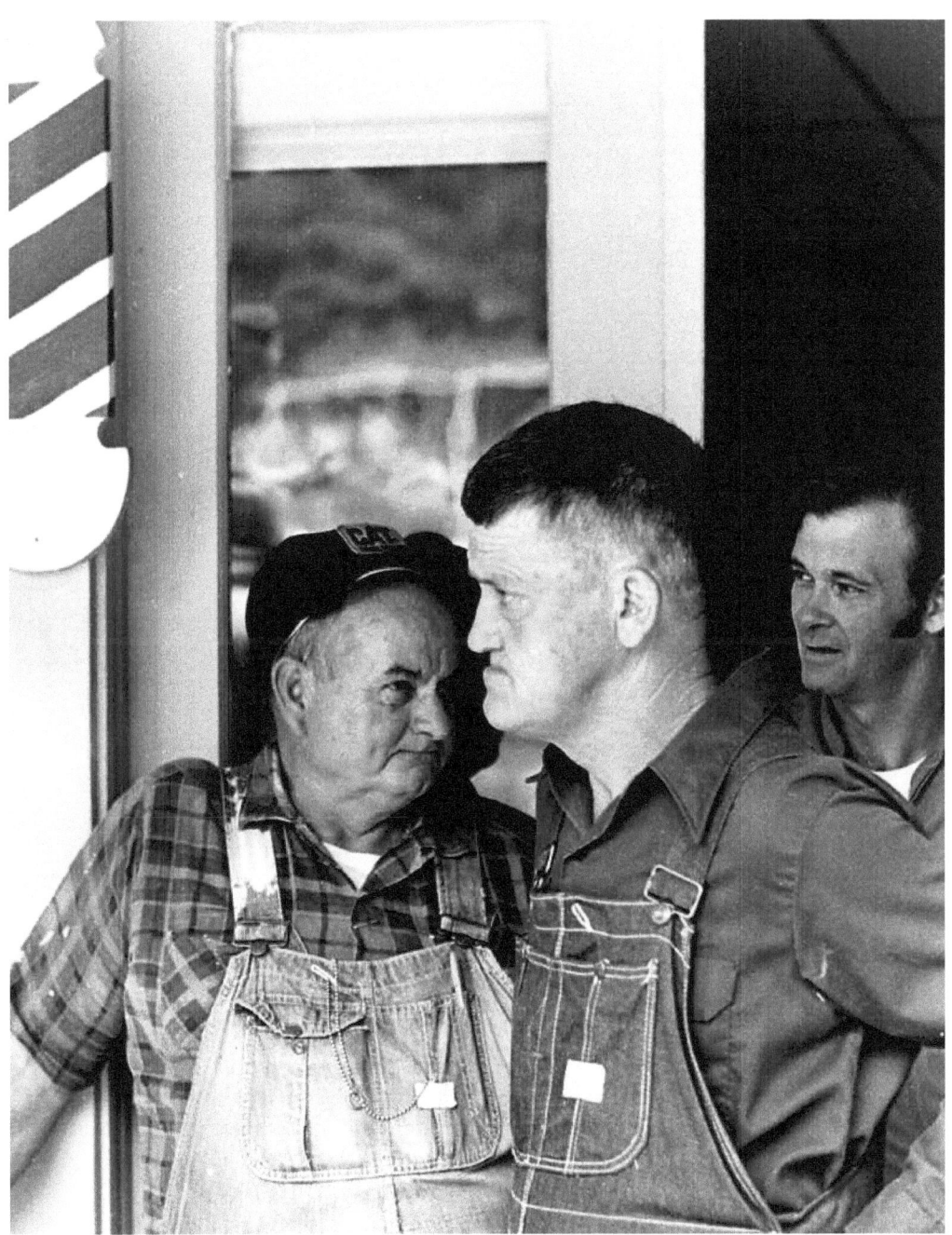

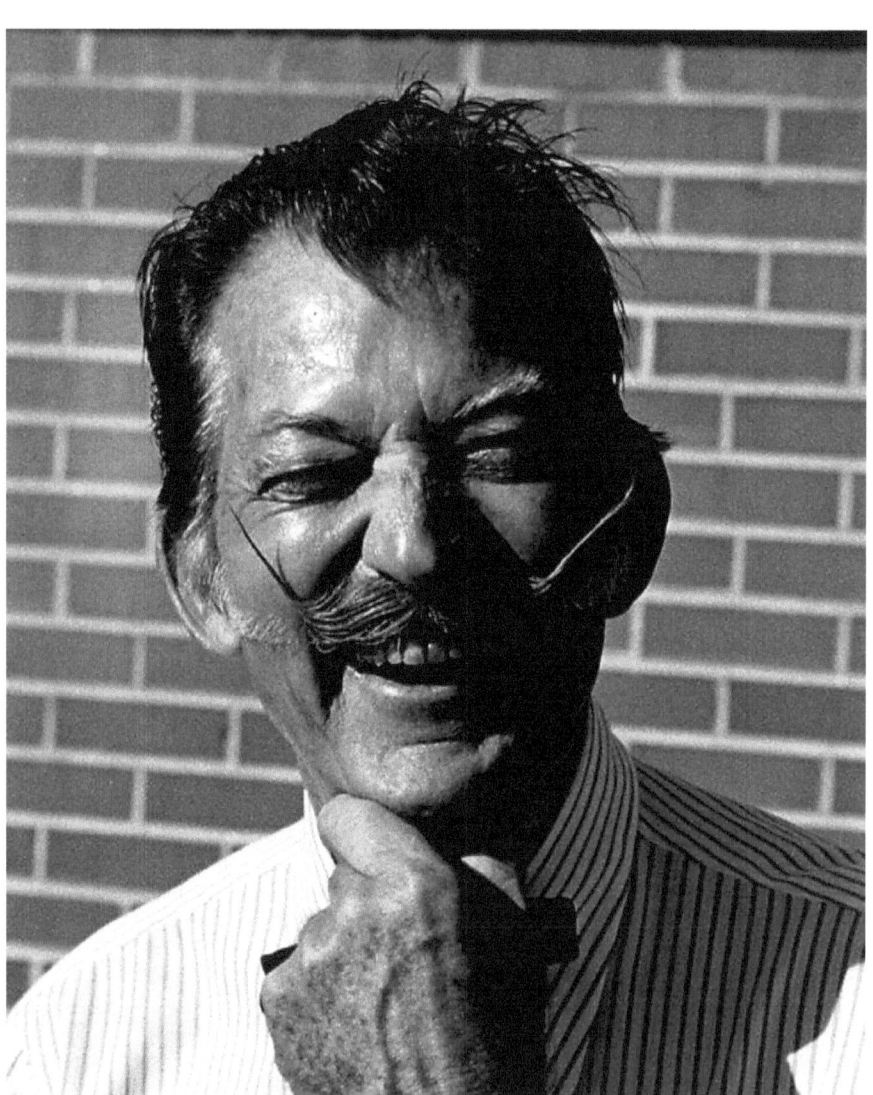

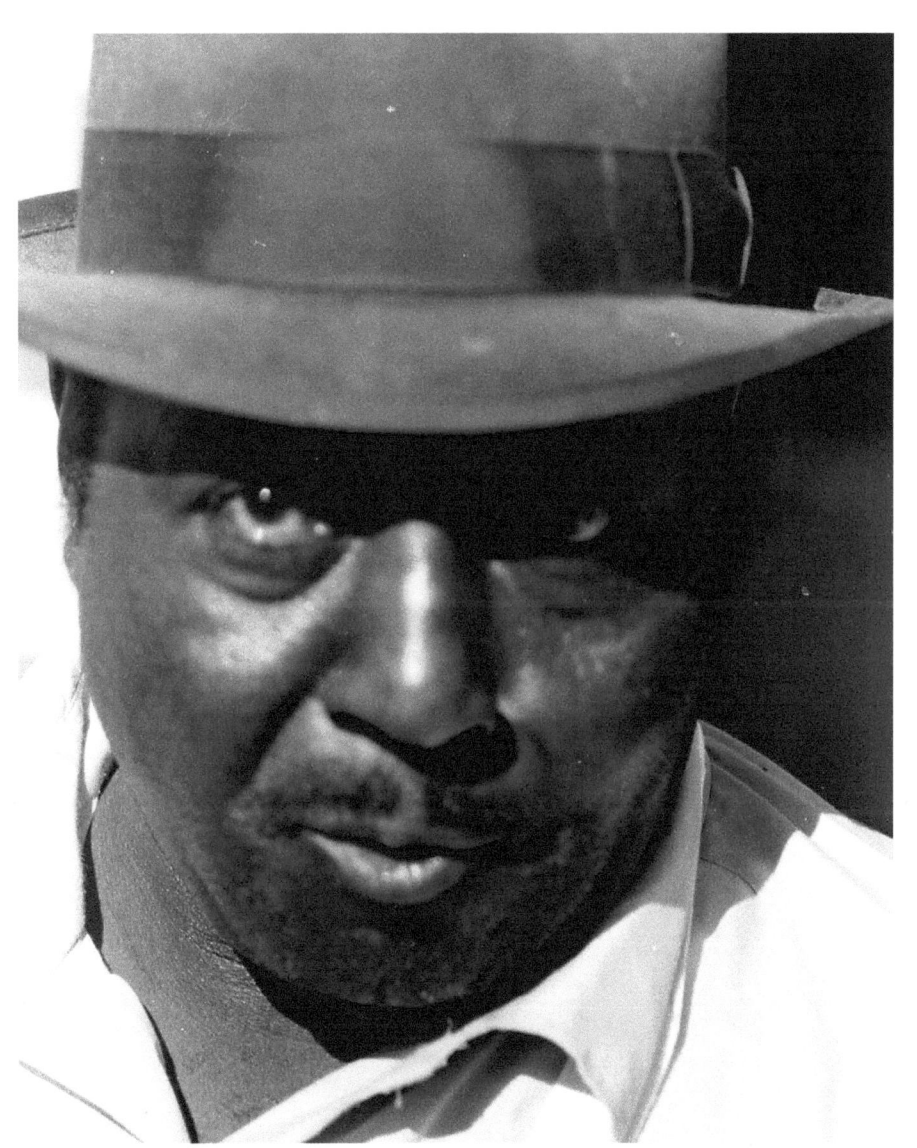

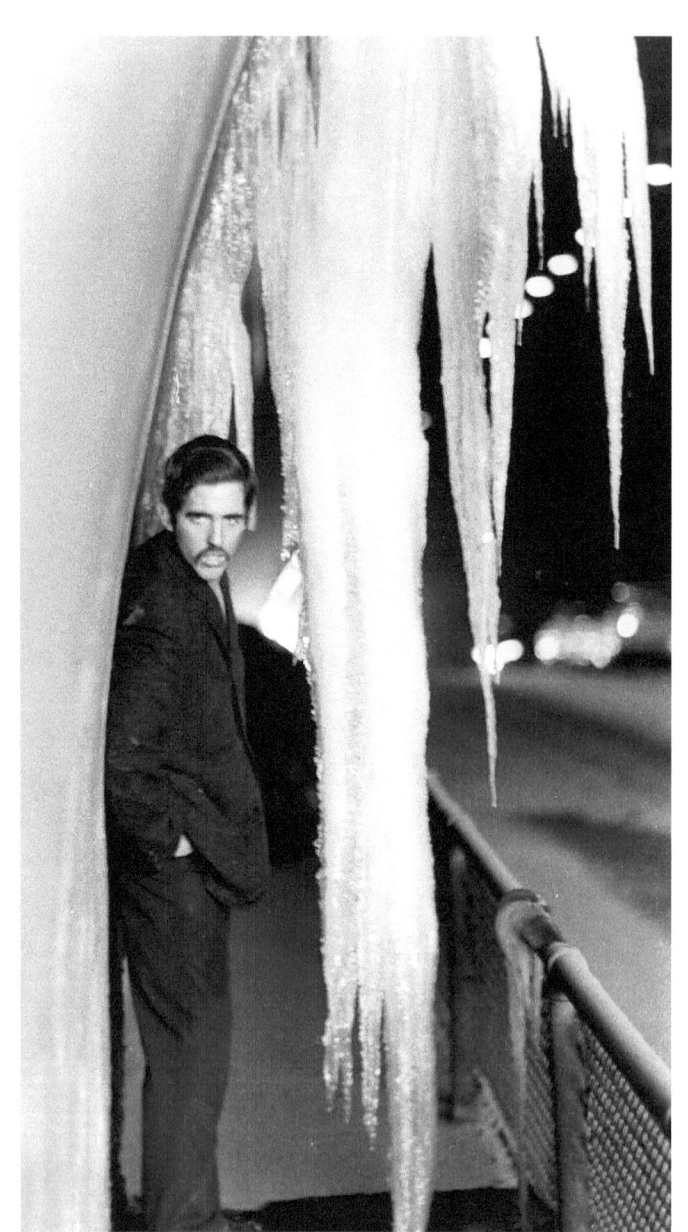

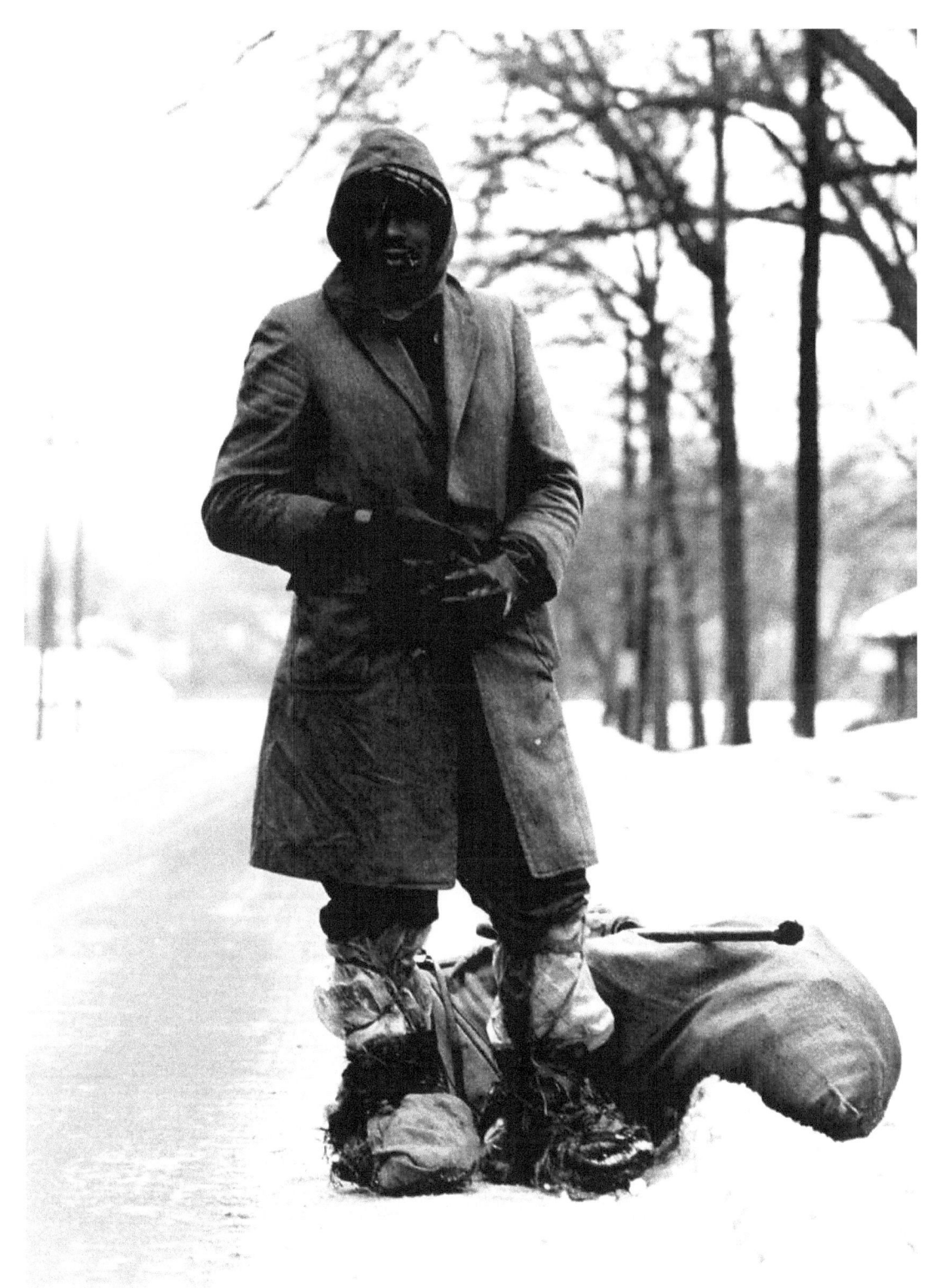

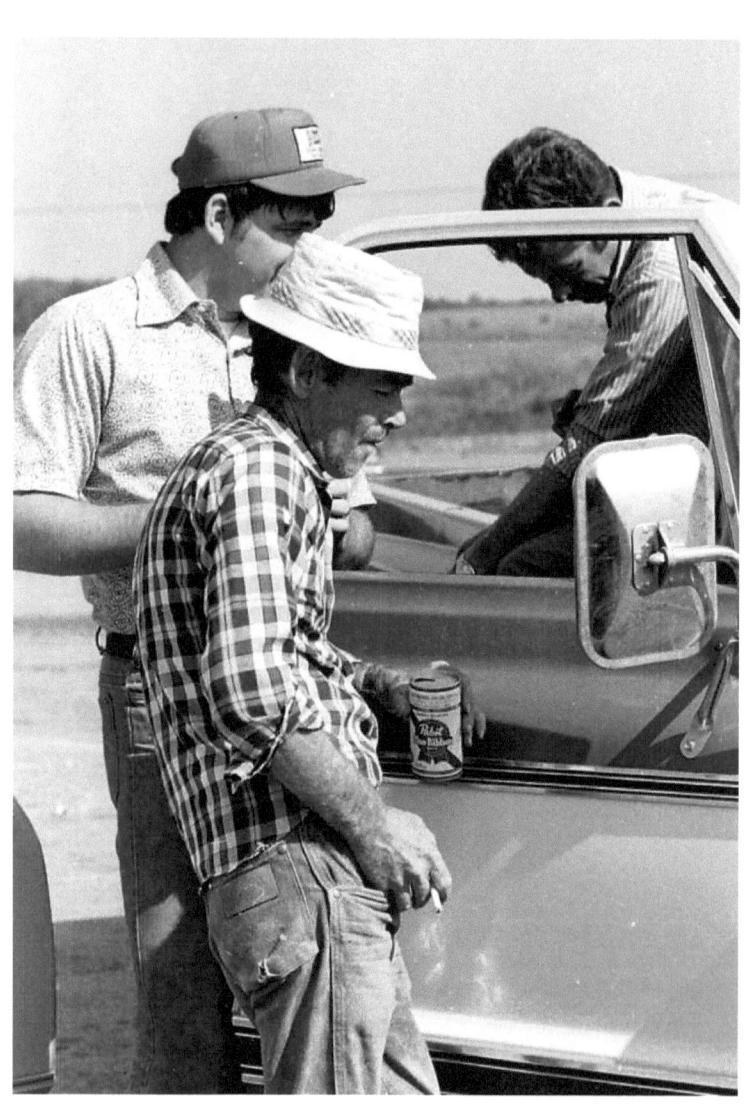

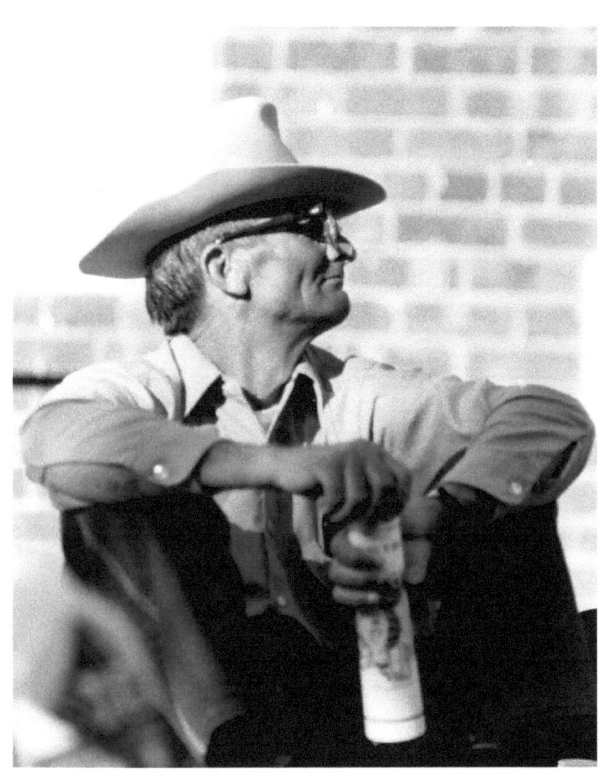

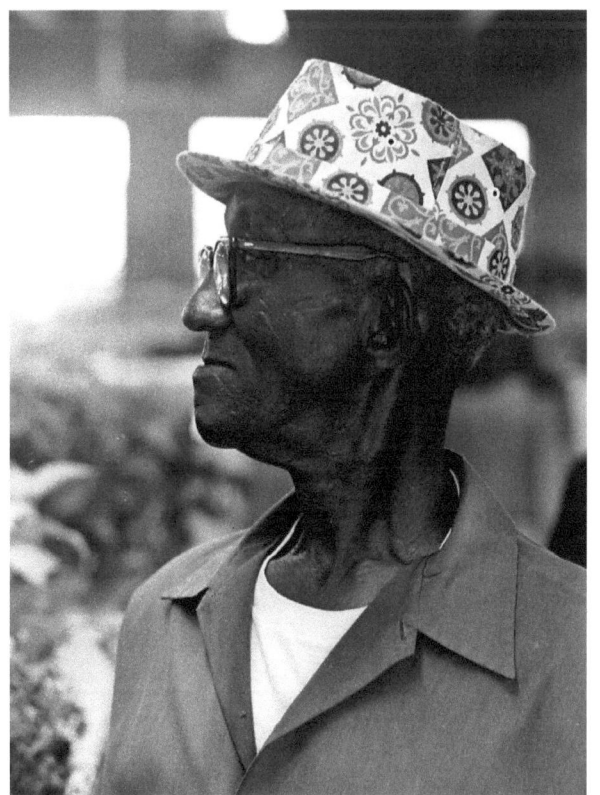

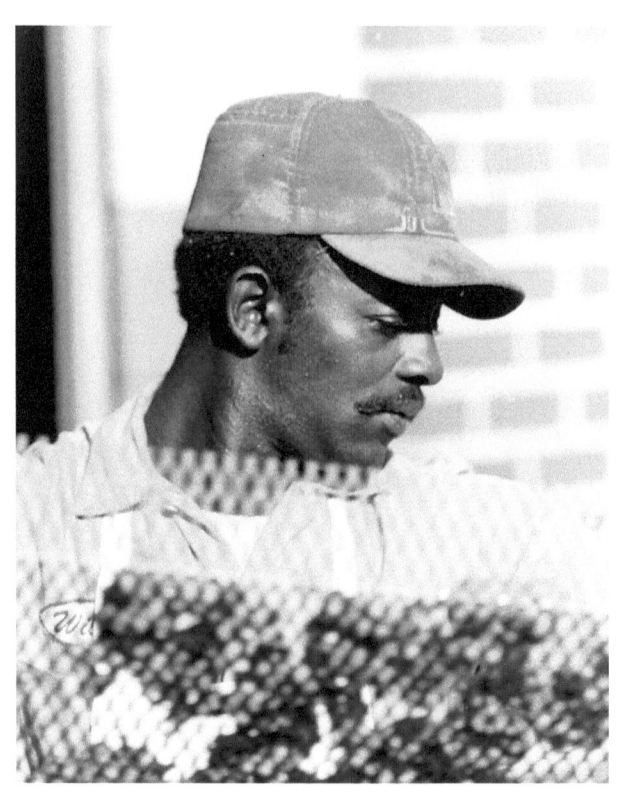

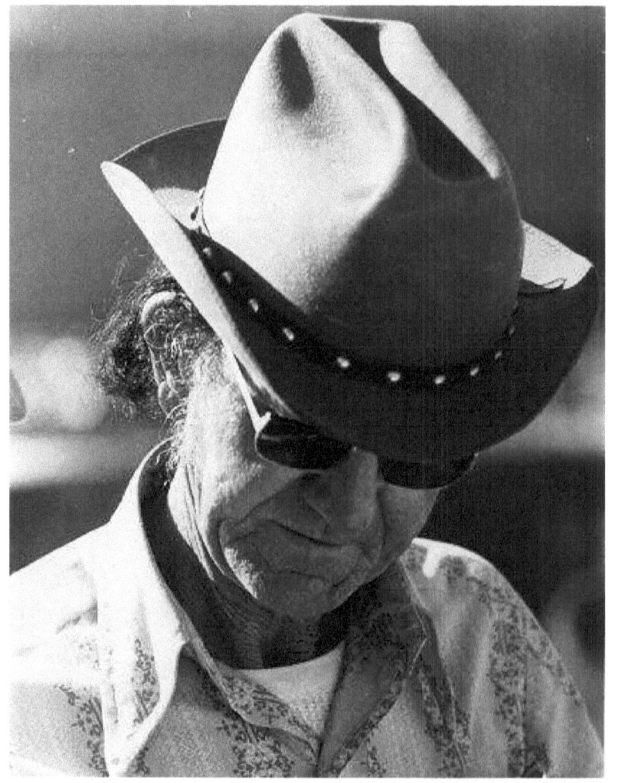

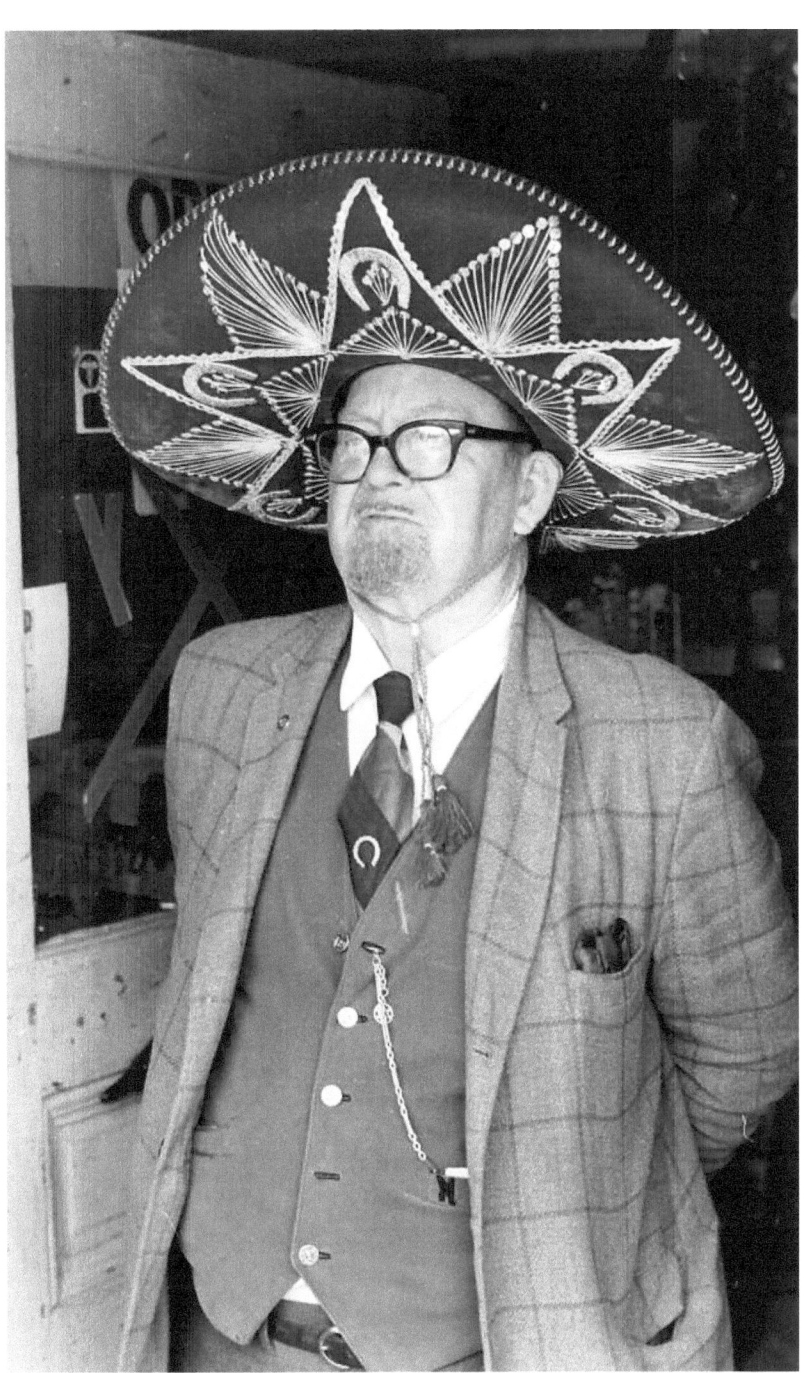

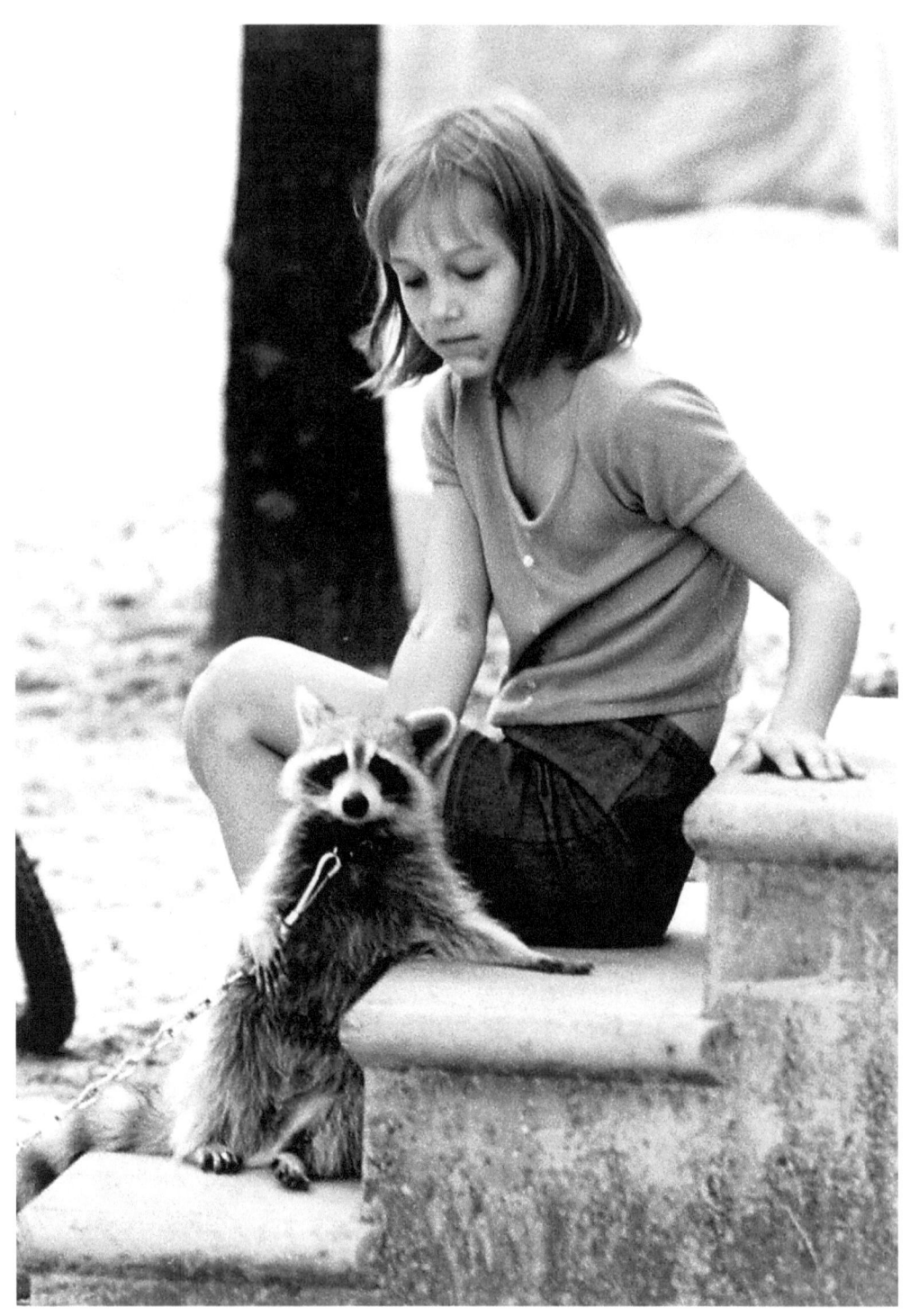

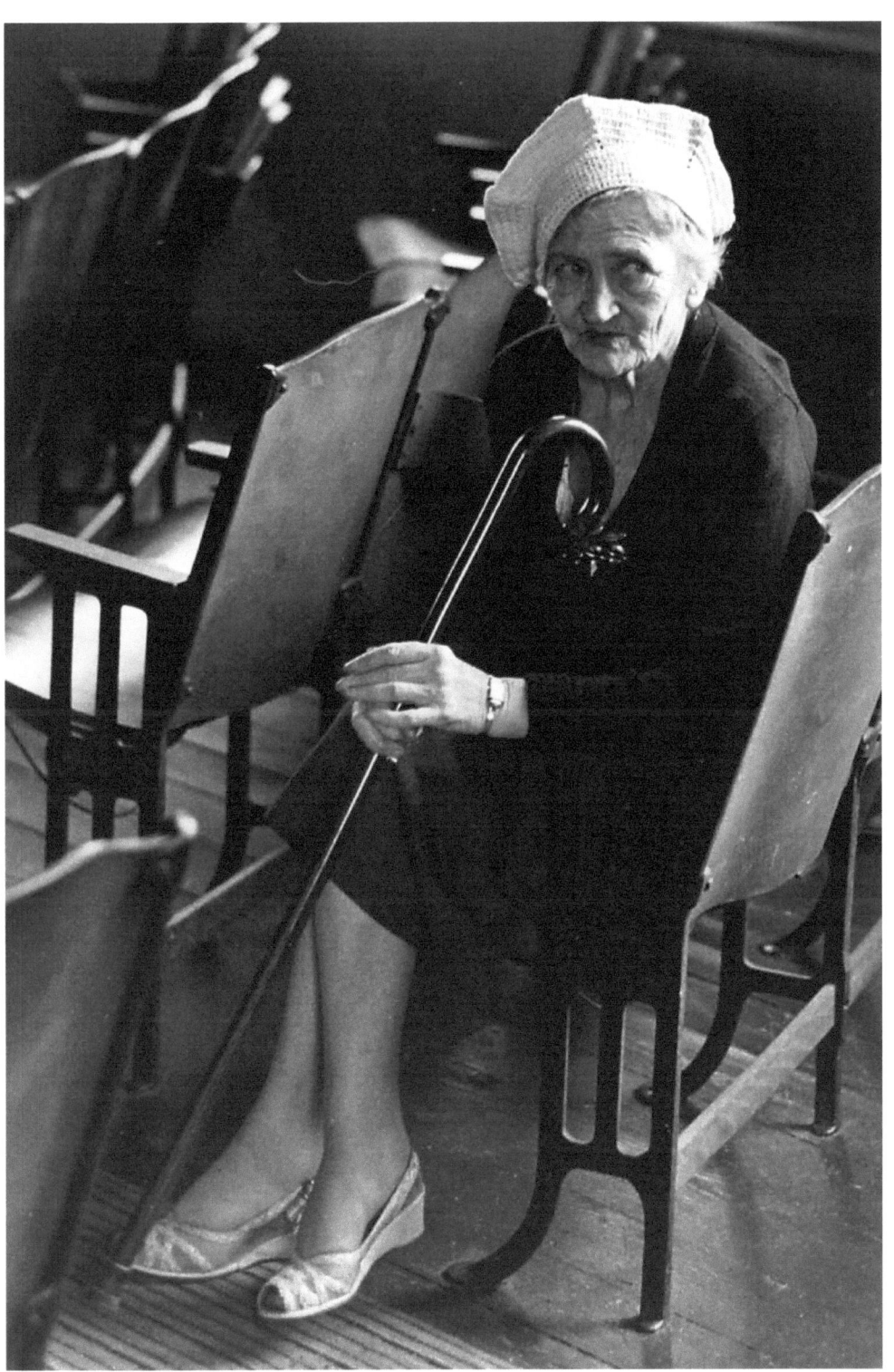

II

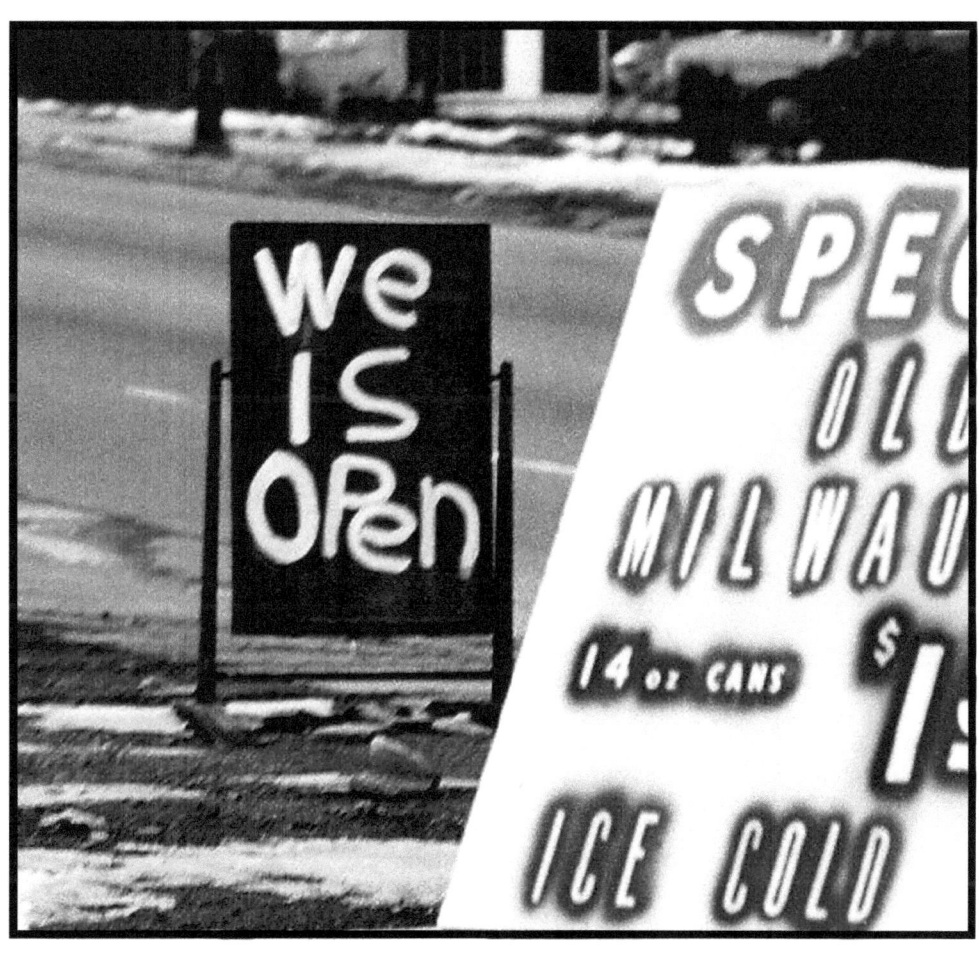

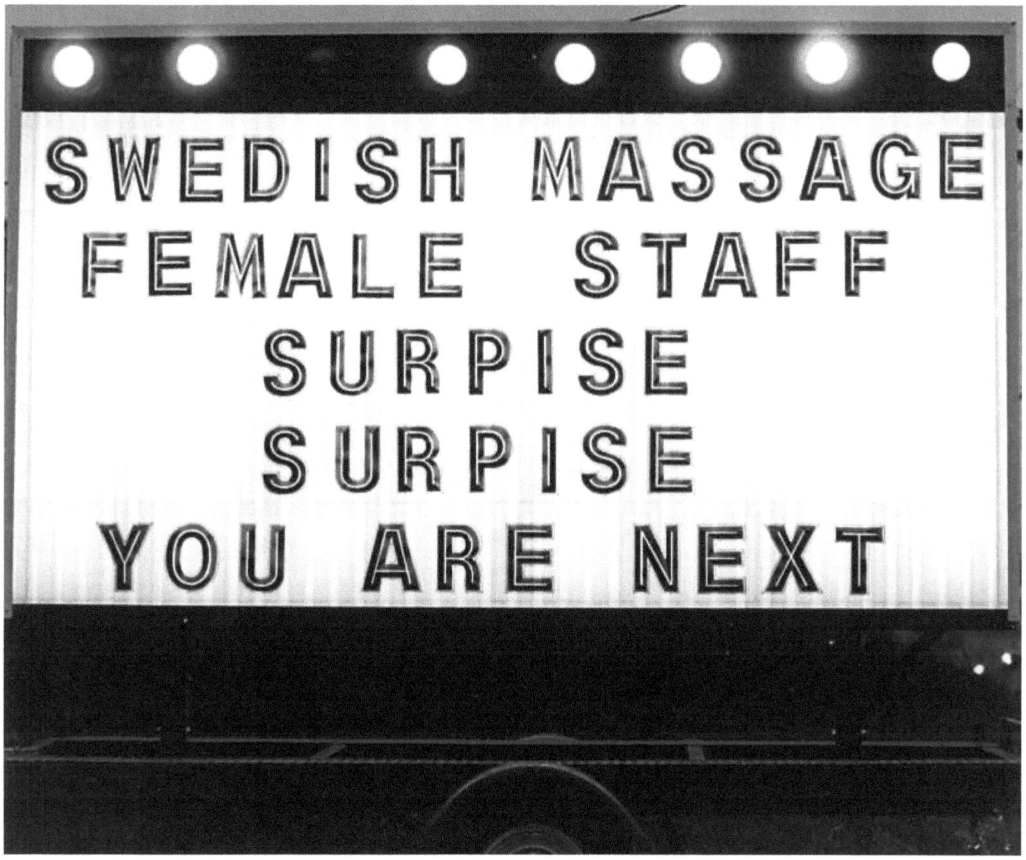
SWEDISH MASSAGE
FEMALE STAFF
SURPISE
SURPISE
YOU ARE NEXT

GREENVILLE
PRINTS · ORIGINAL OI

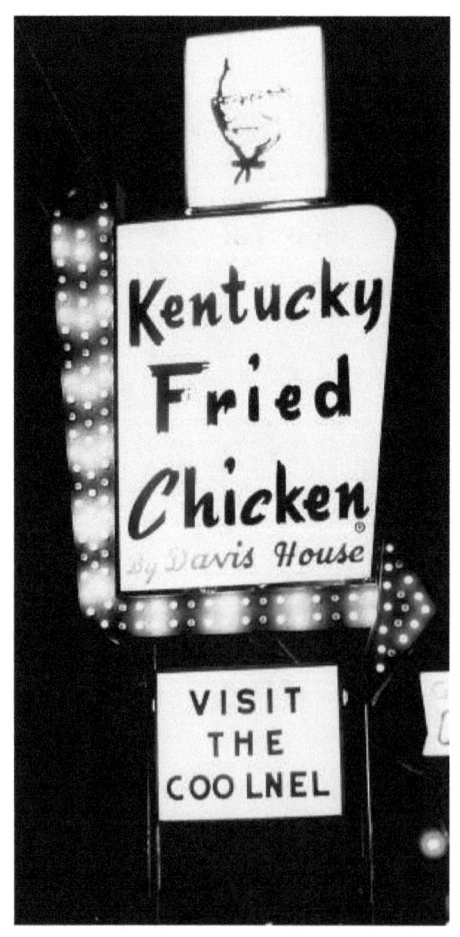

Kentucky
Fried
Chicken
By Davis House

VISIT
THE
COO LNEL

FRAME CENTER
LS • NUMBERED ITCHINGS

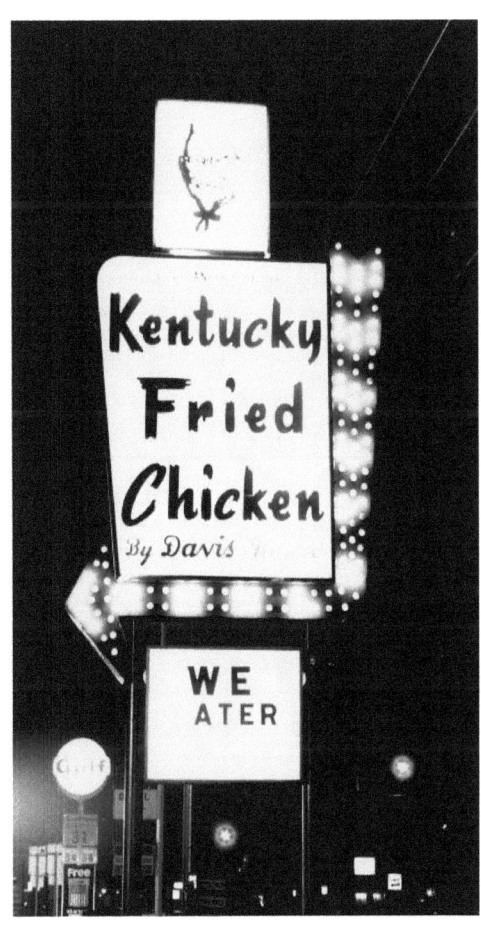

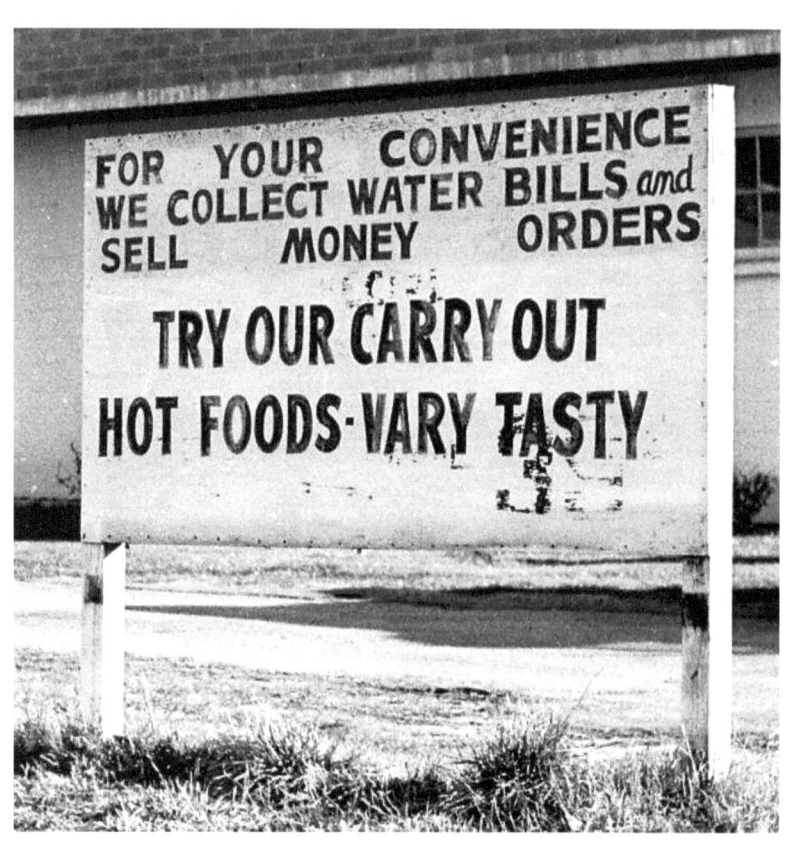

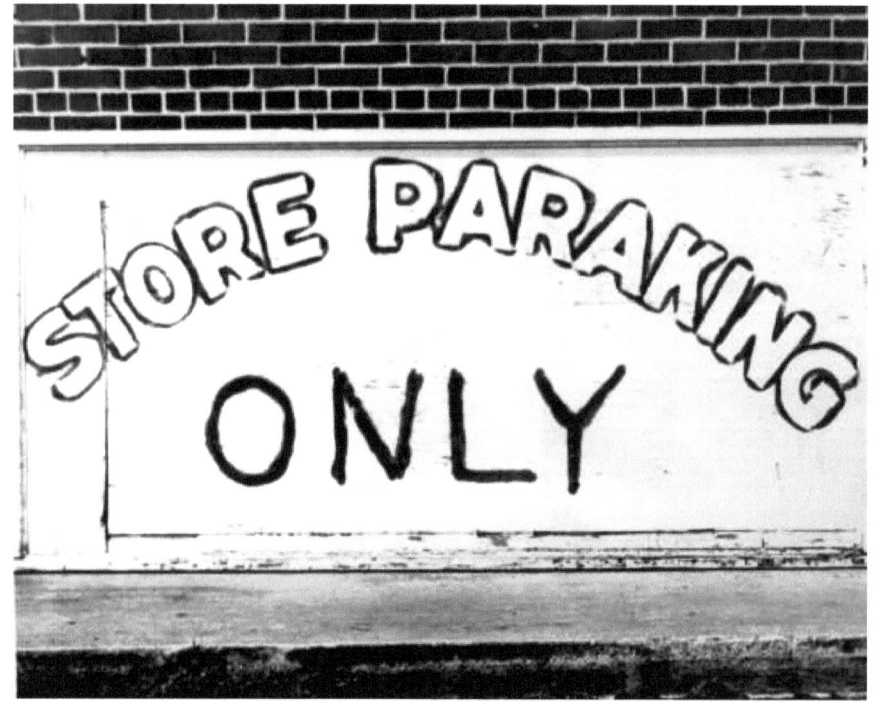

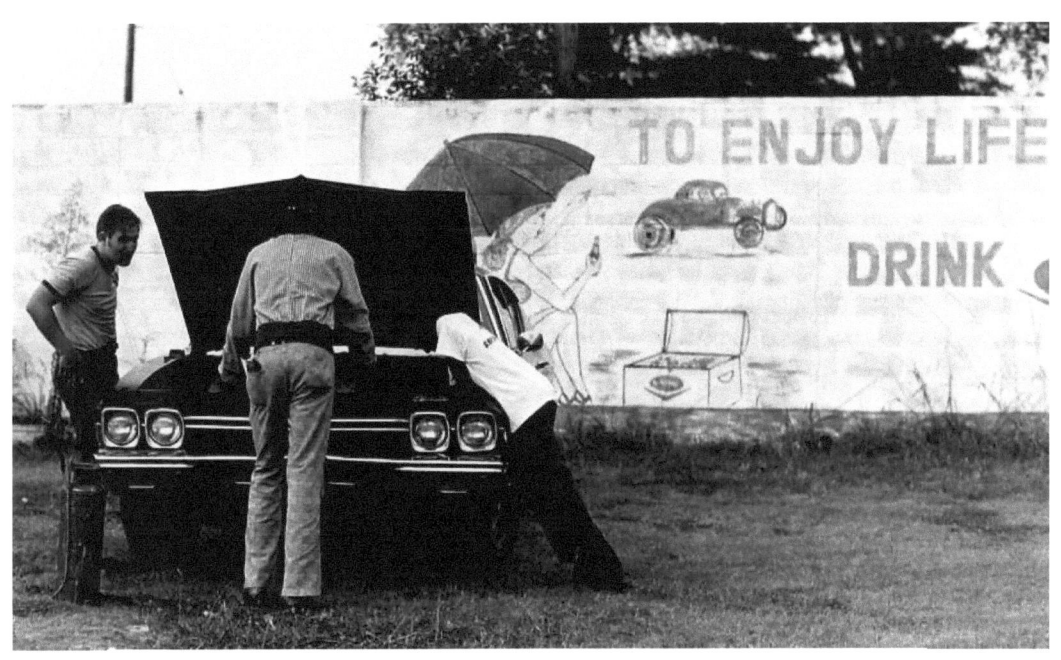

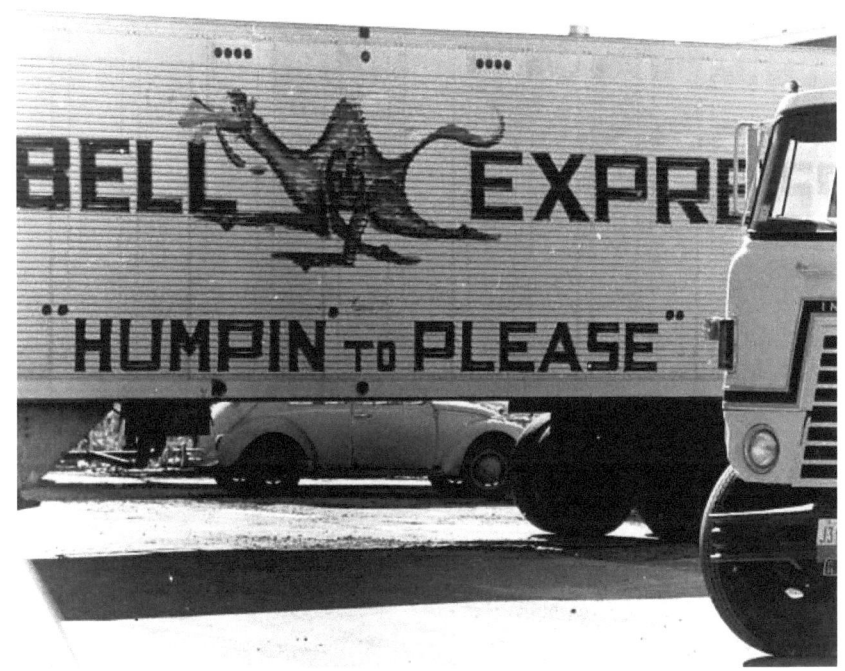

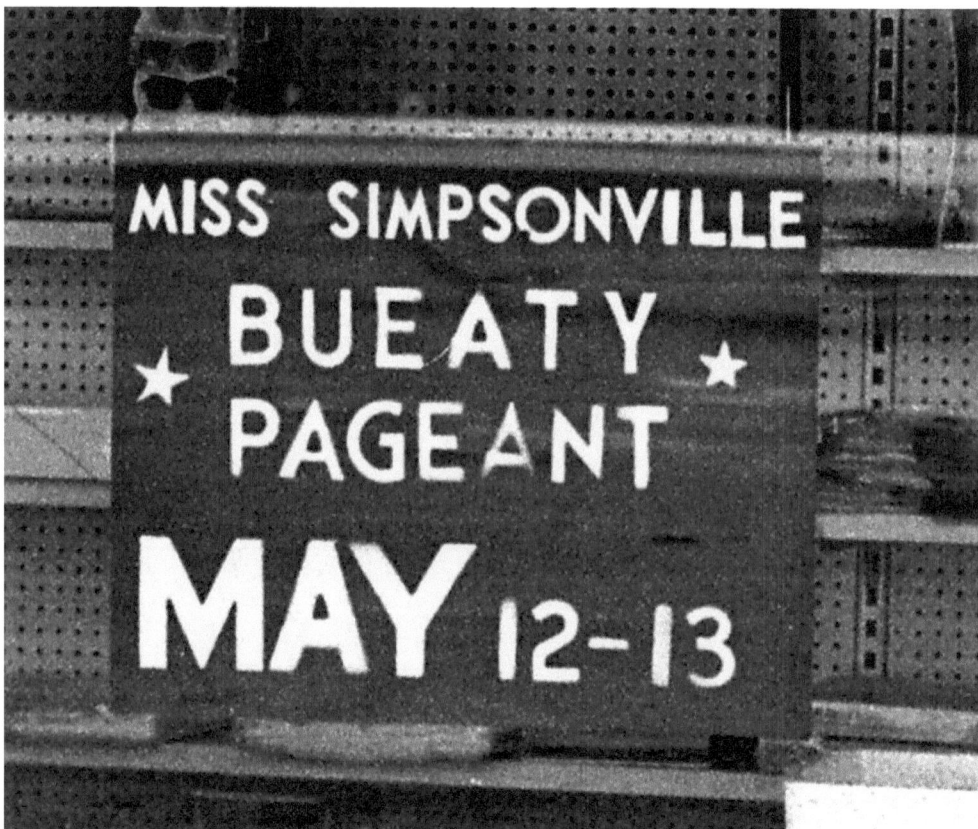

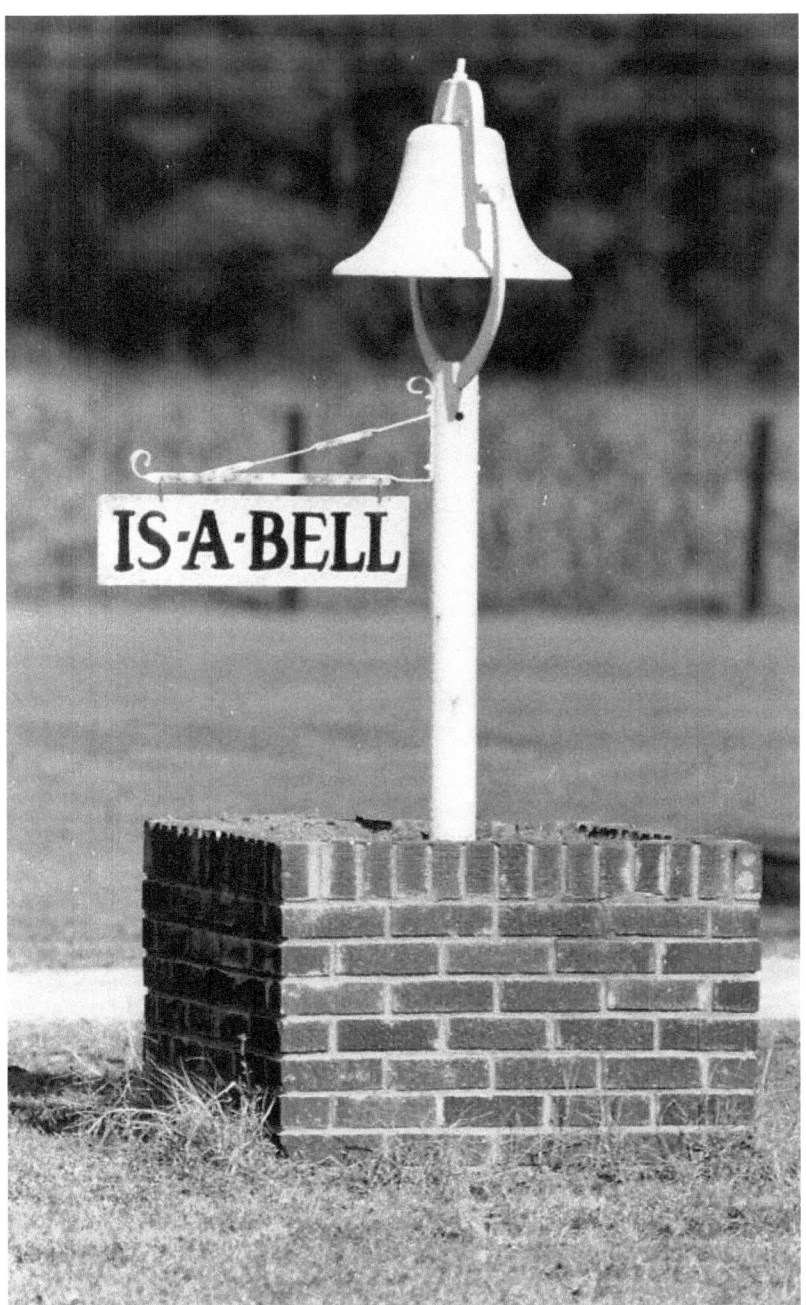

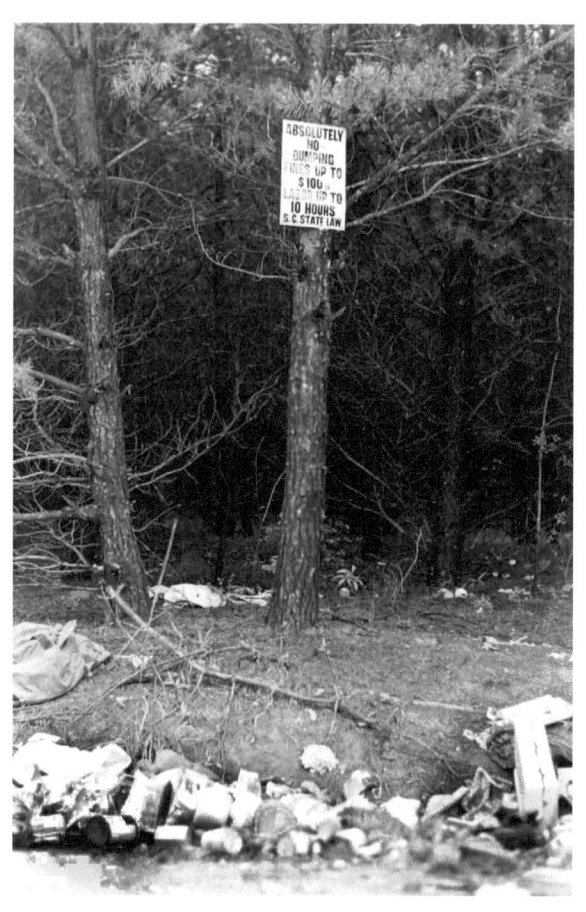

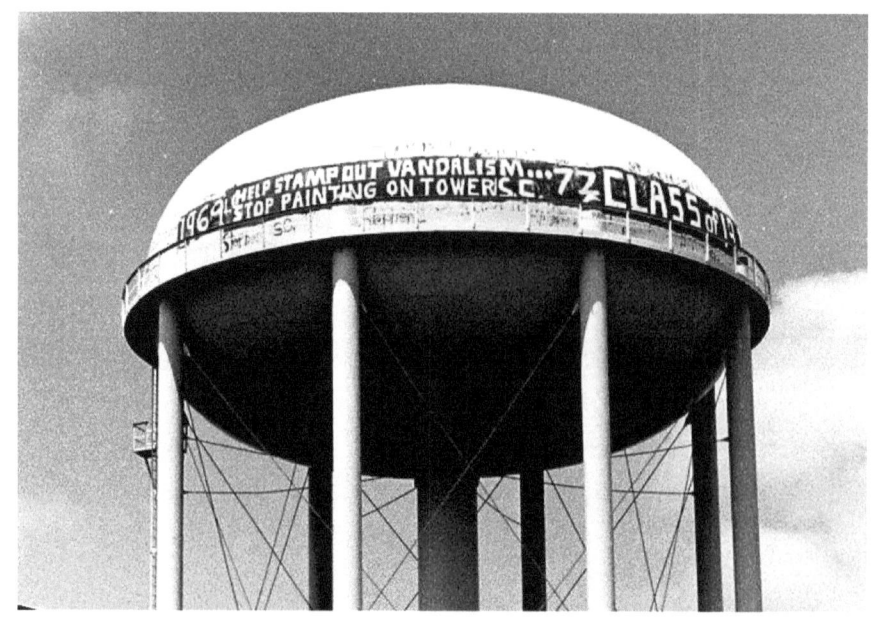

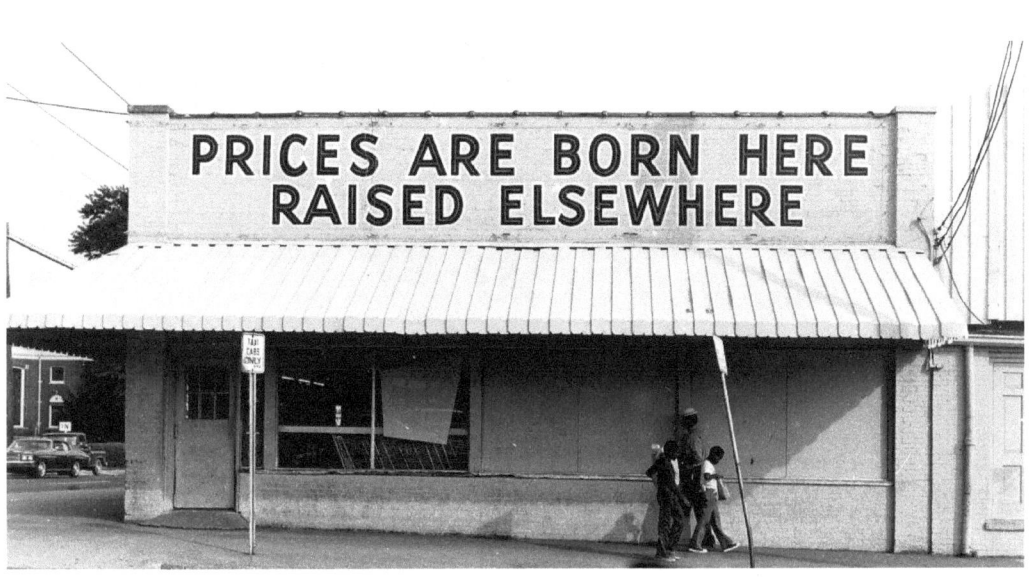

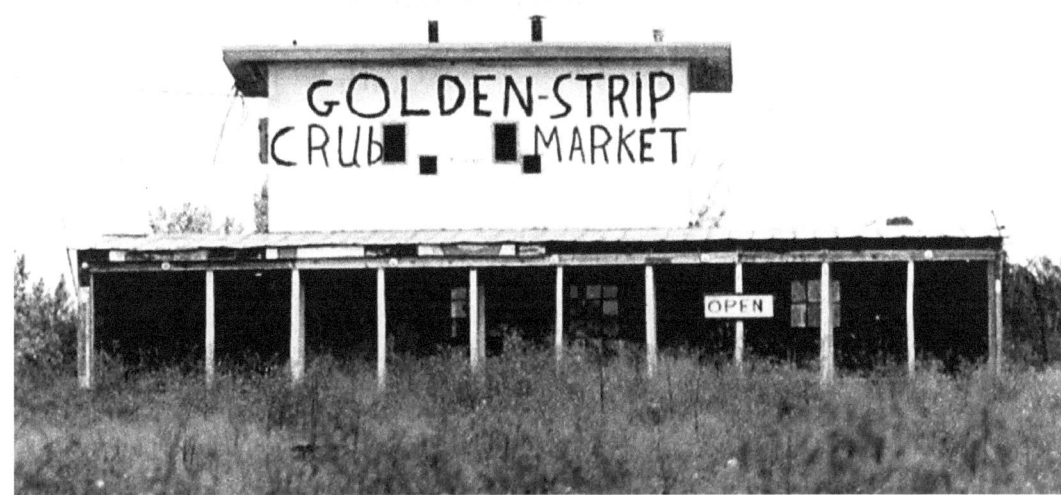

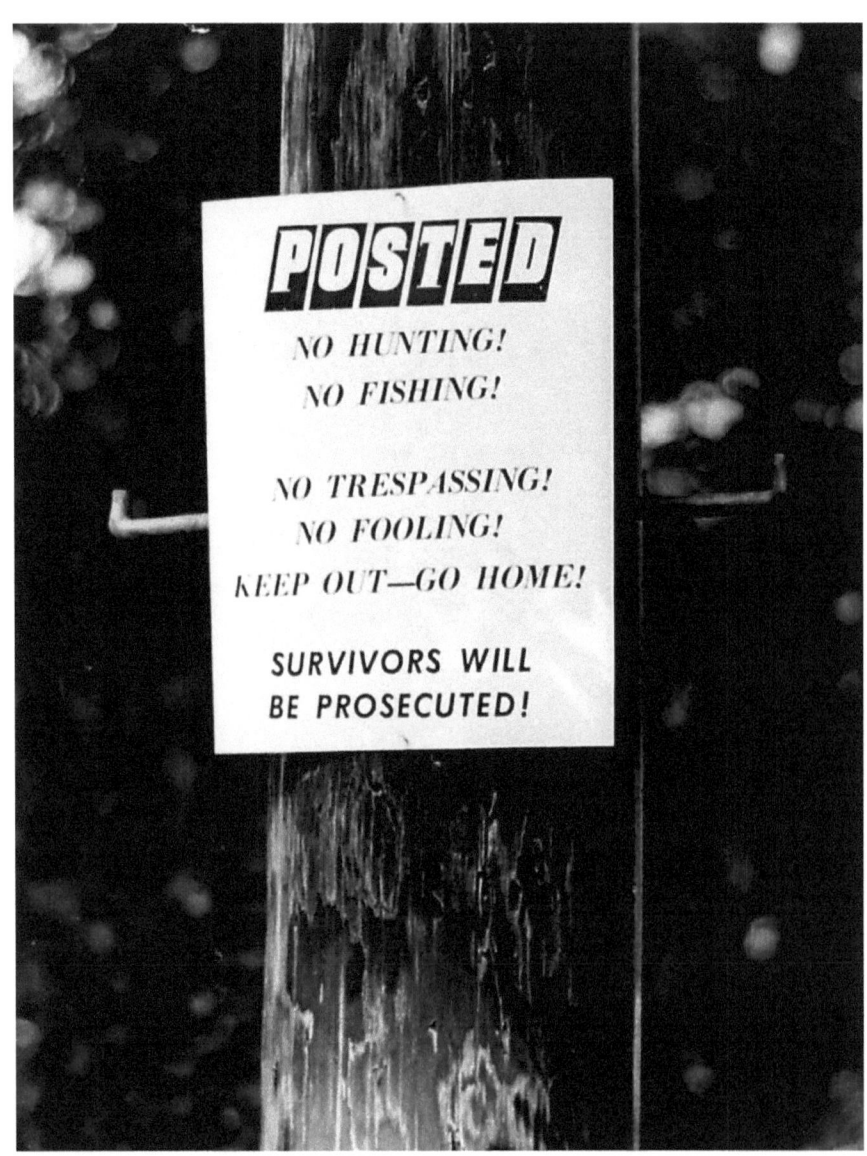

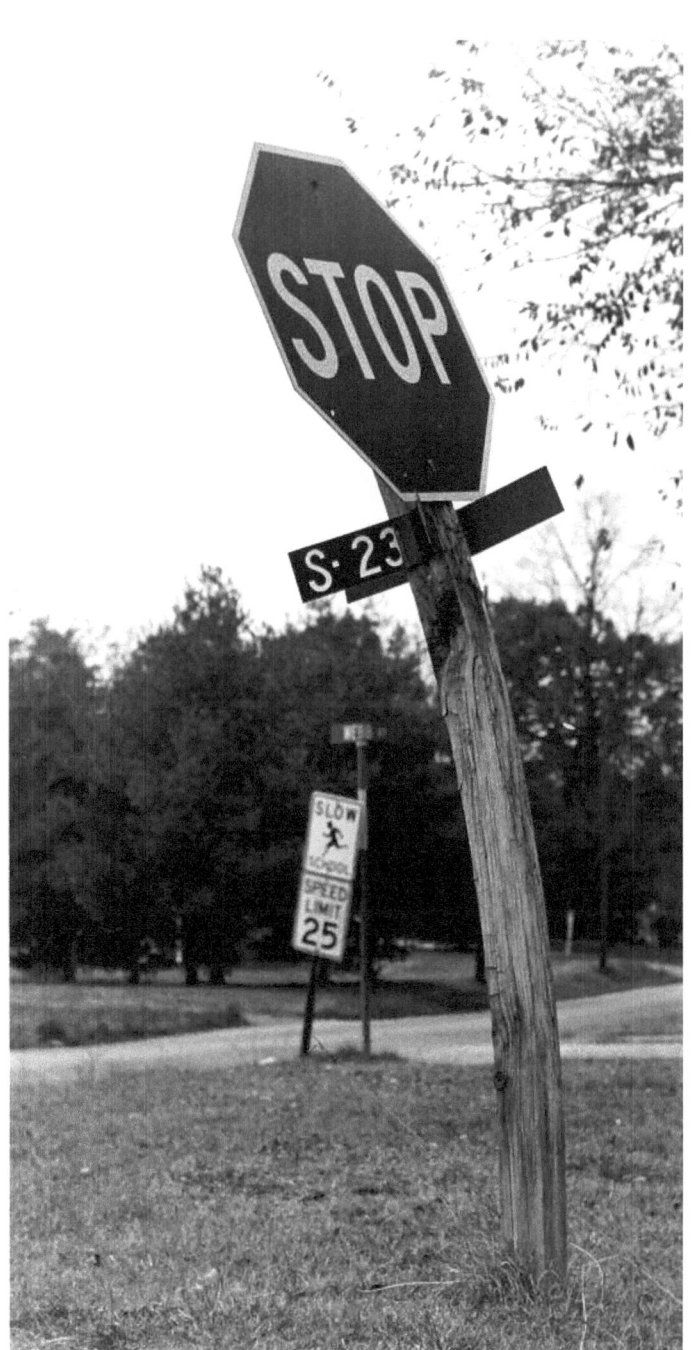

III

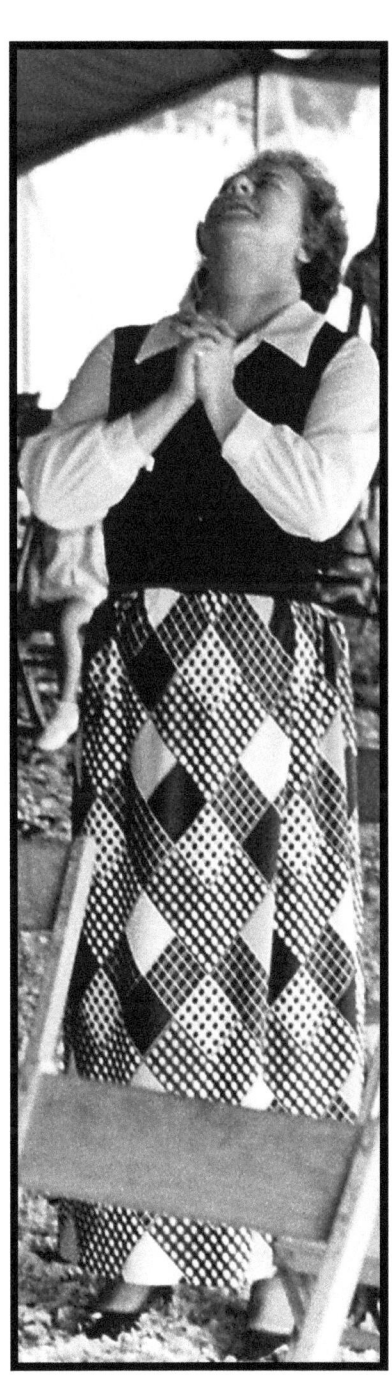

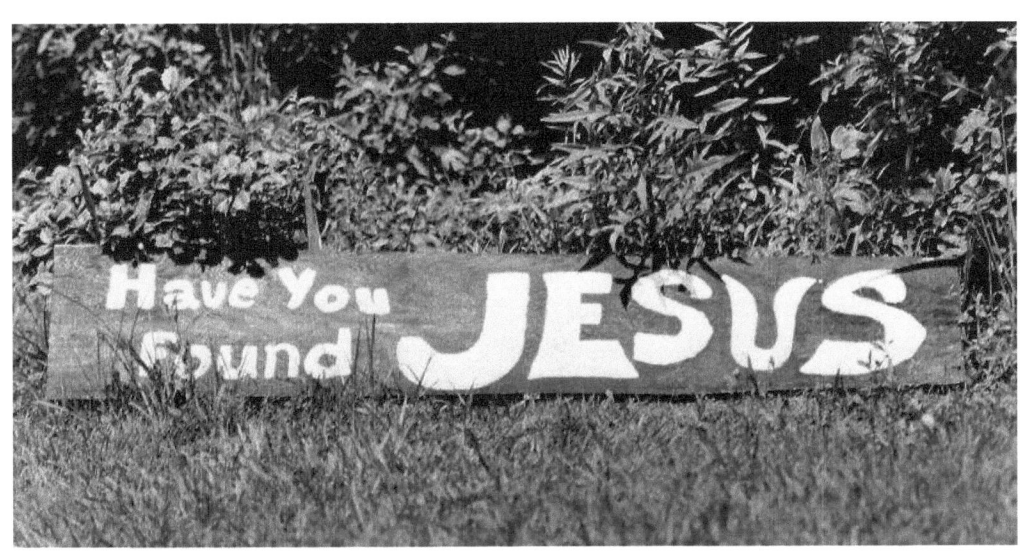

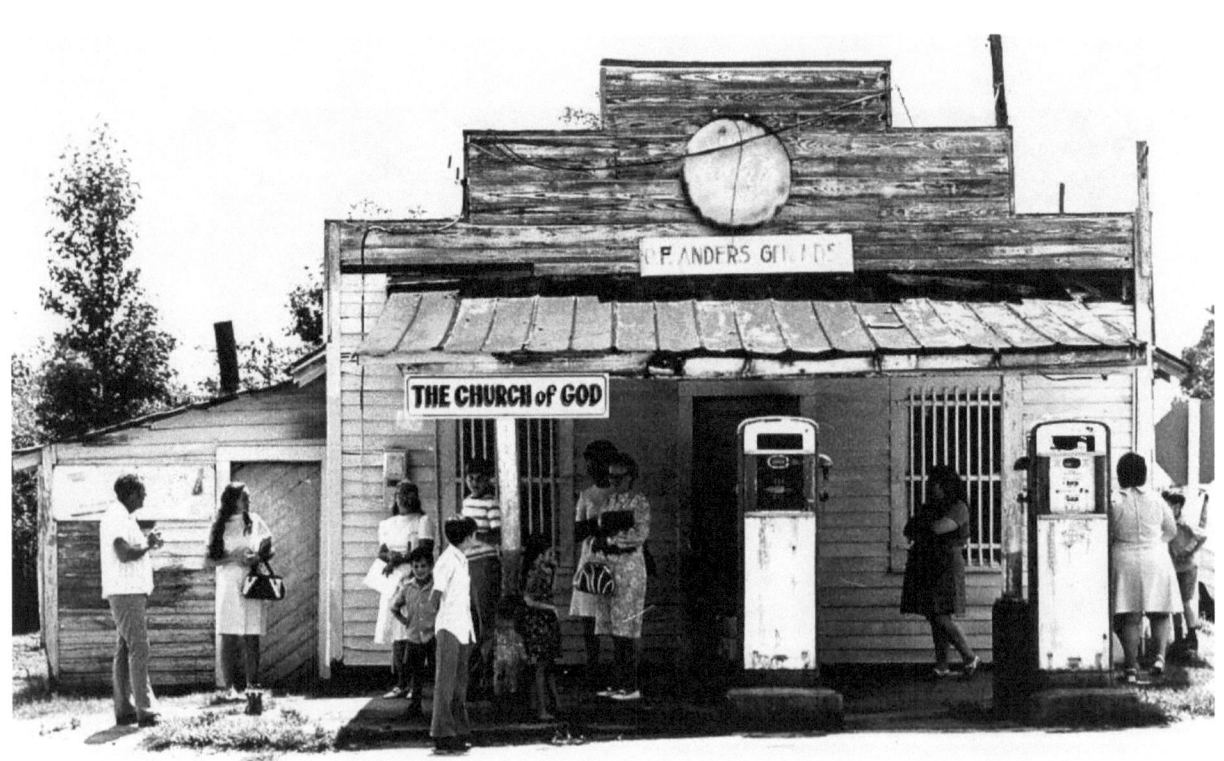

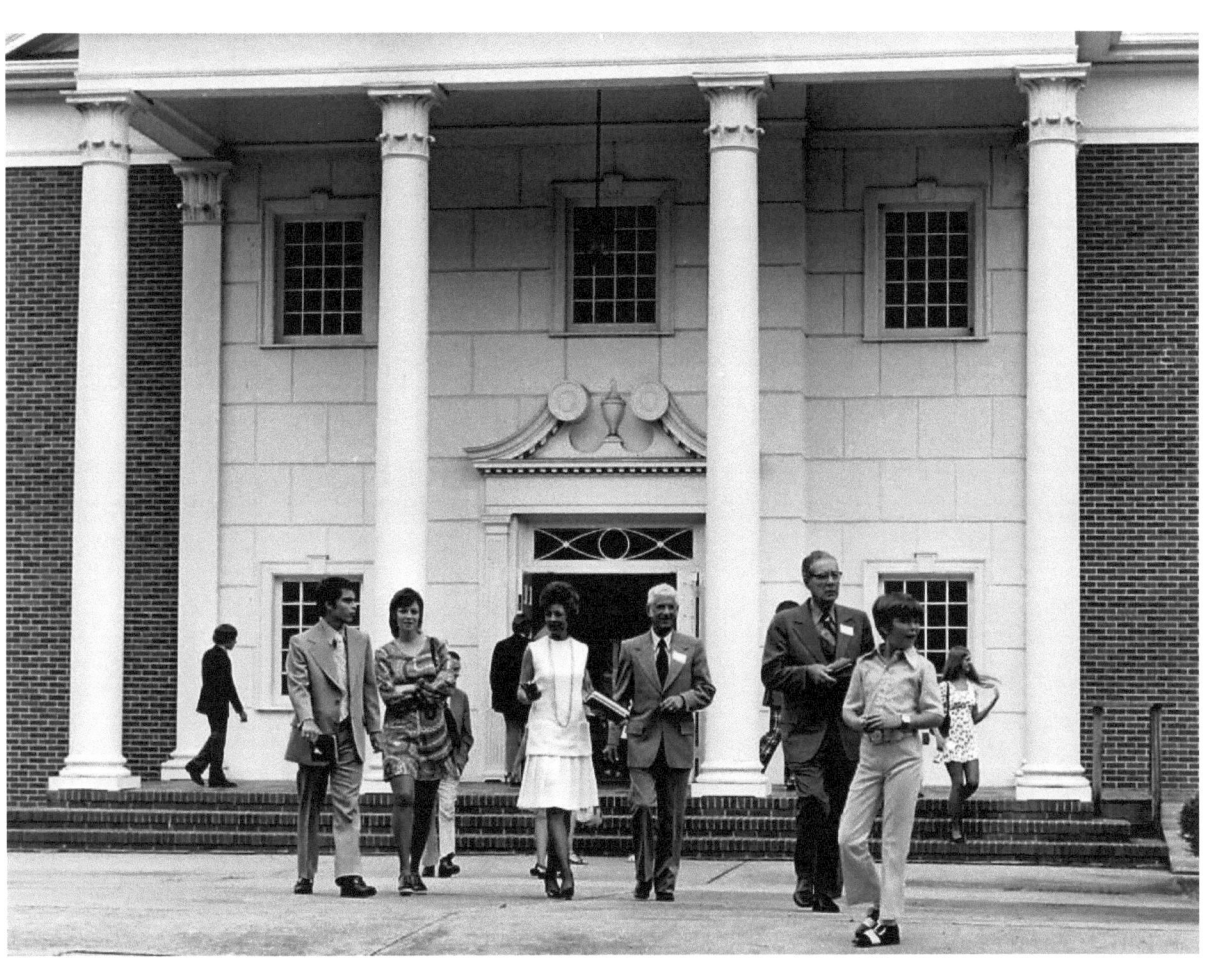

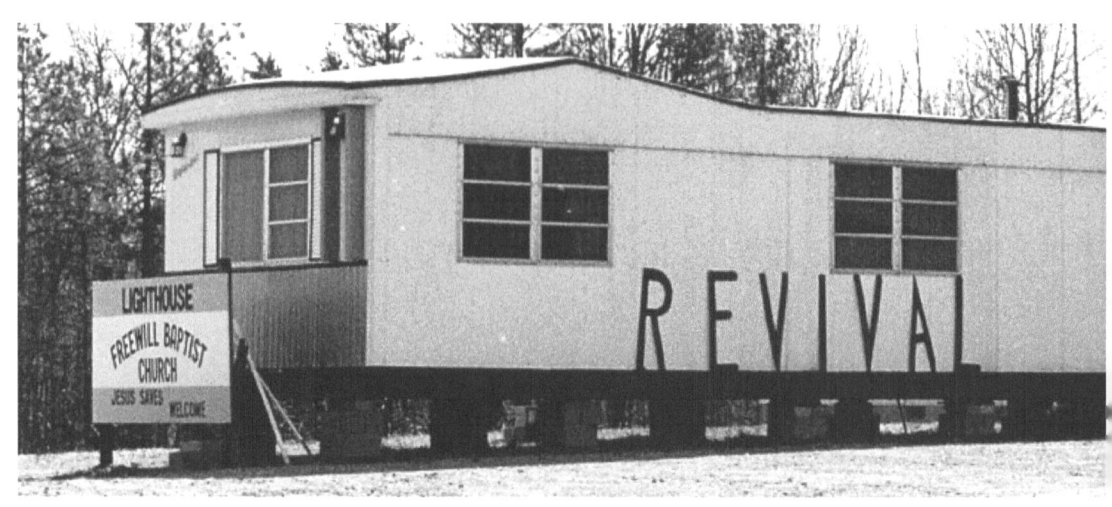

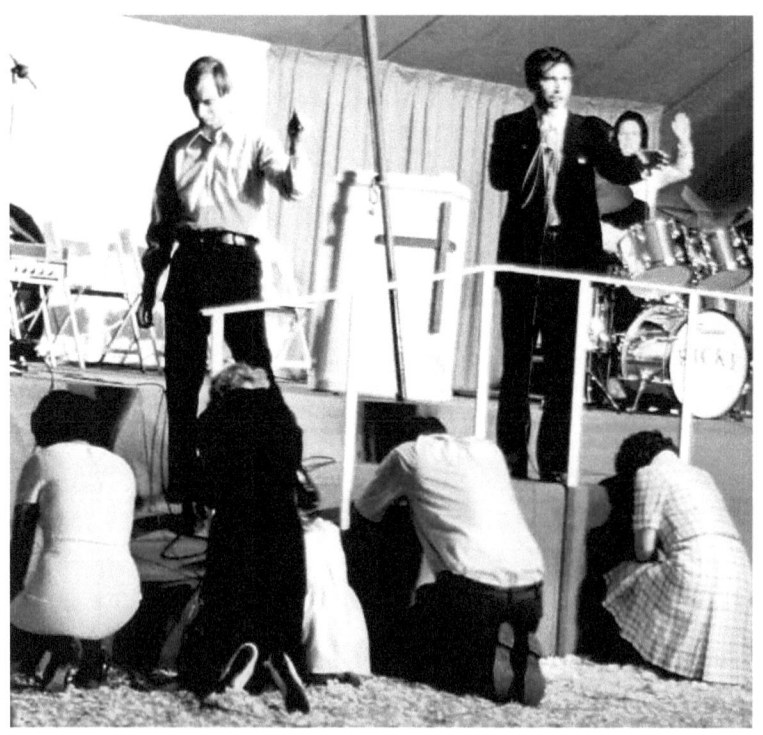

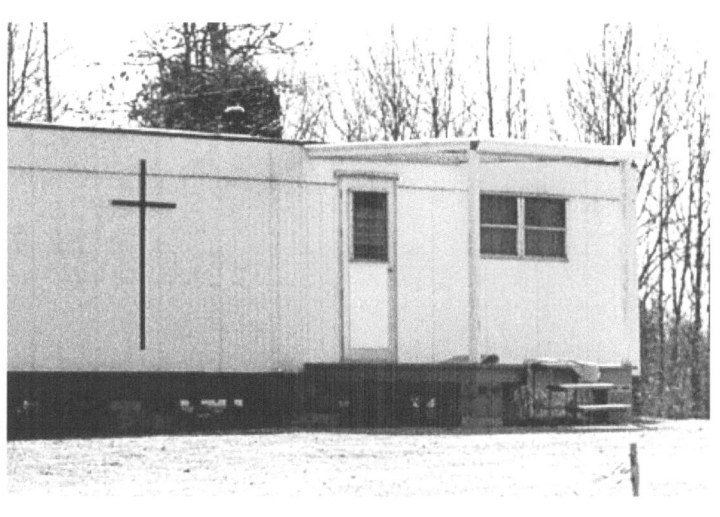

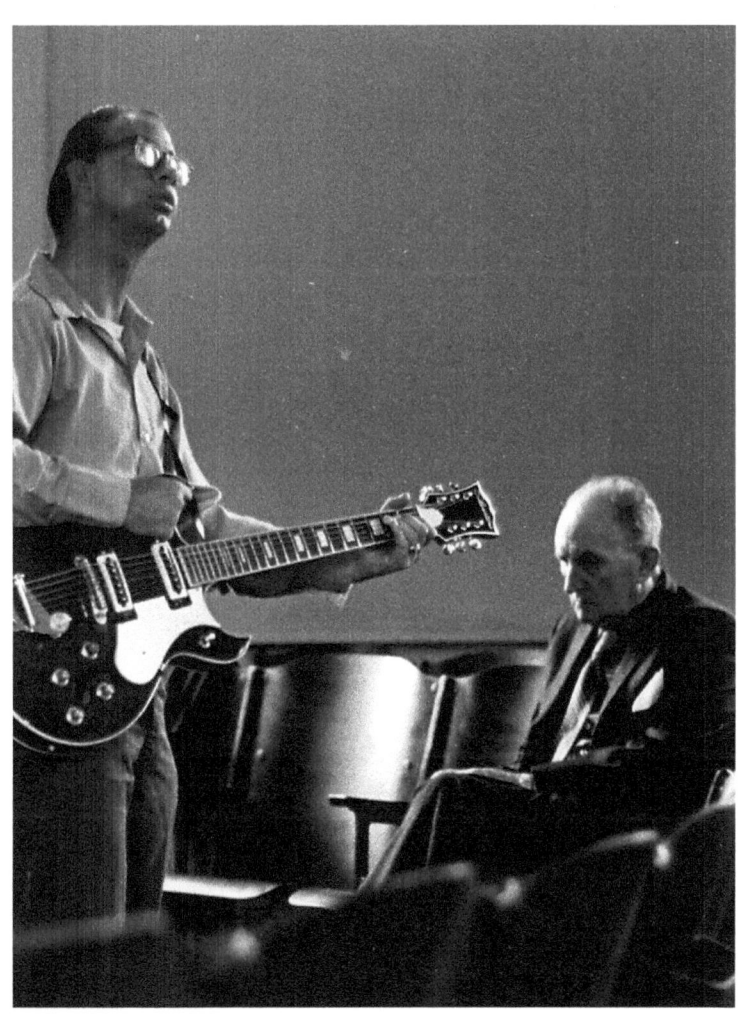

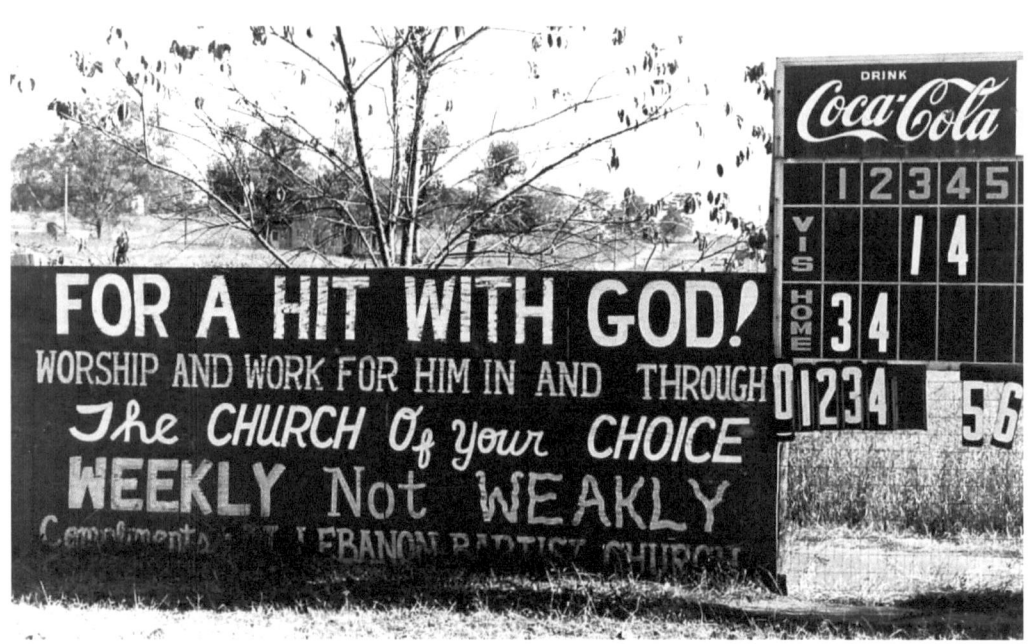

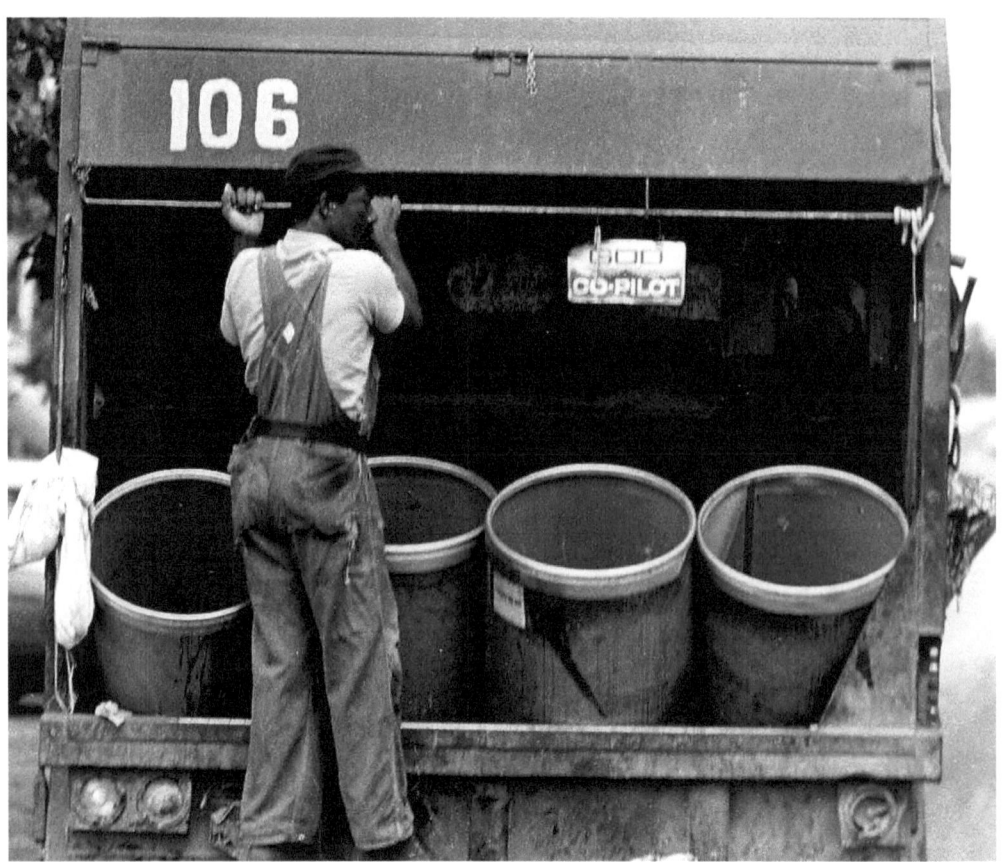

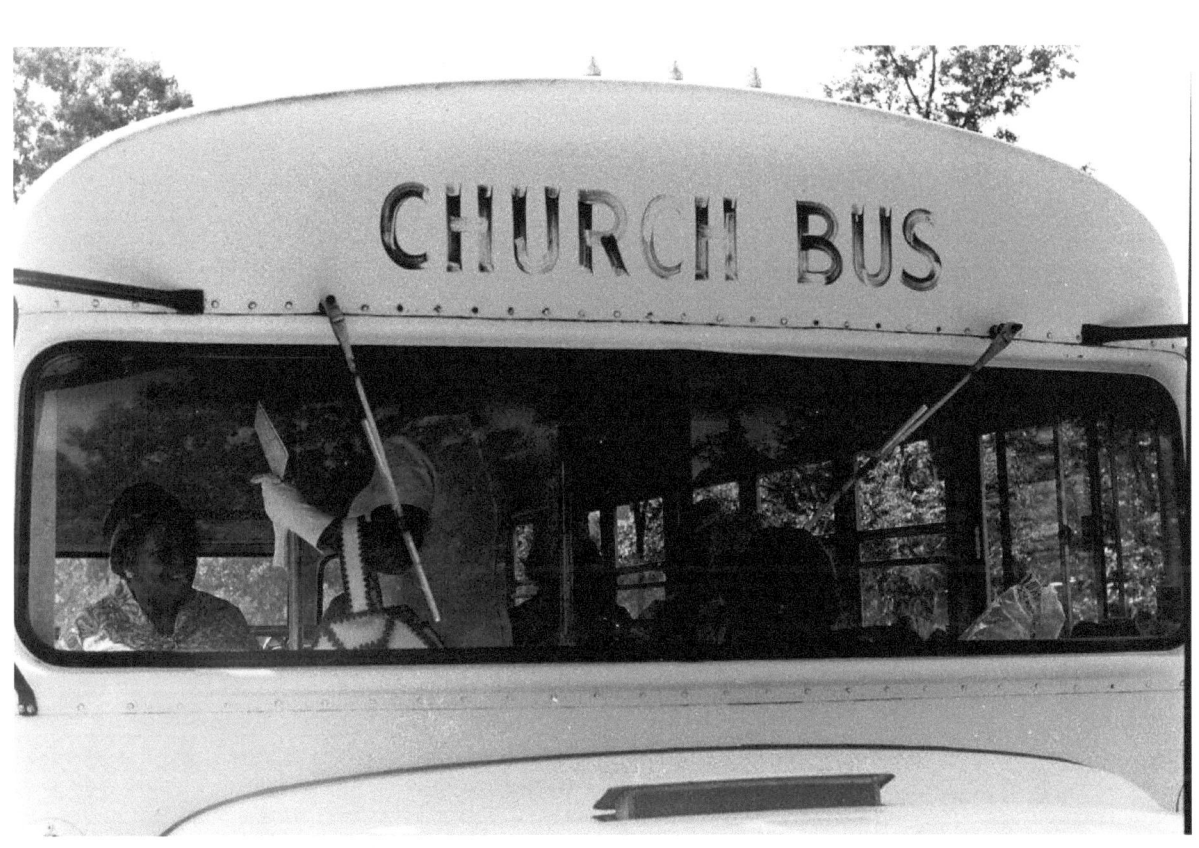

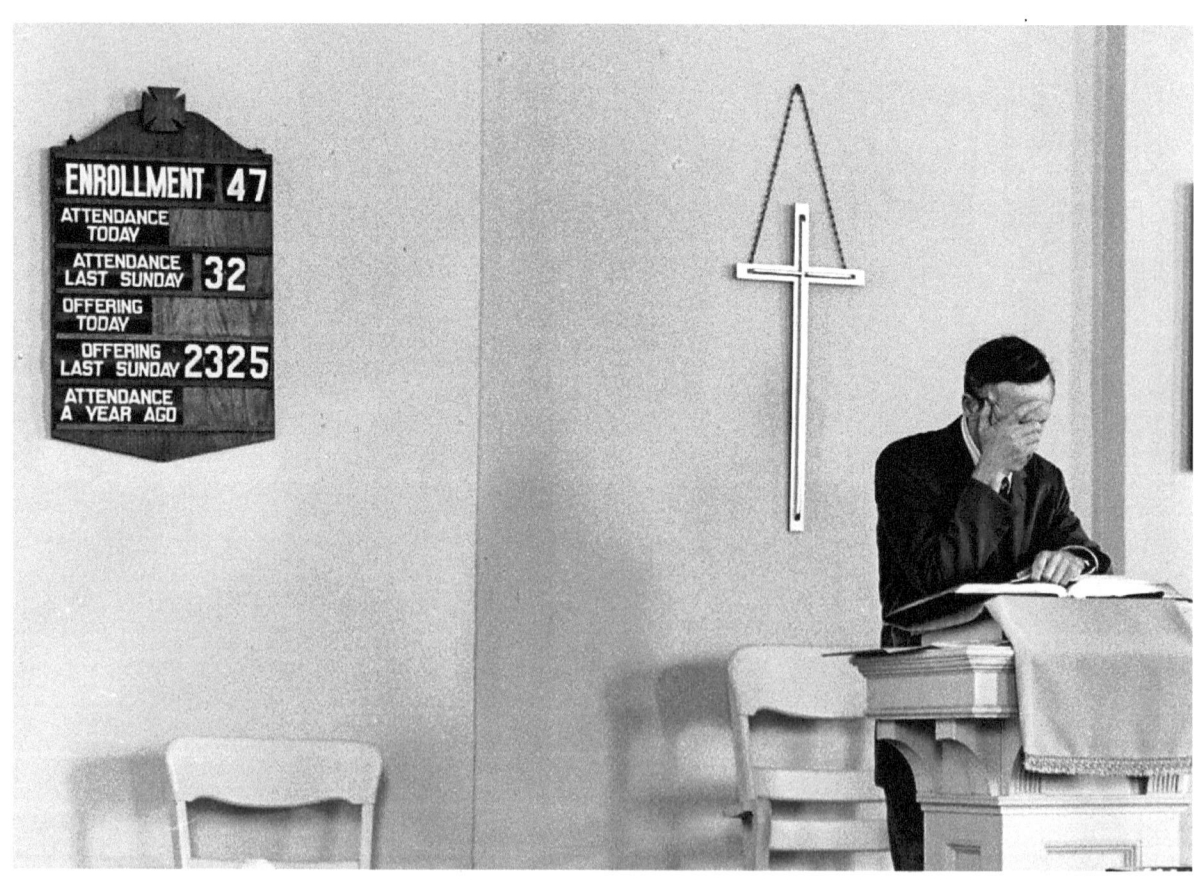

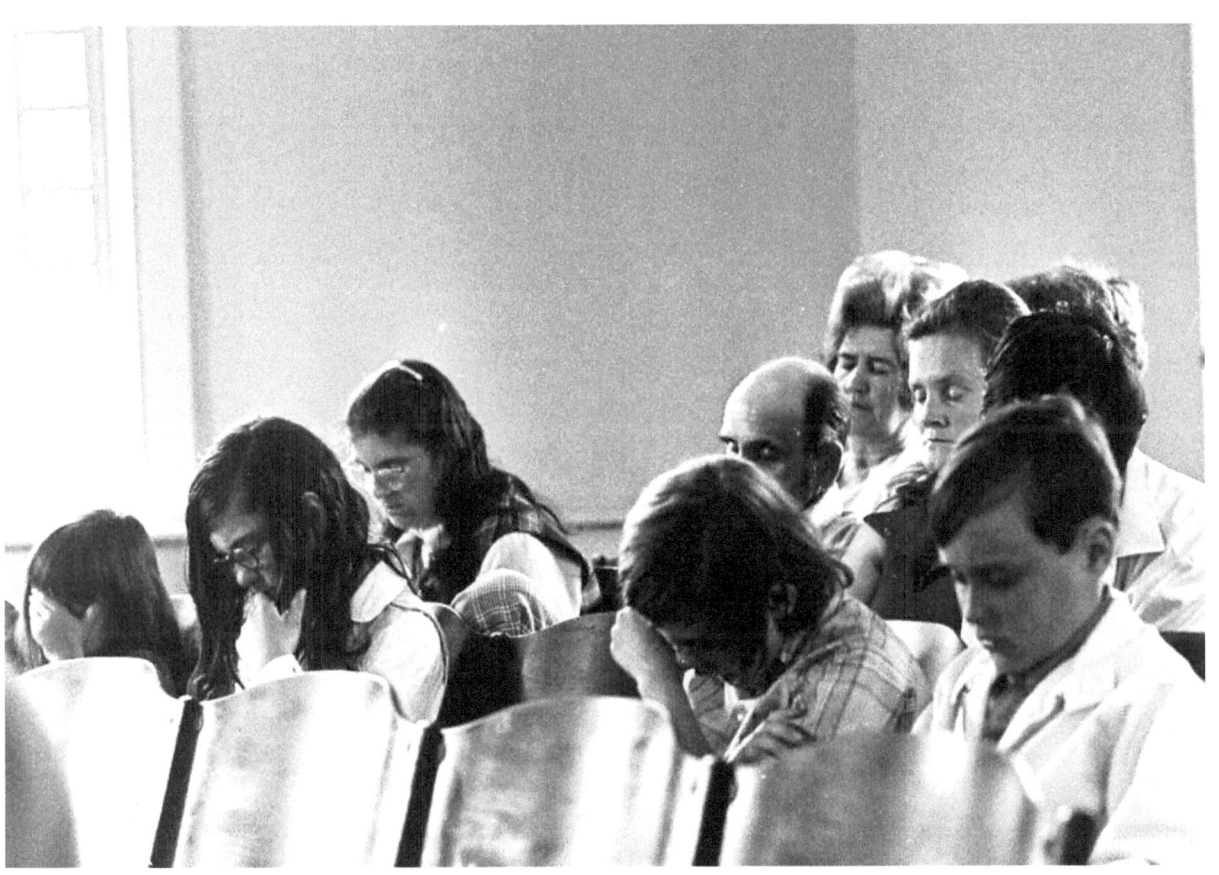

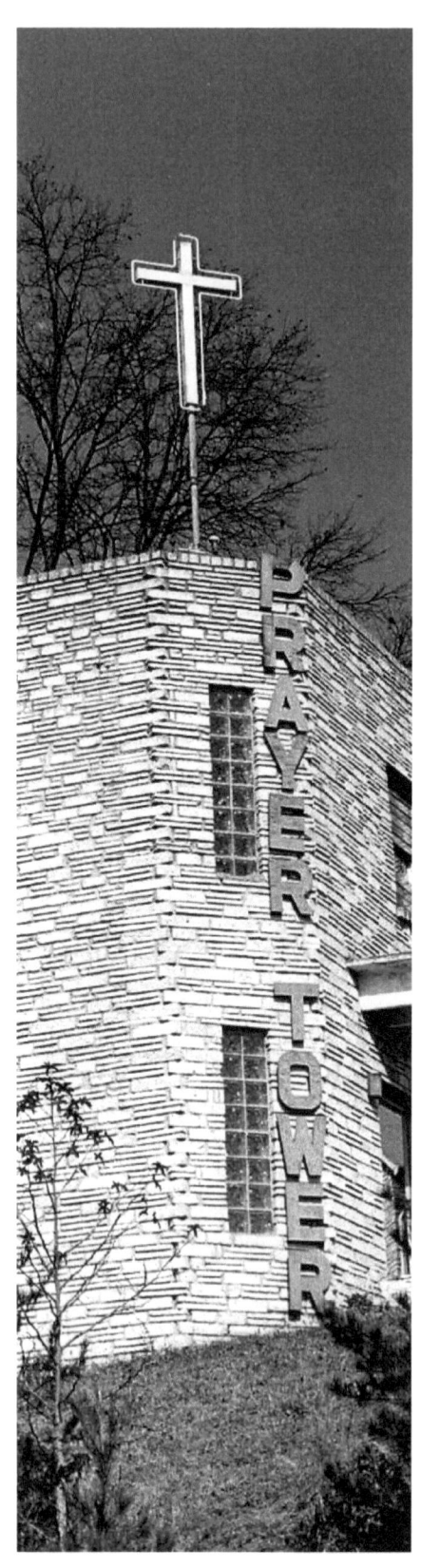

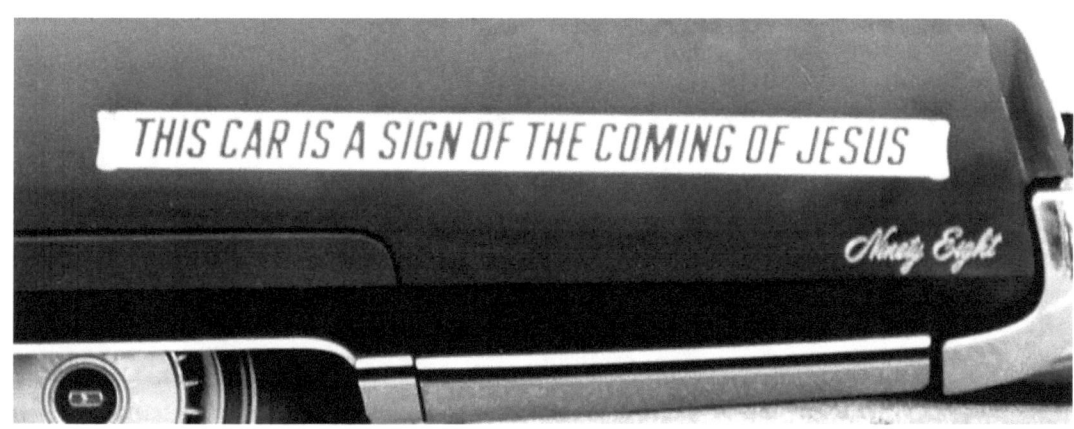

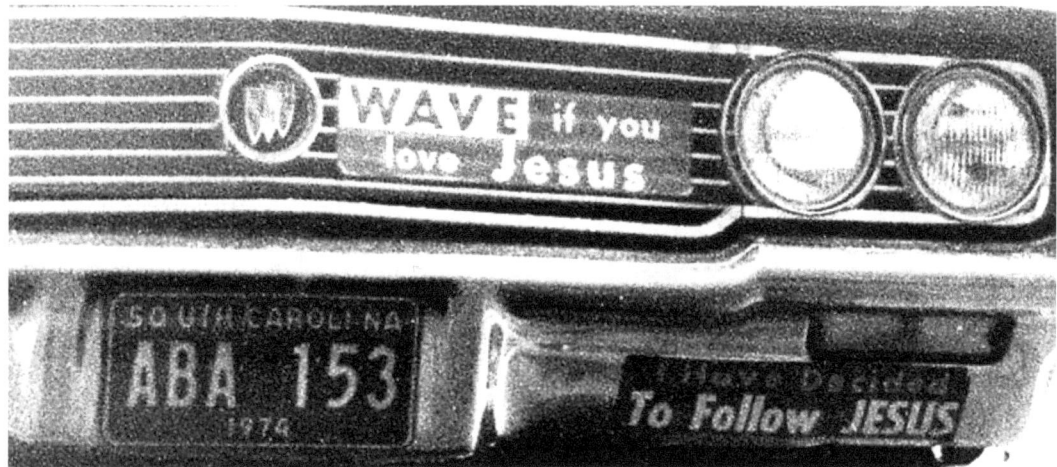

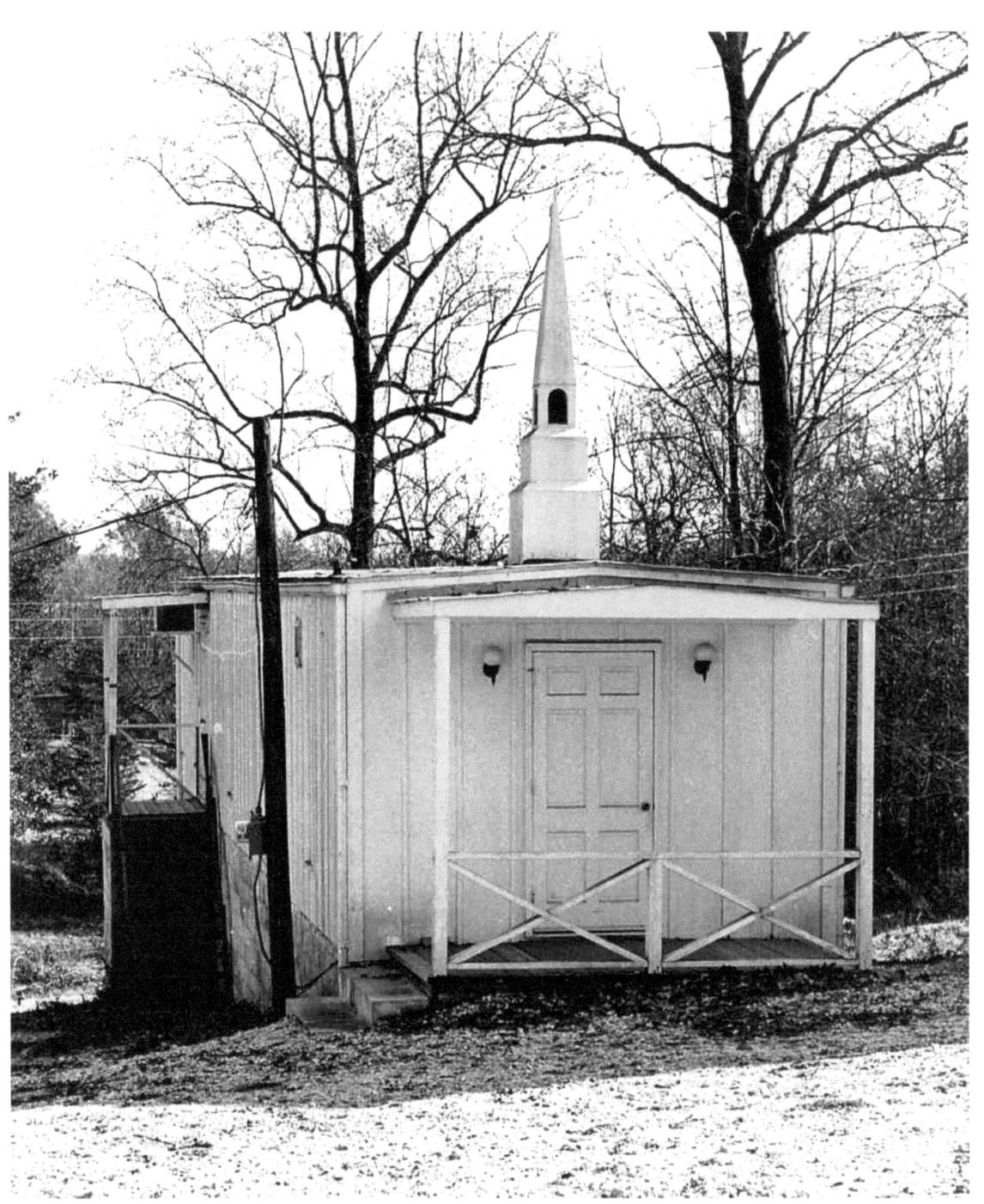

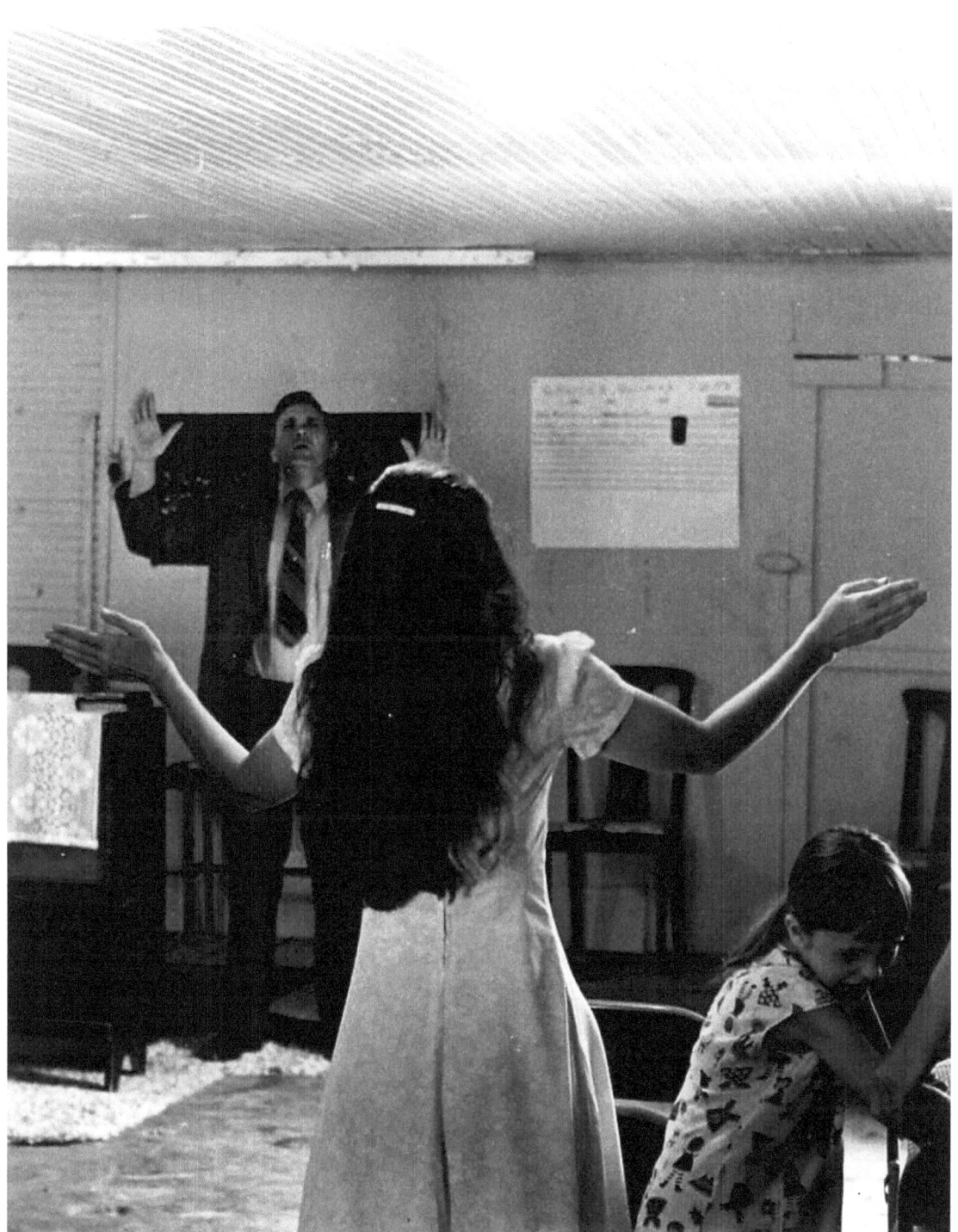

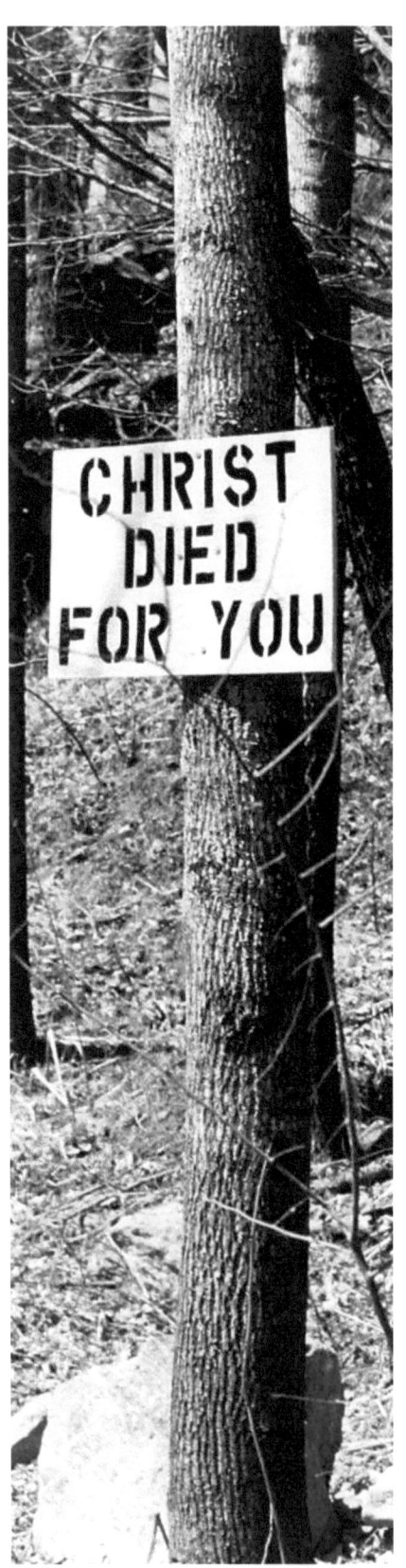
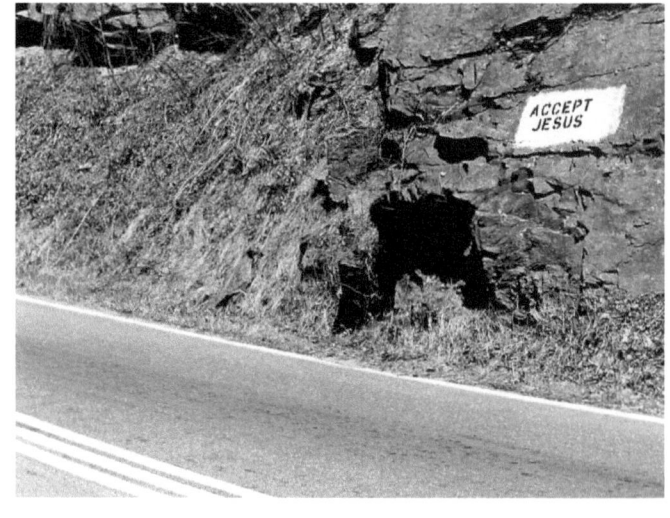

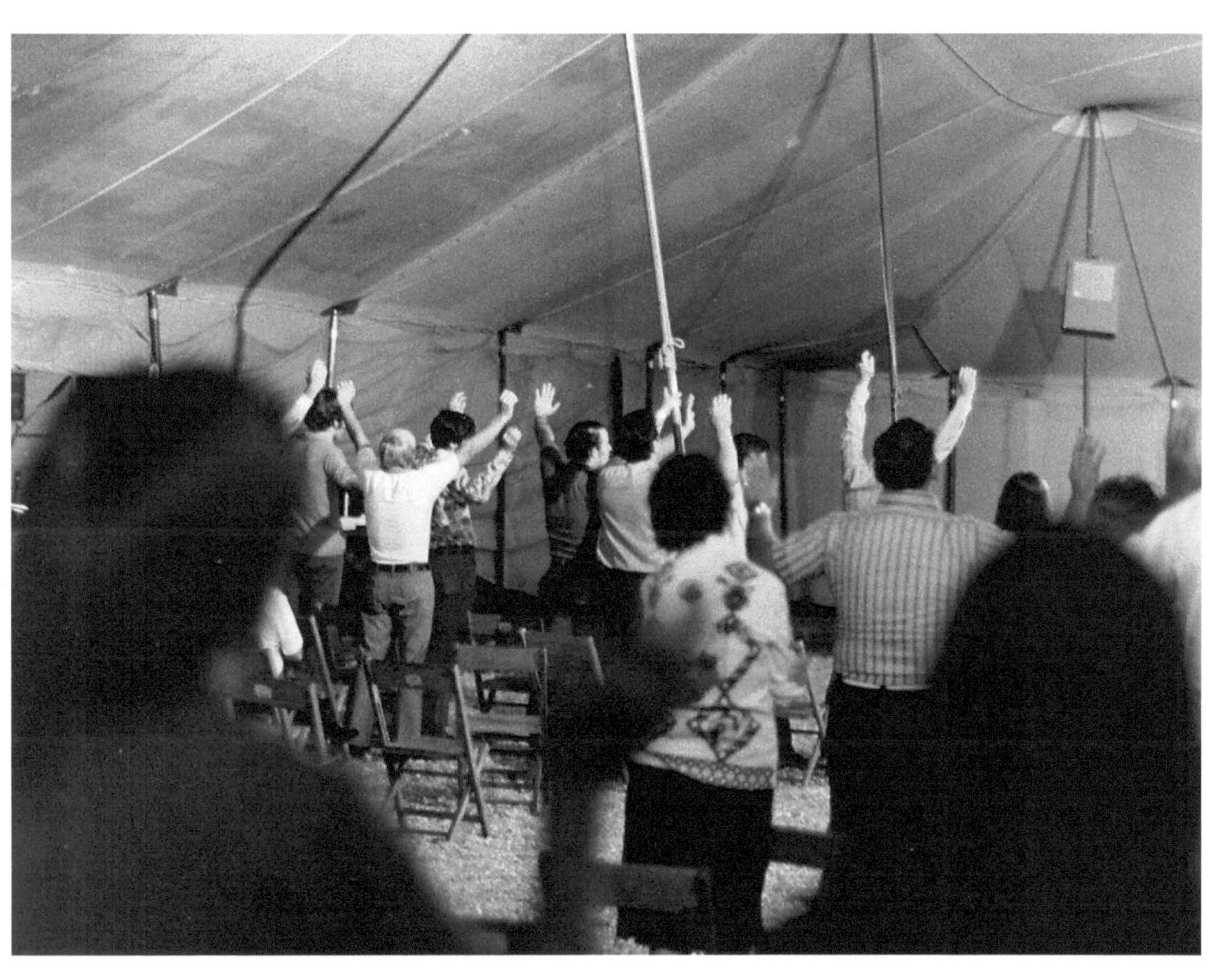

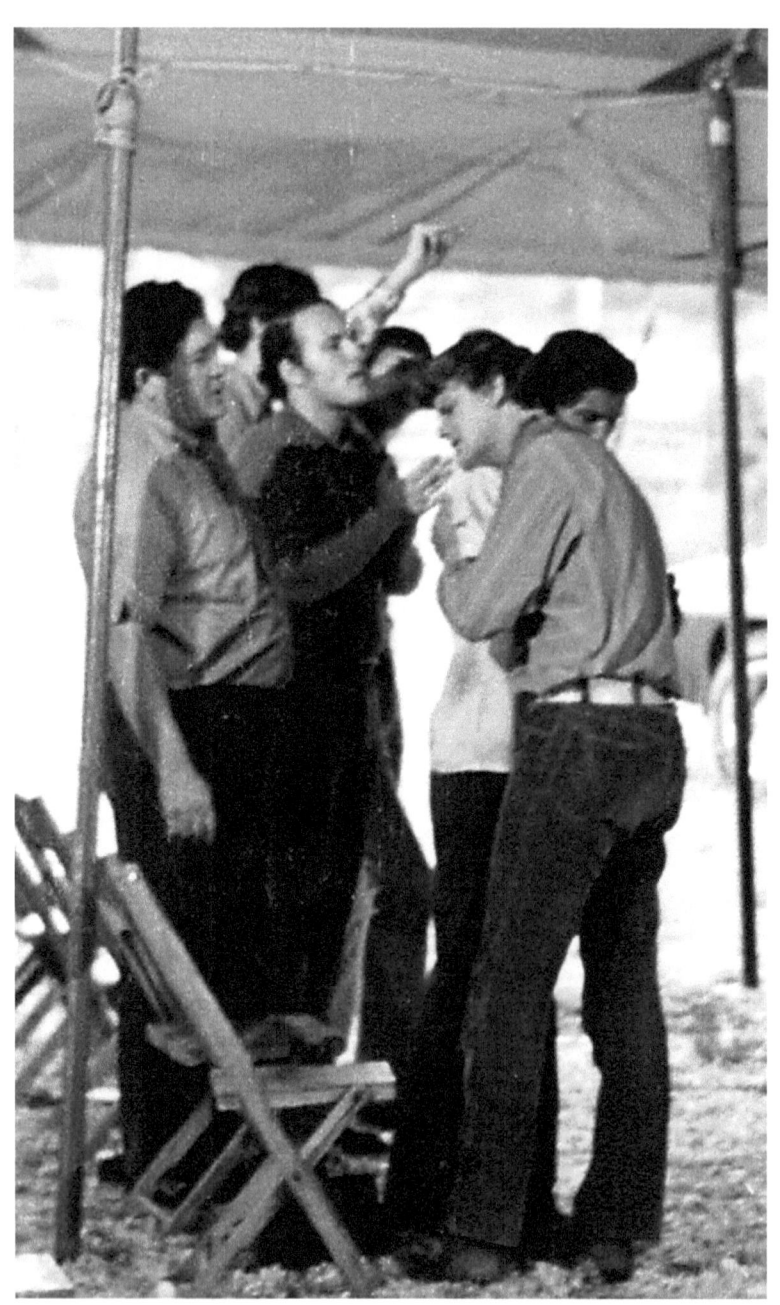

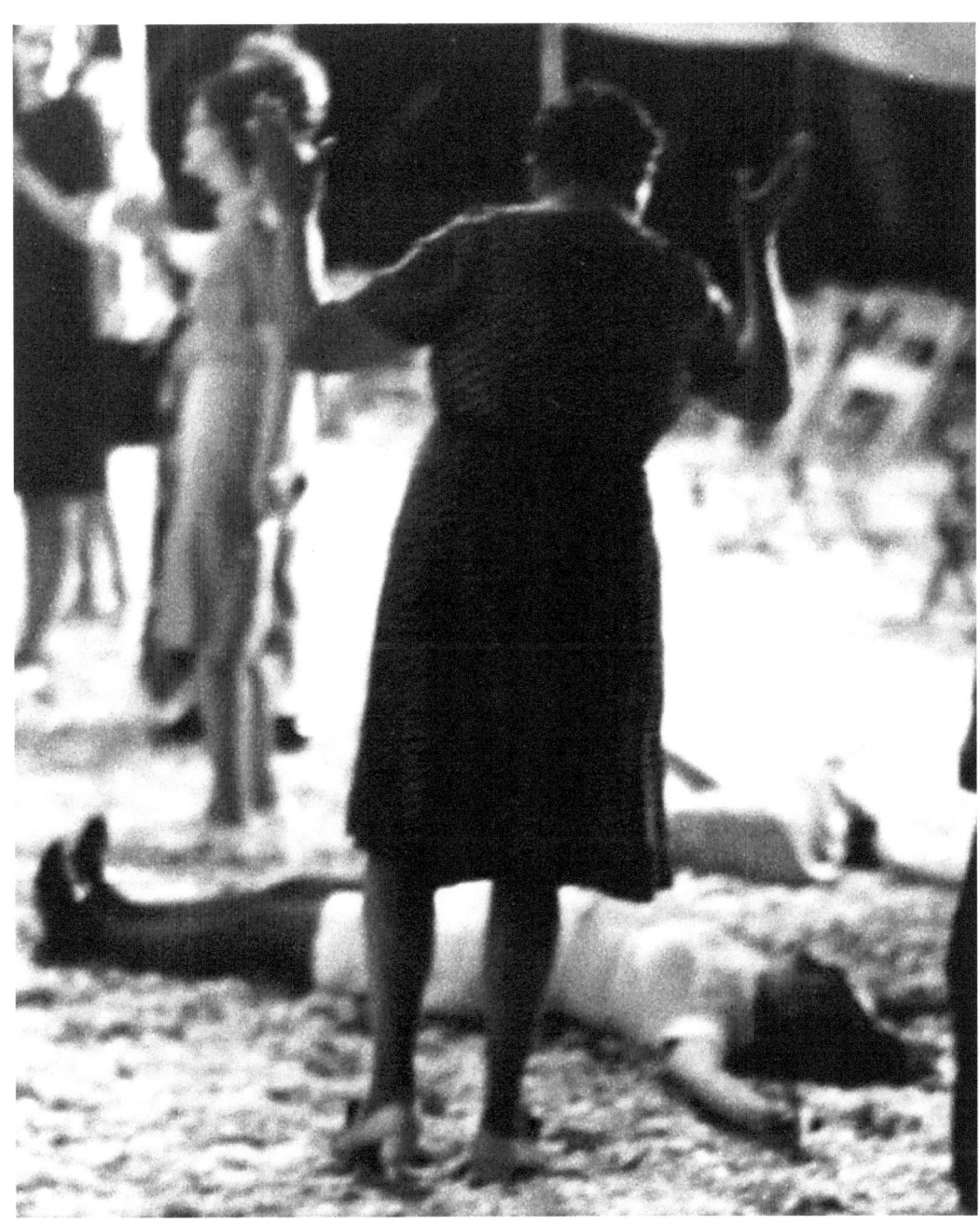

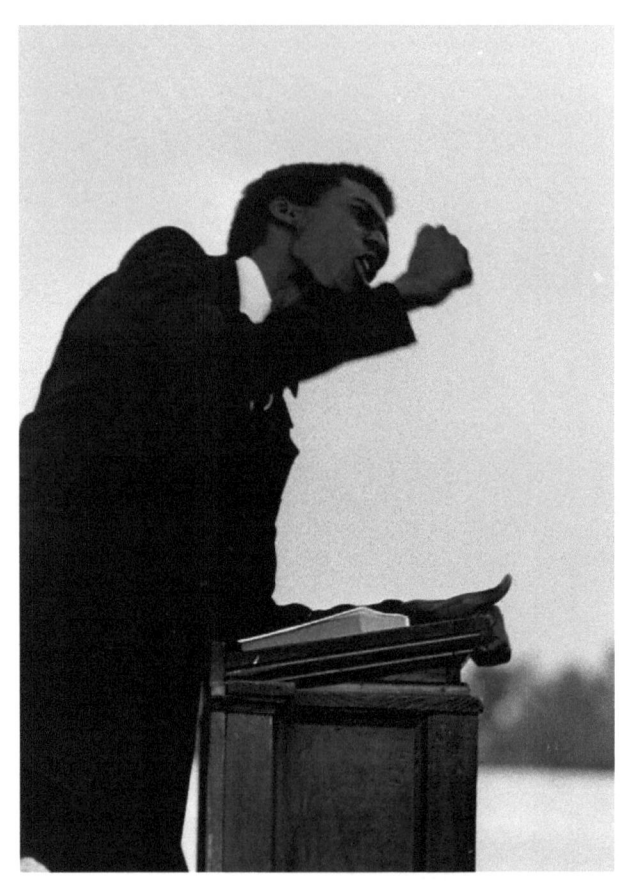
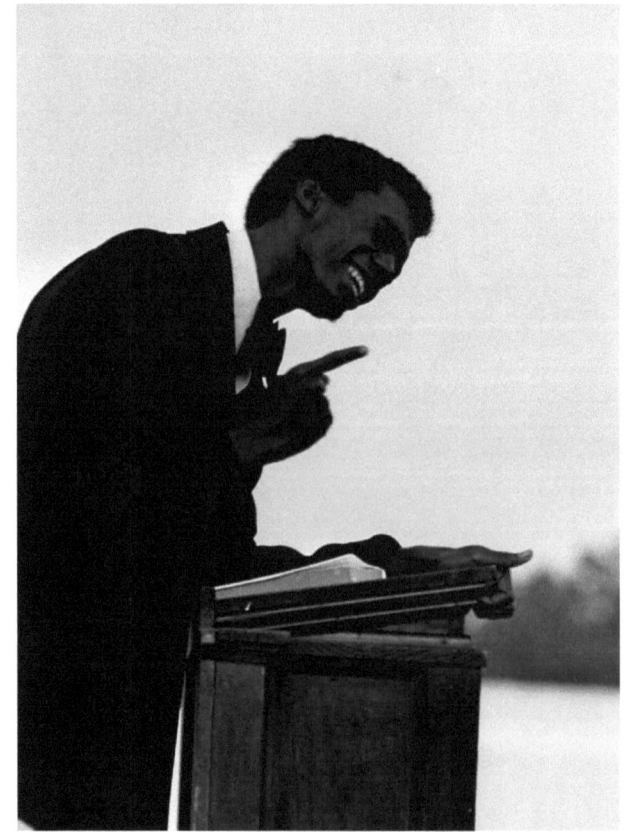

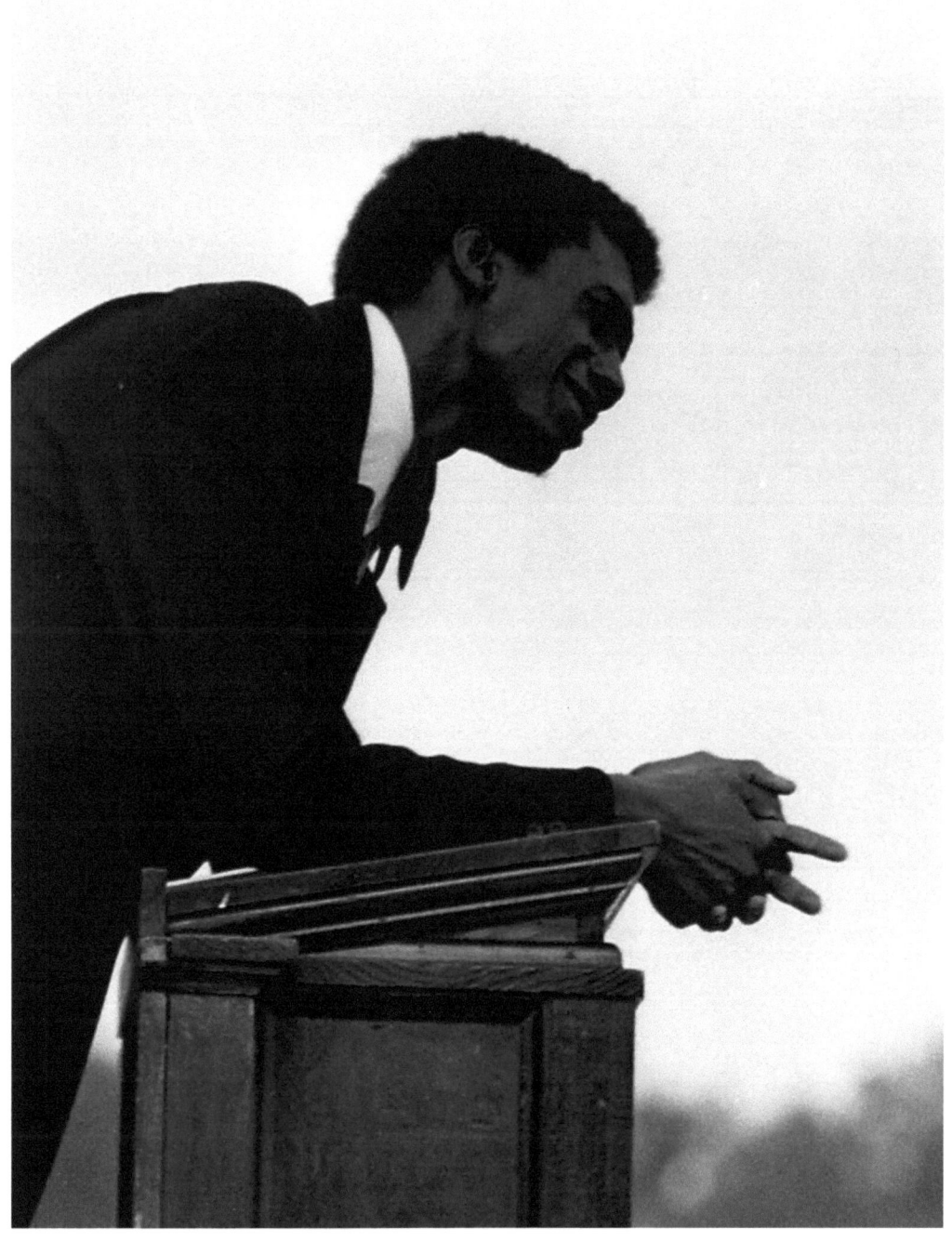

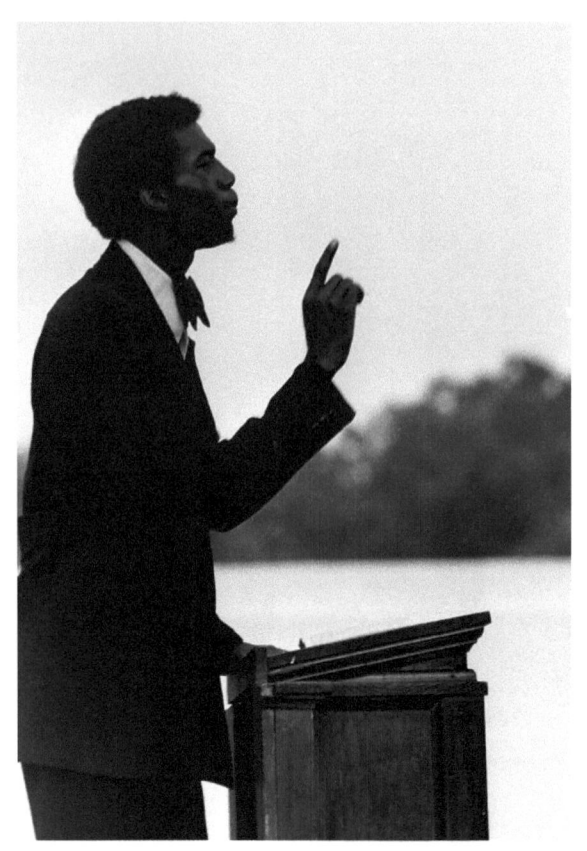
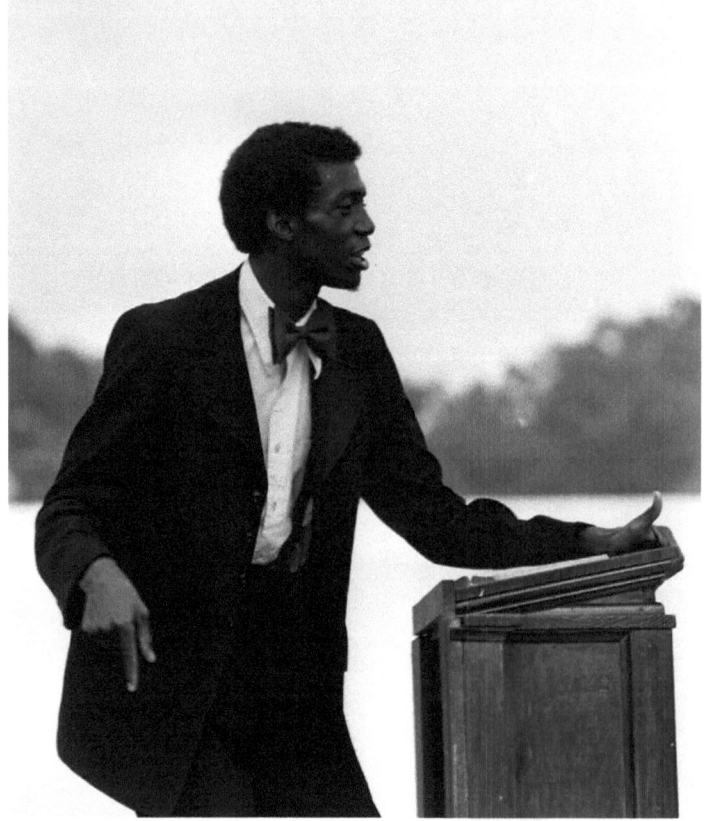

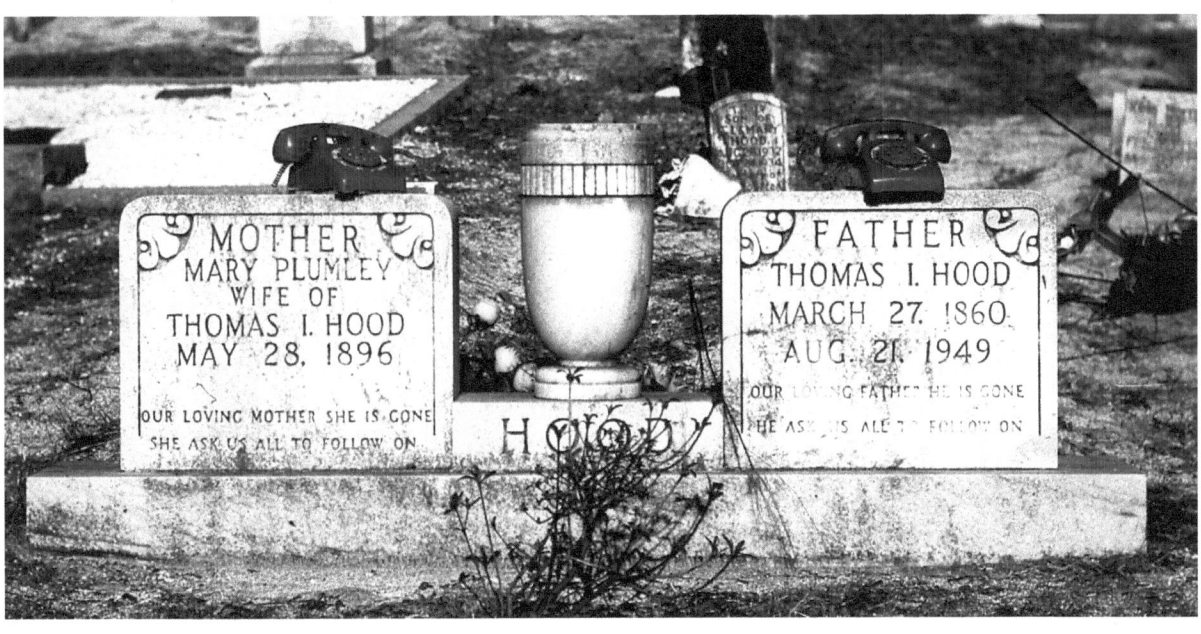

IV

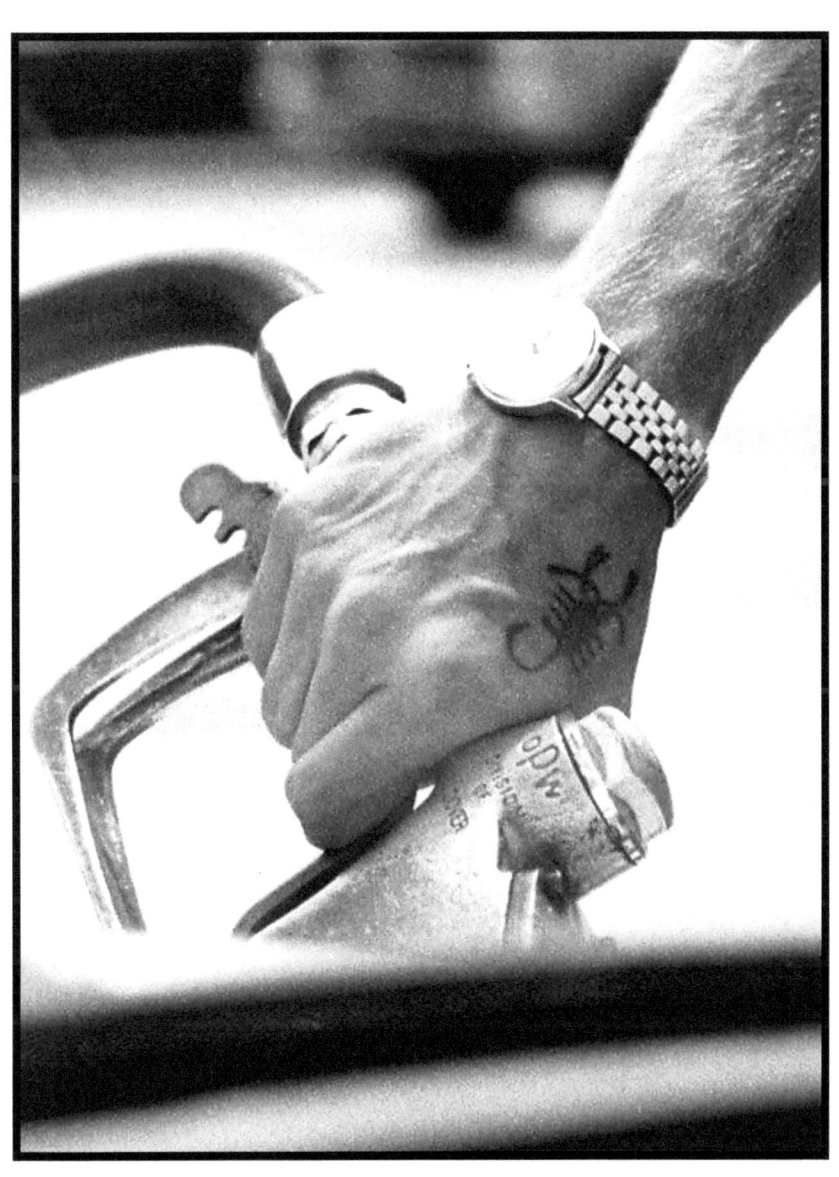

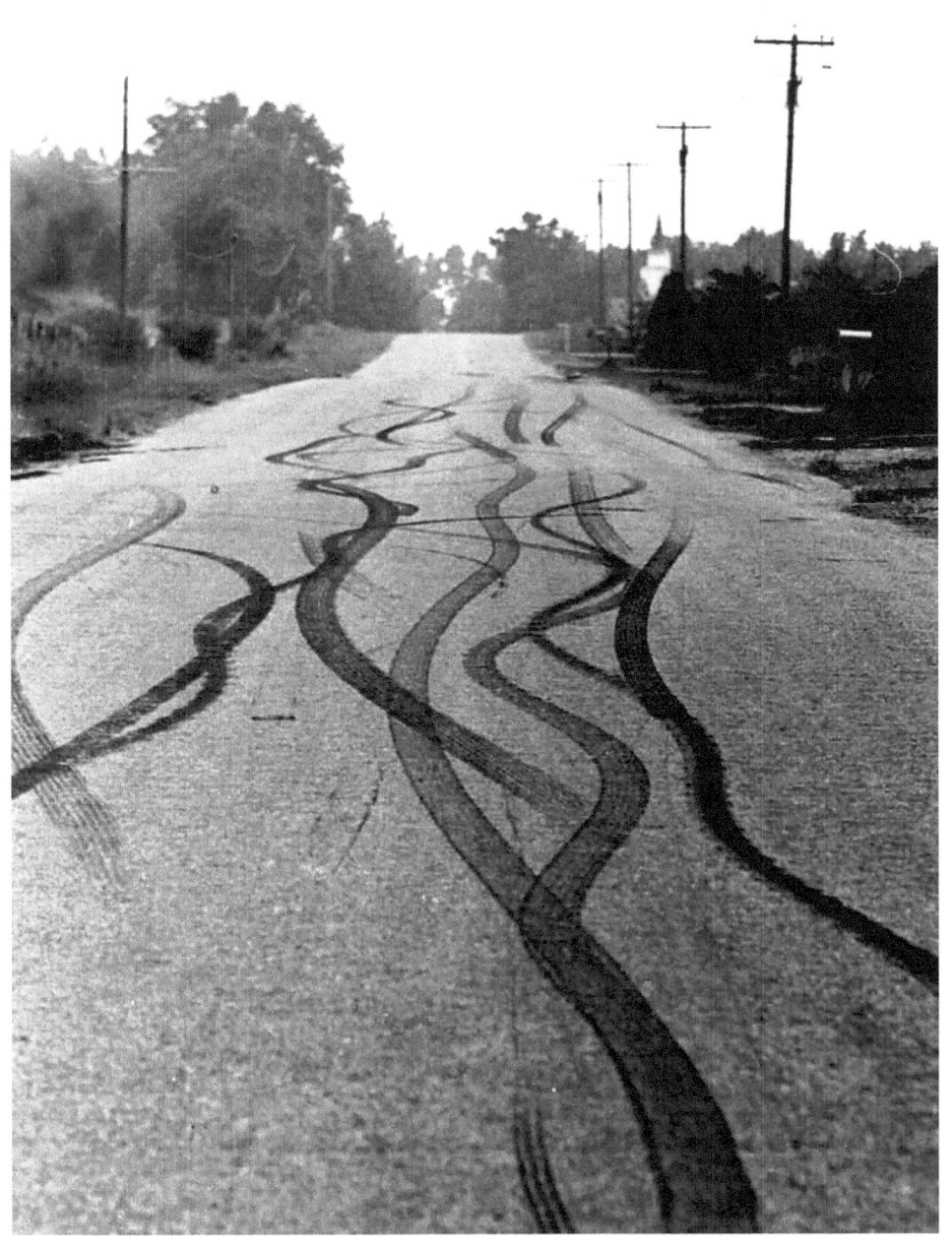

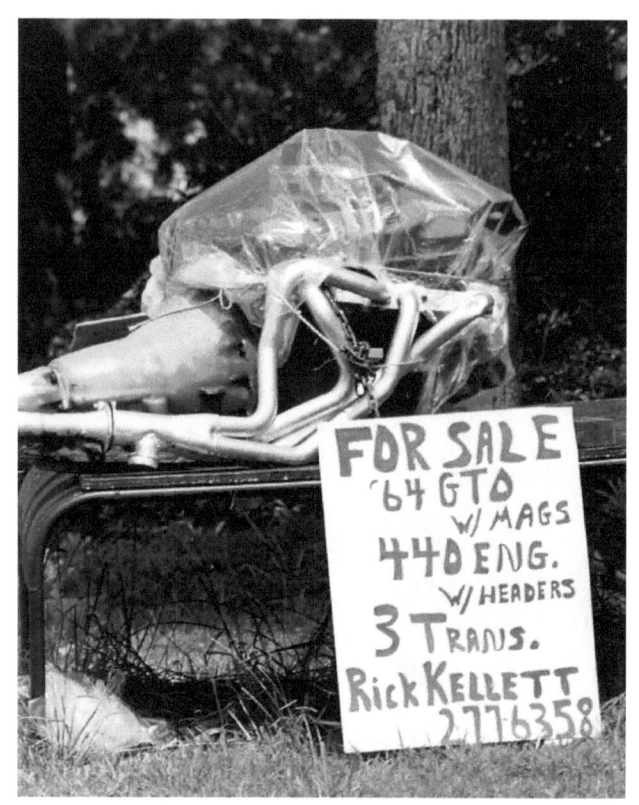

FOR SALE
'64 GTO
W/ MAGS
440 ENG.
W/ HEADERS
3 TRANS.
Rick KELLETT
2776358

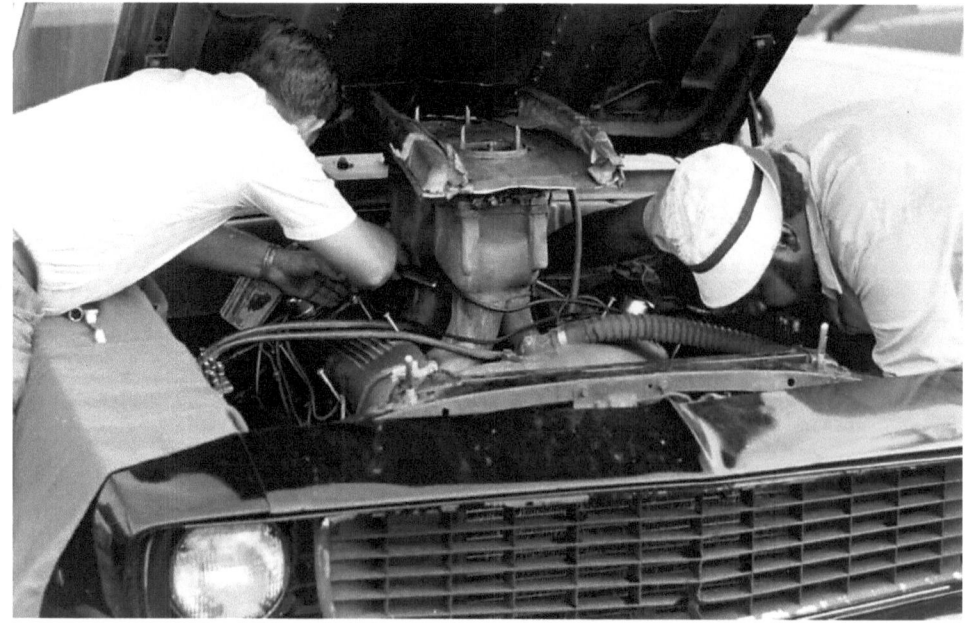

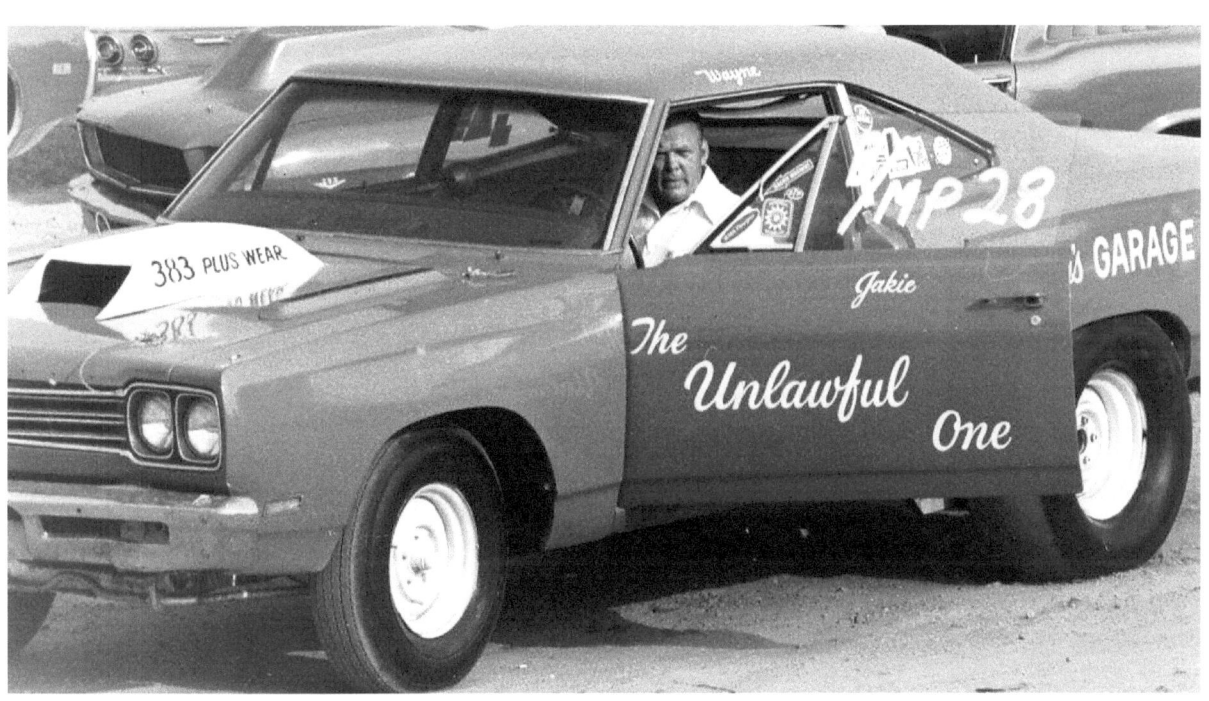

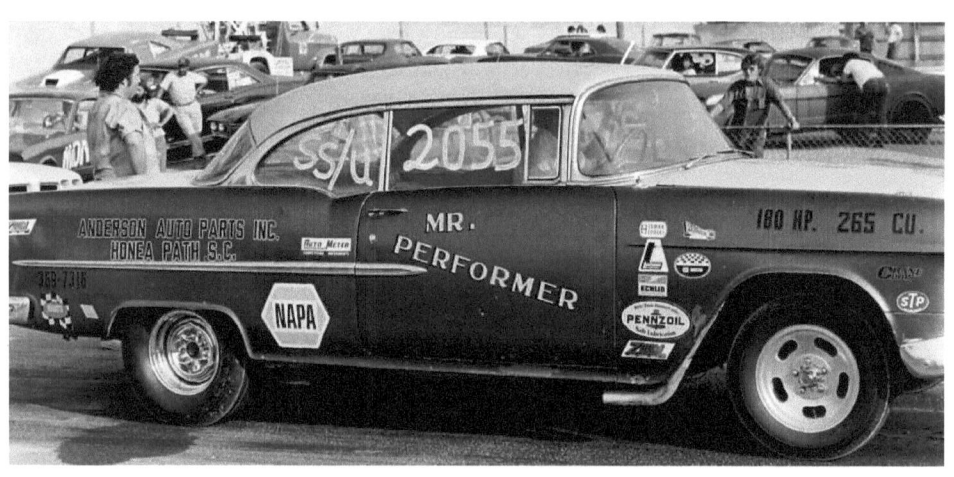

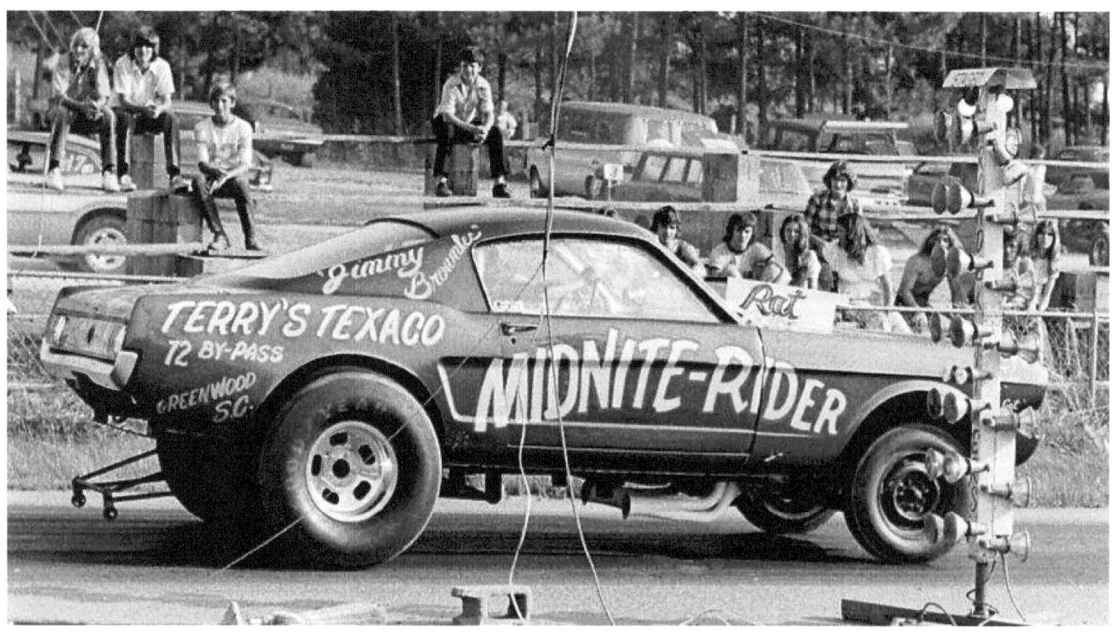

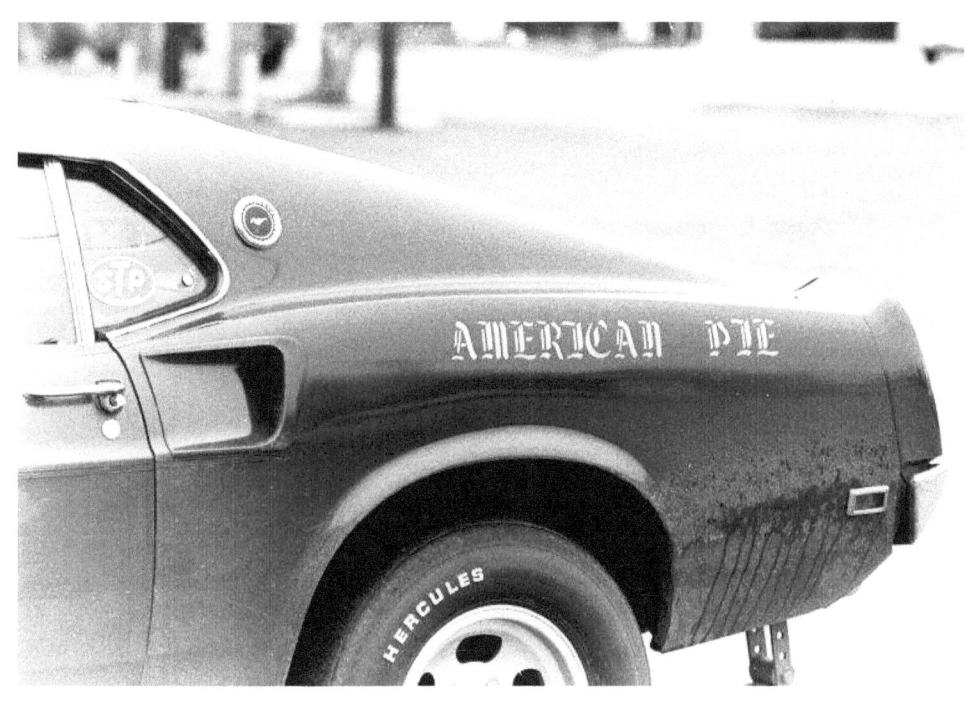

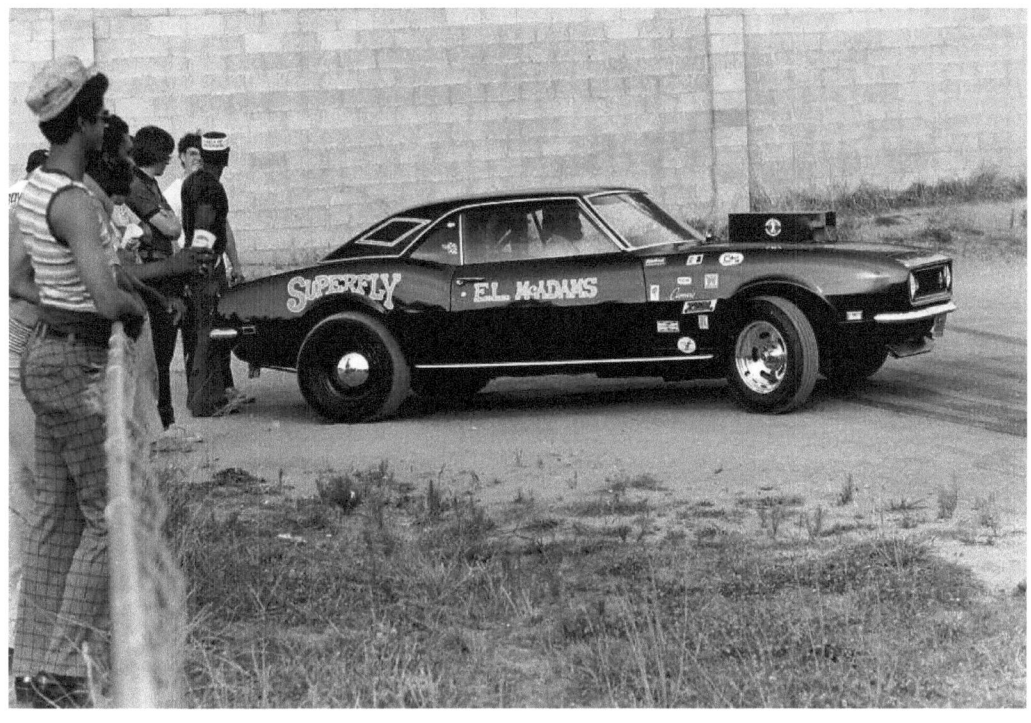

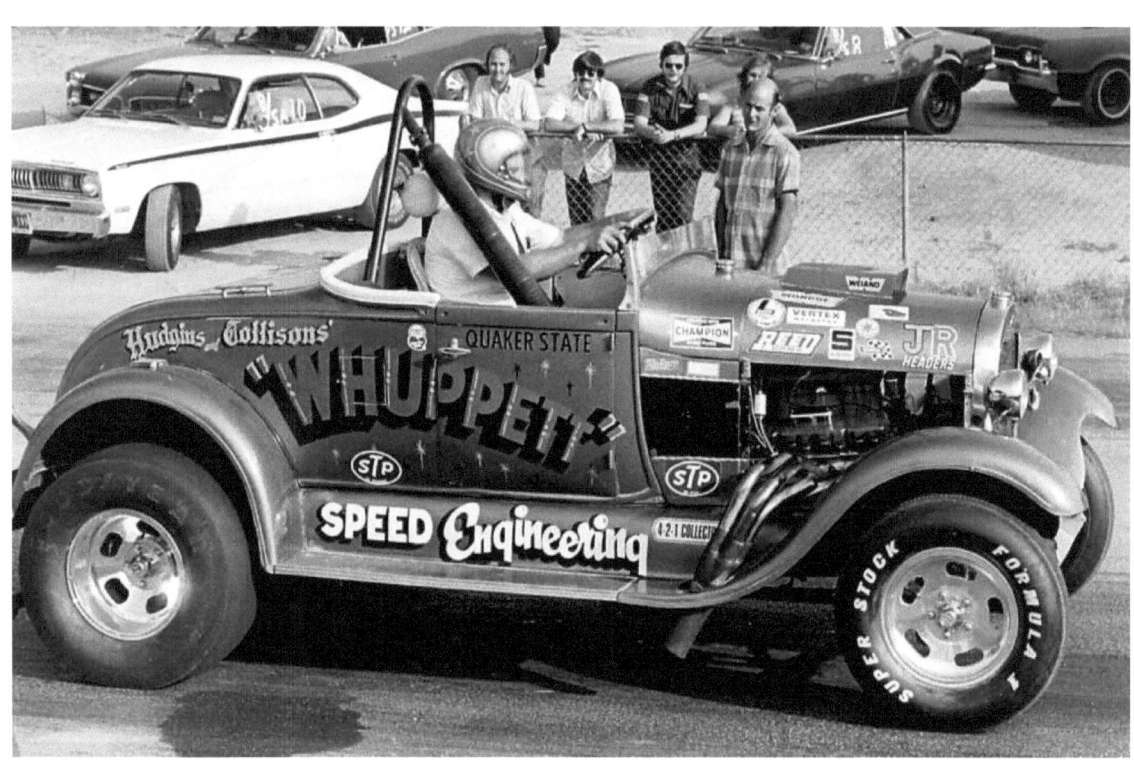

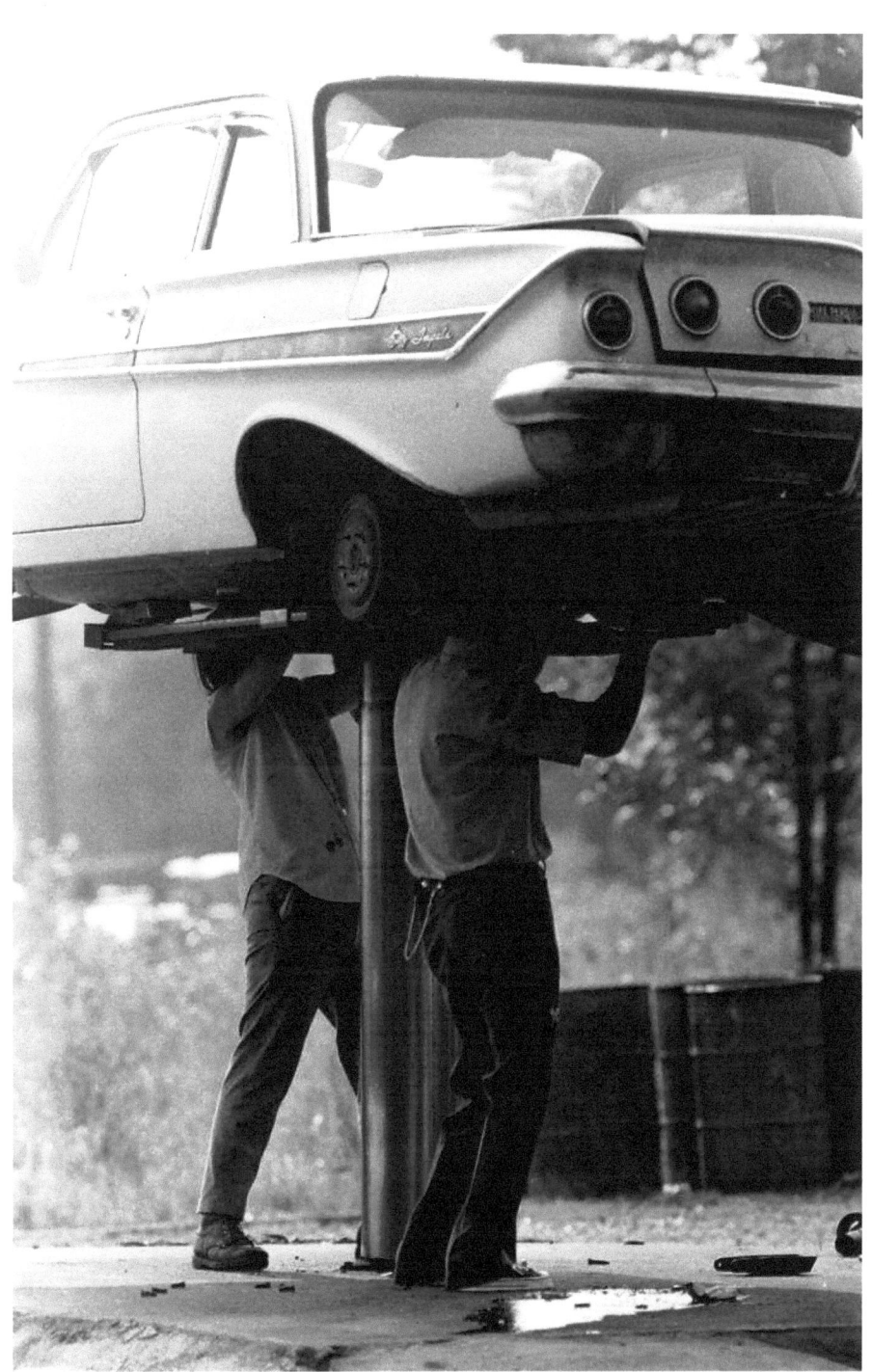

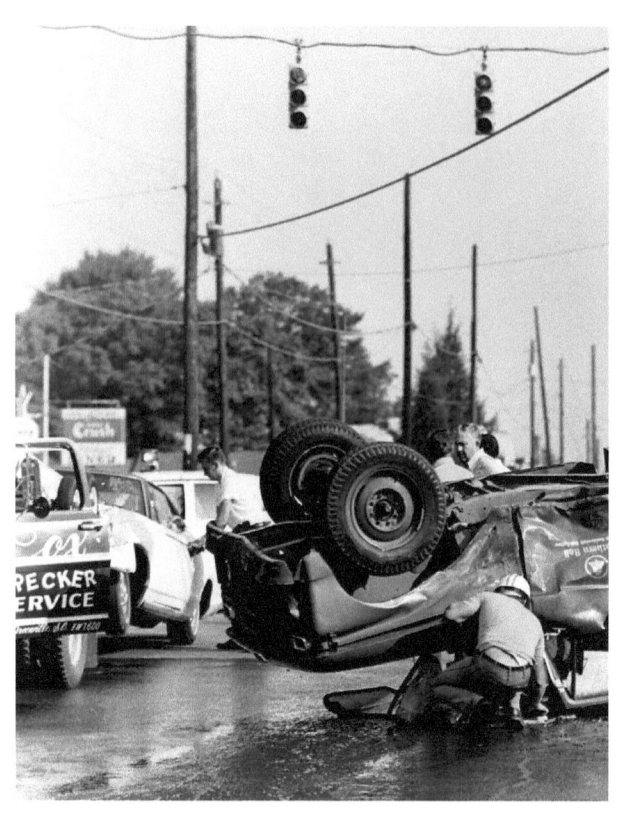

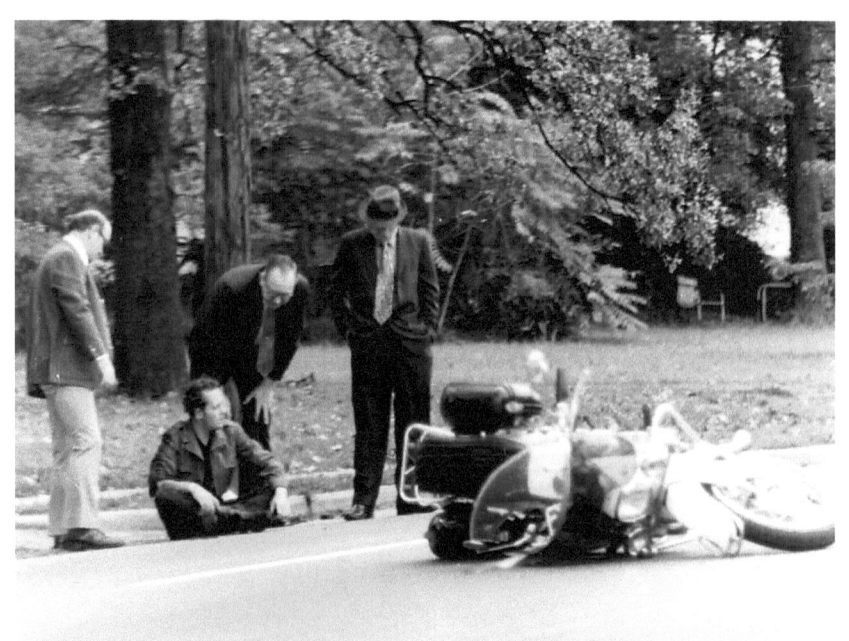

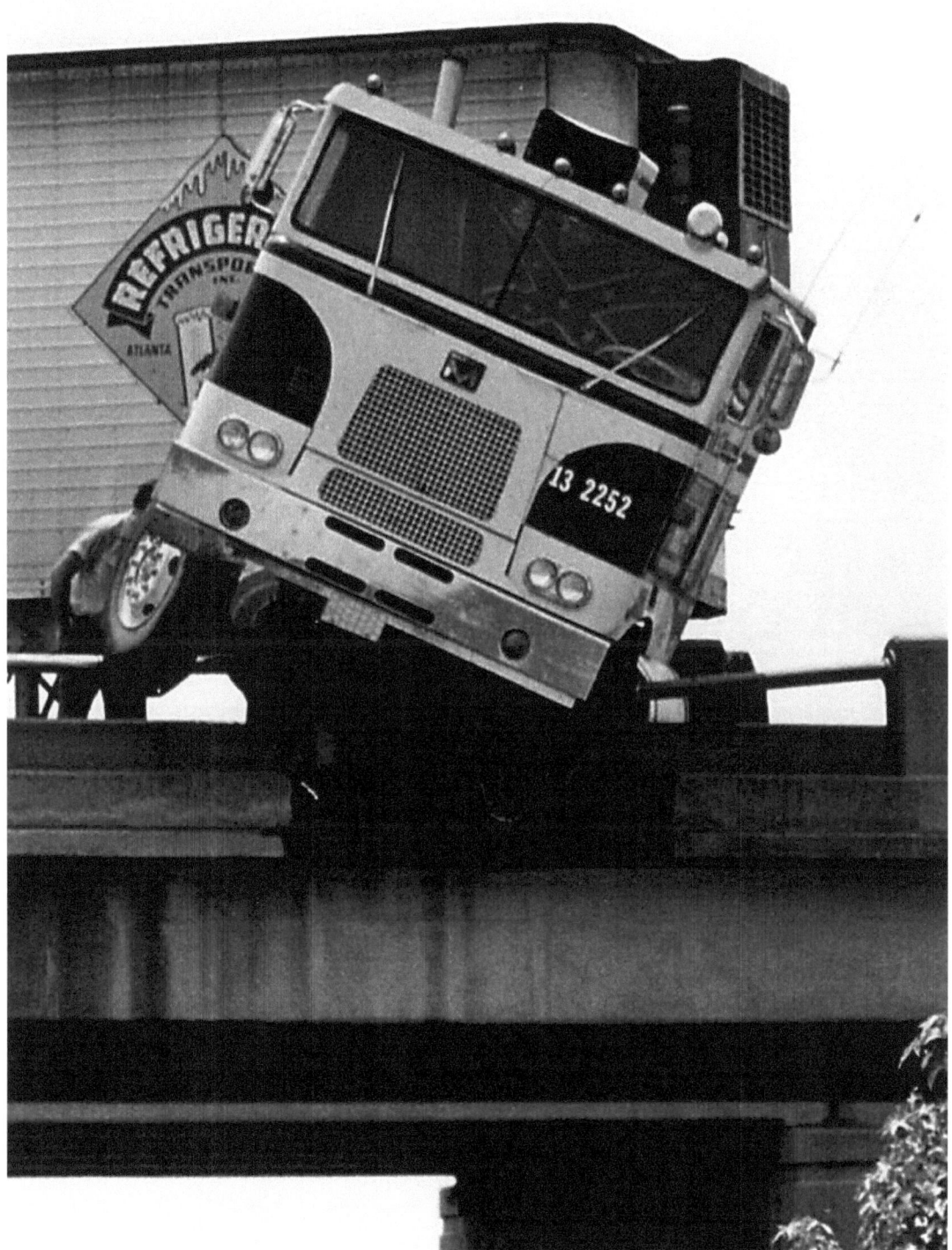

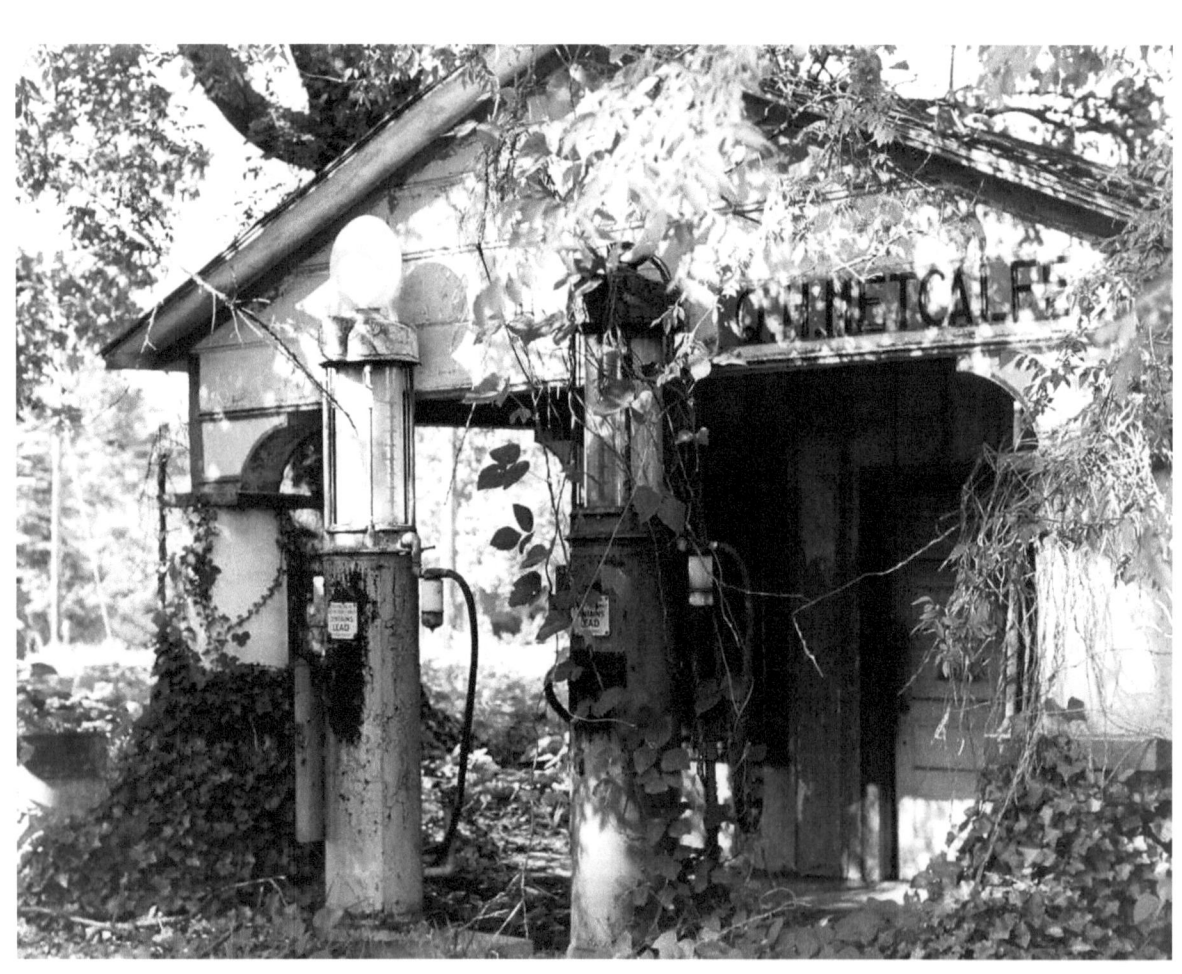

V

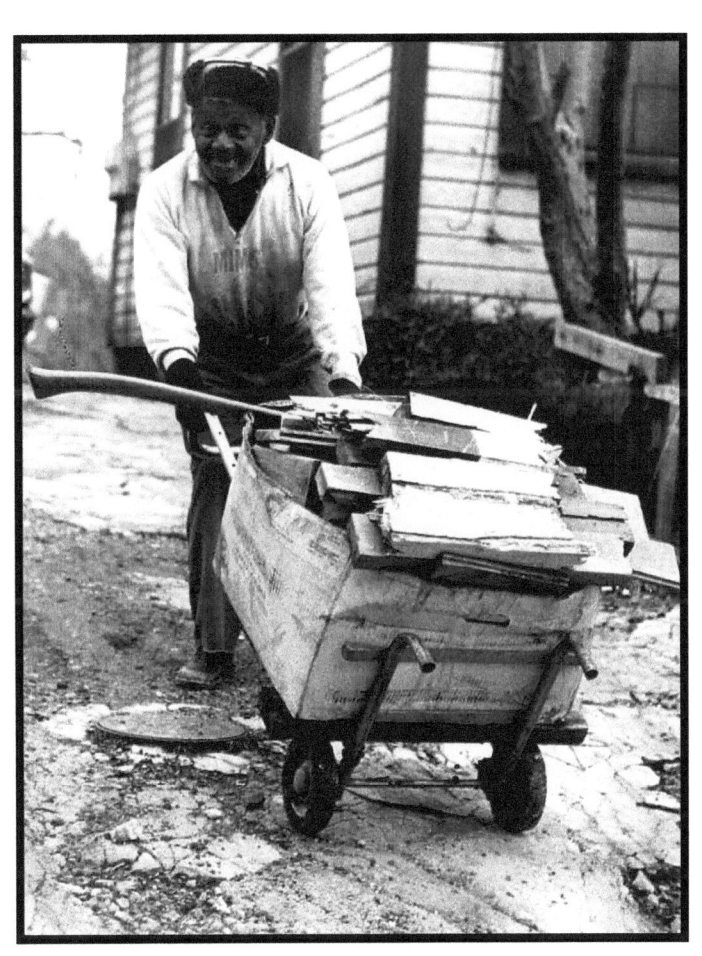

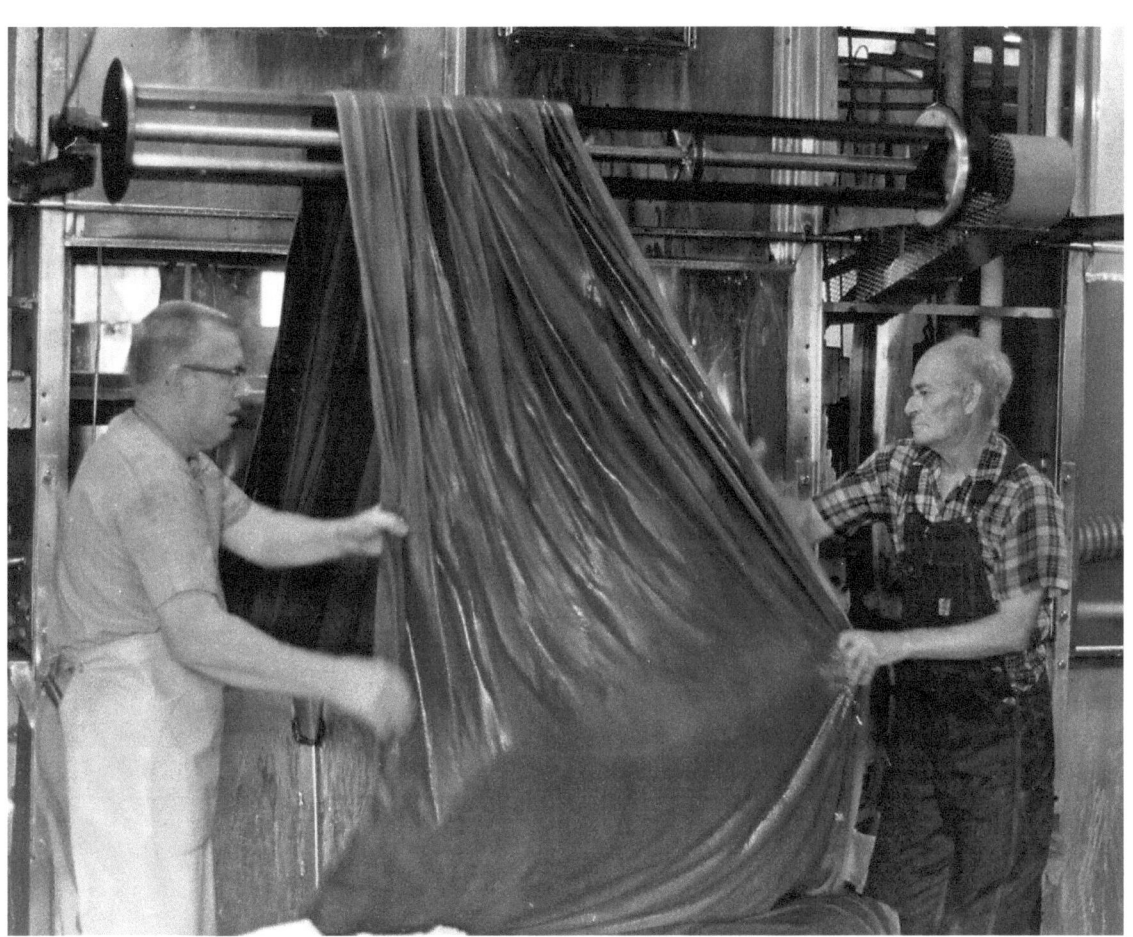

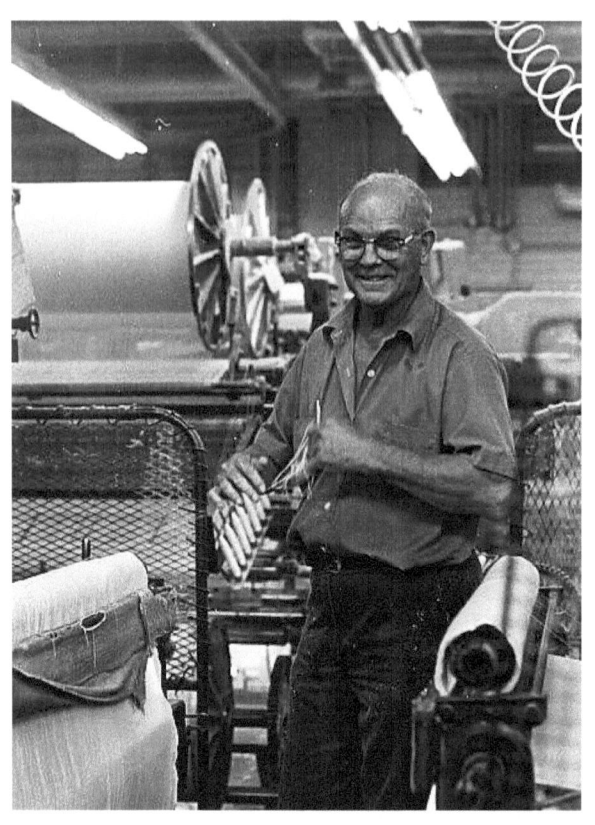

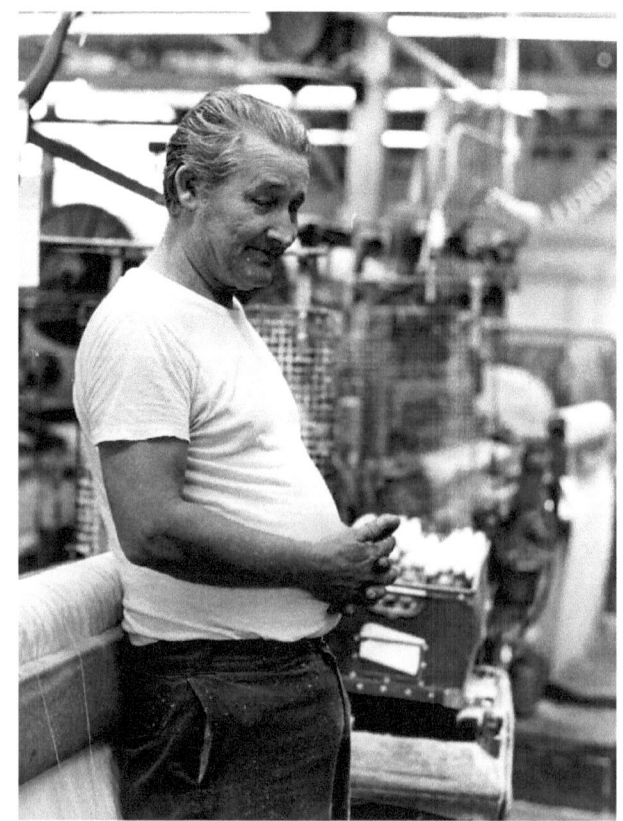

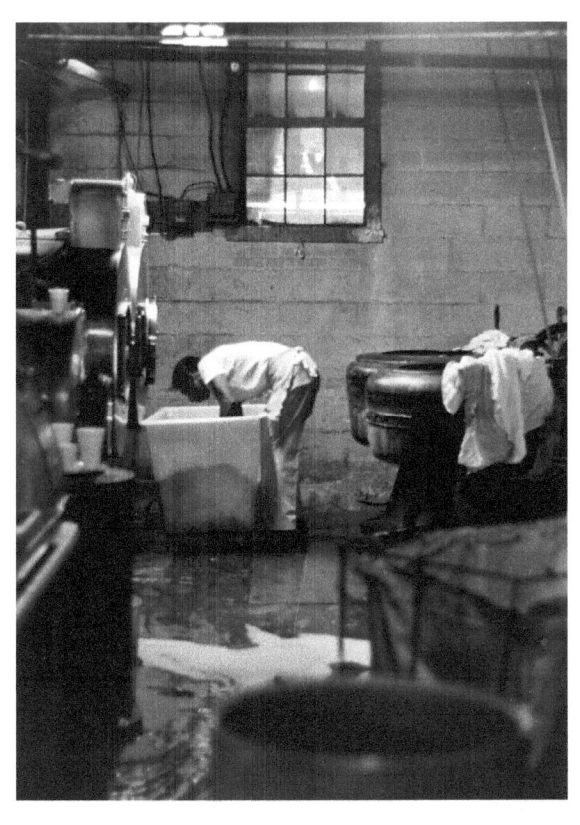

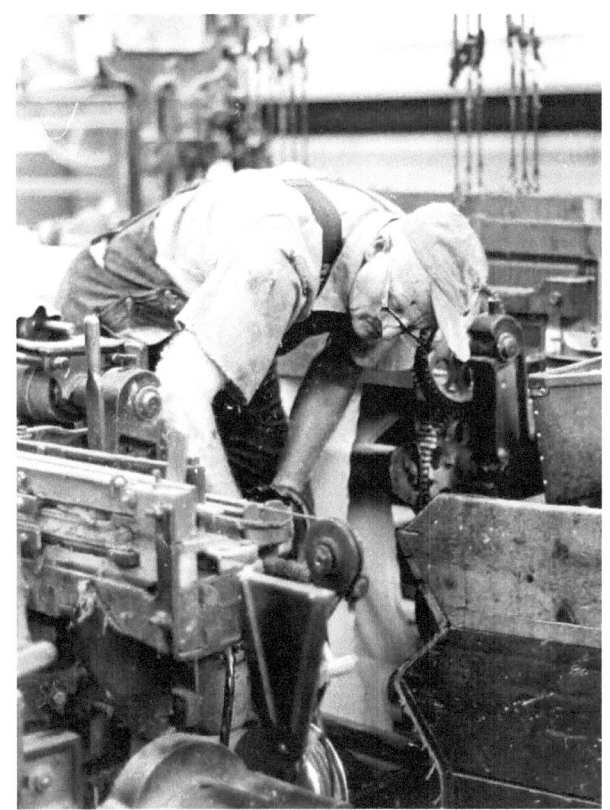

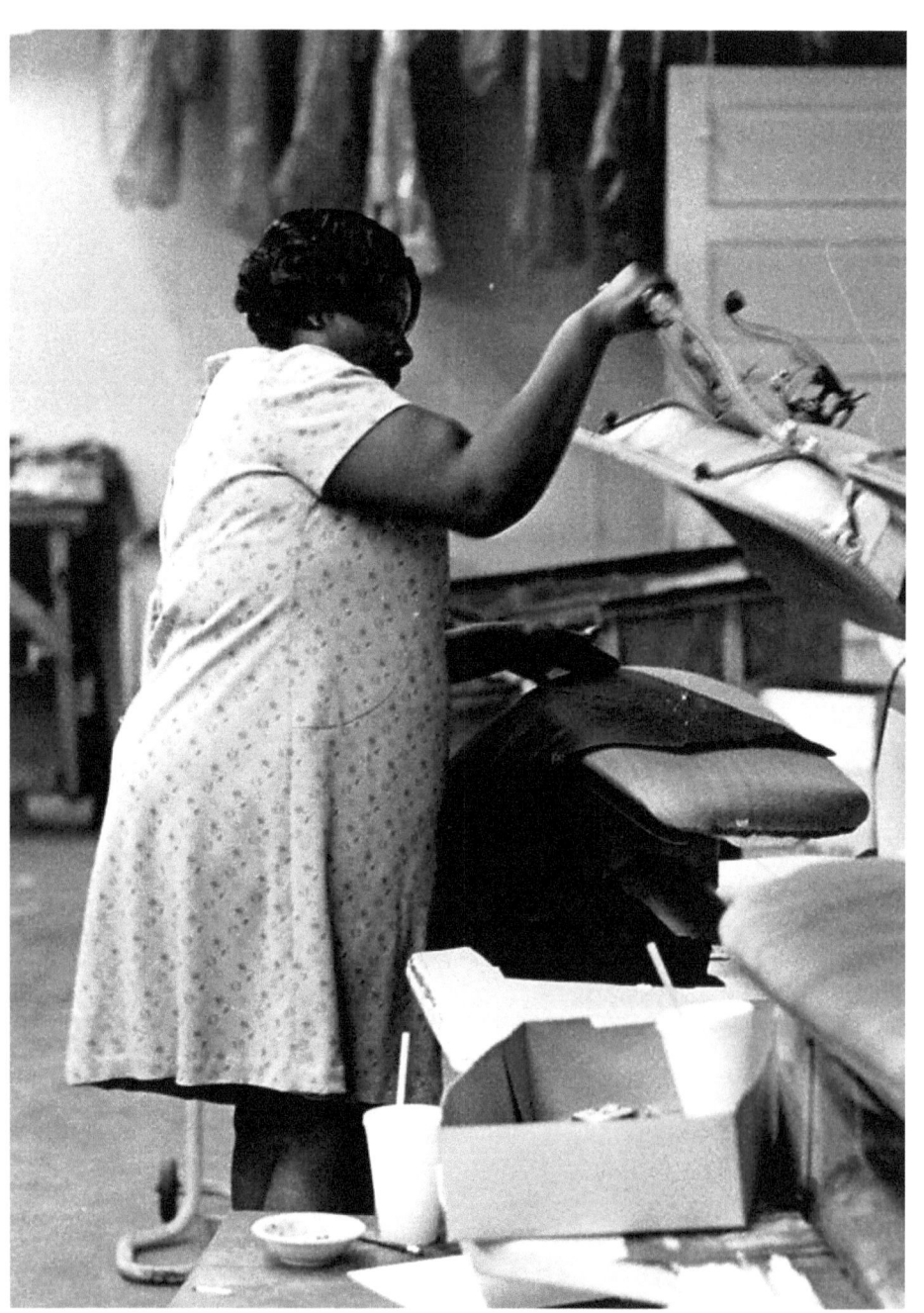

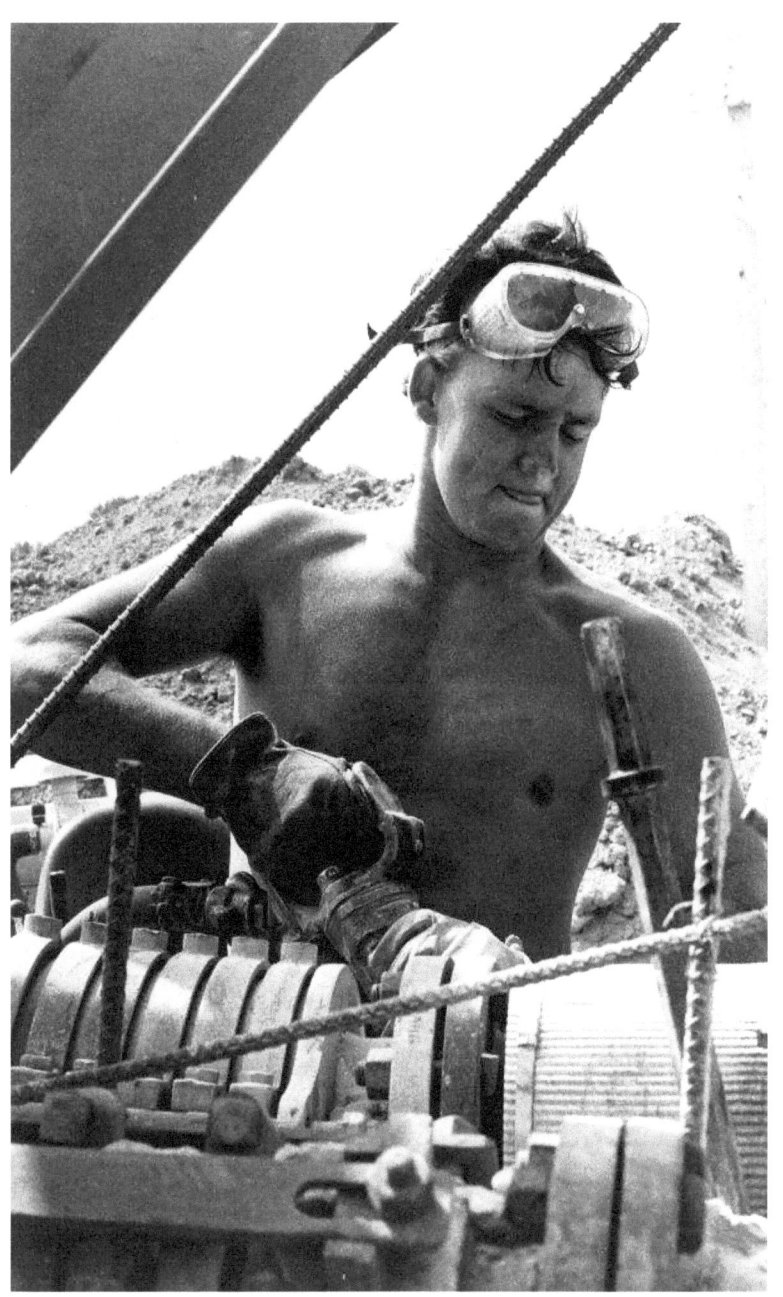

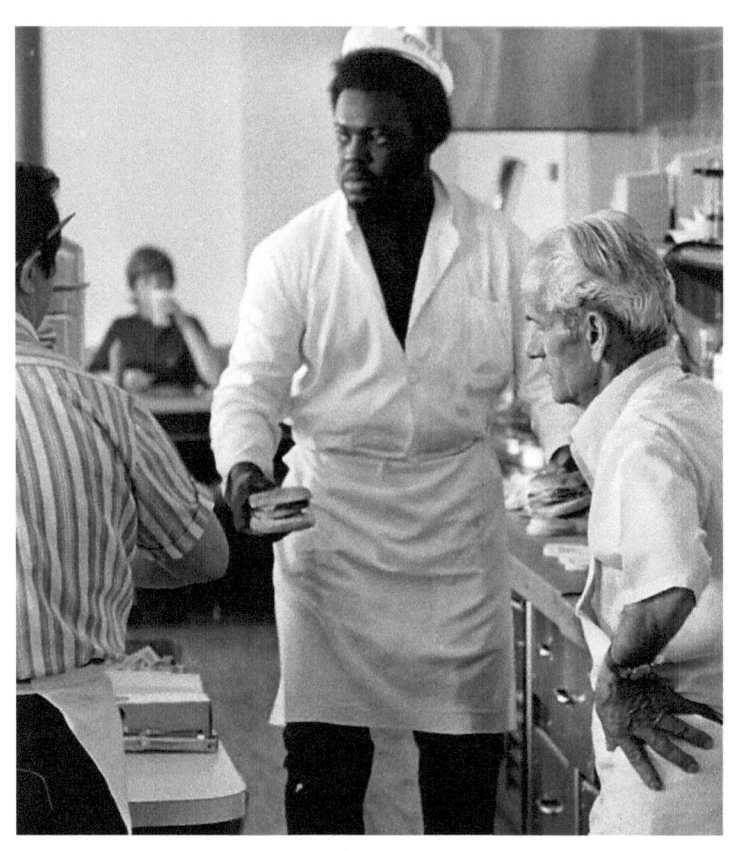

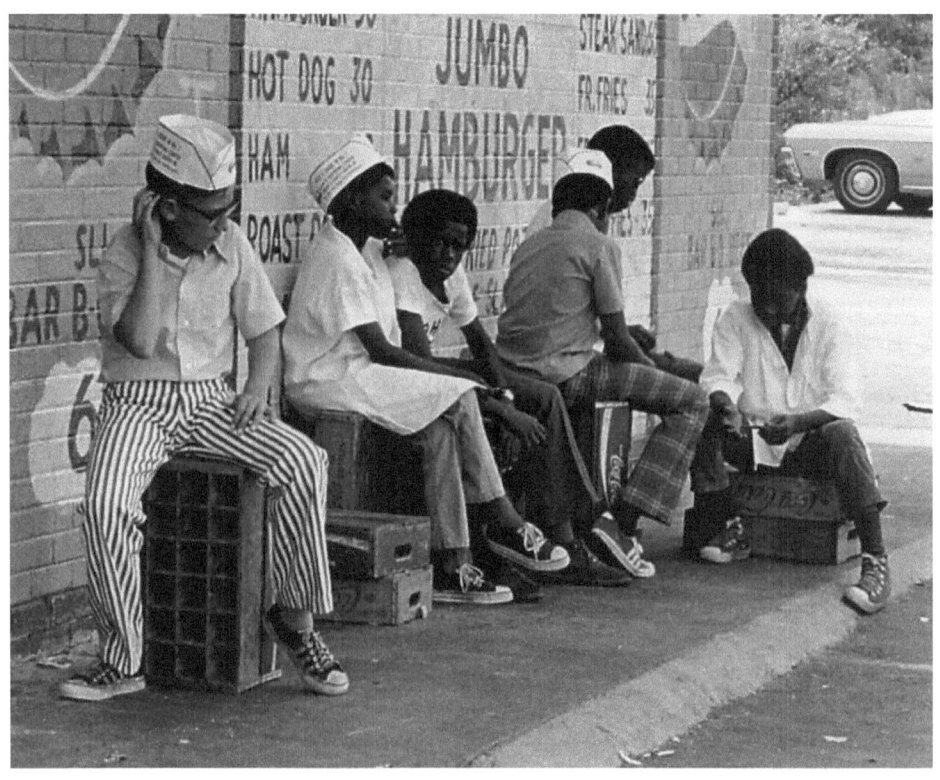

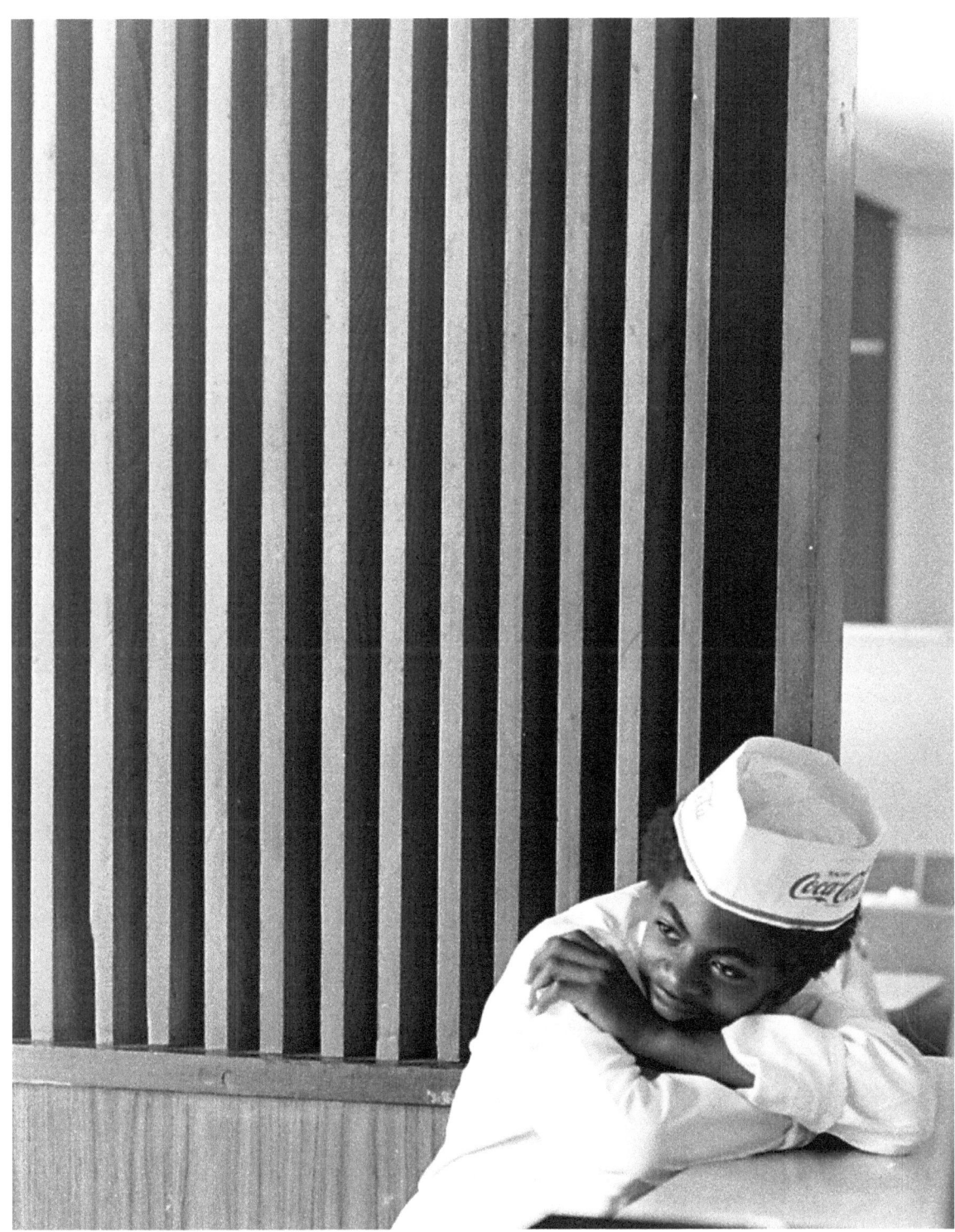

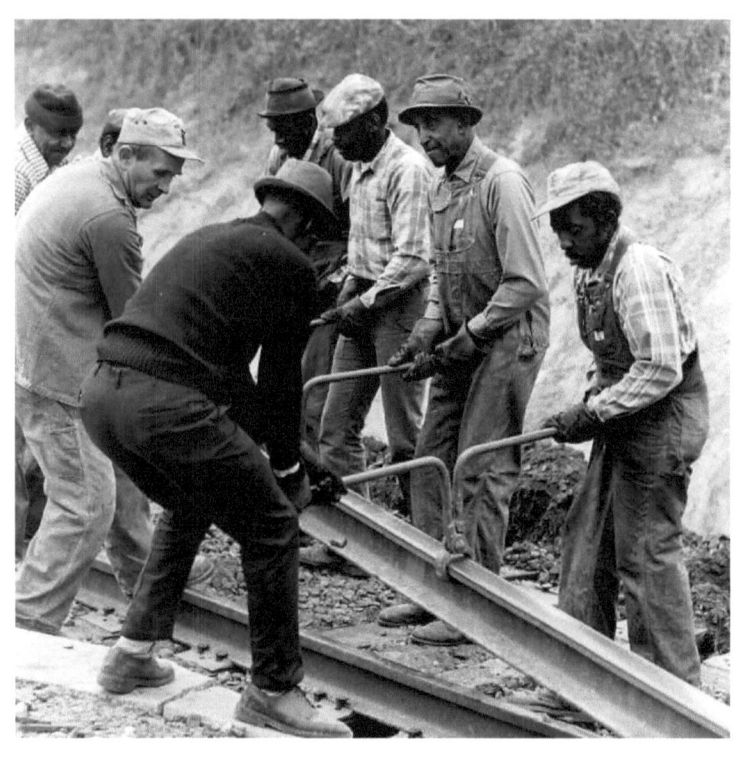

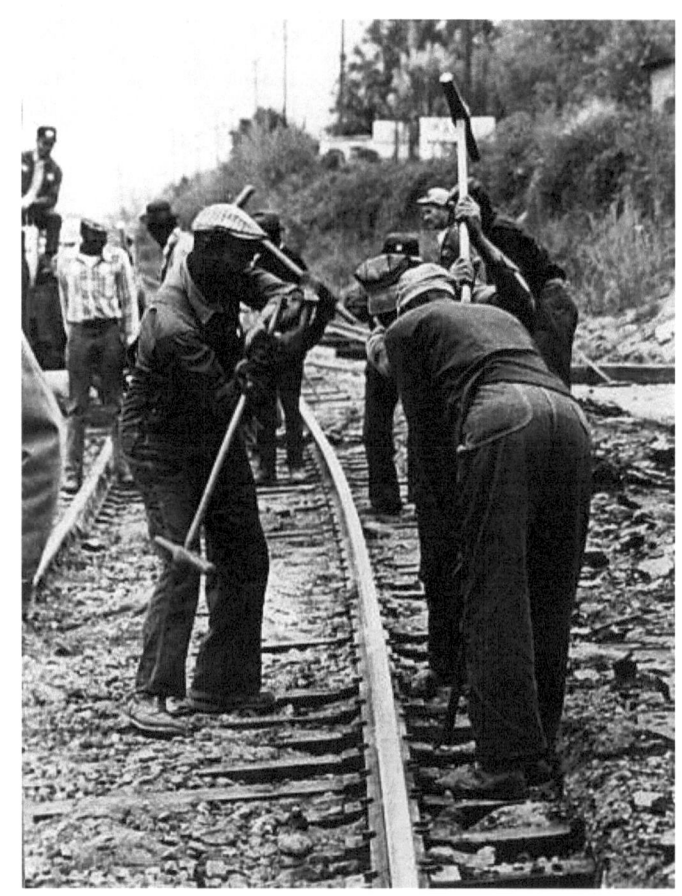

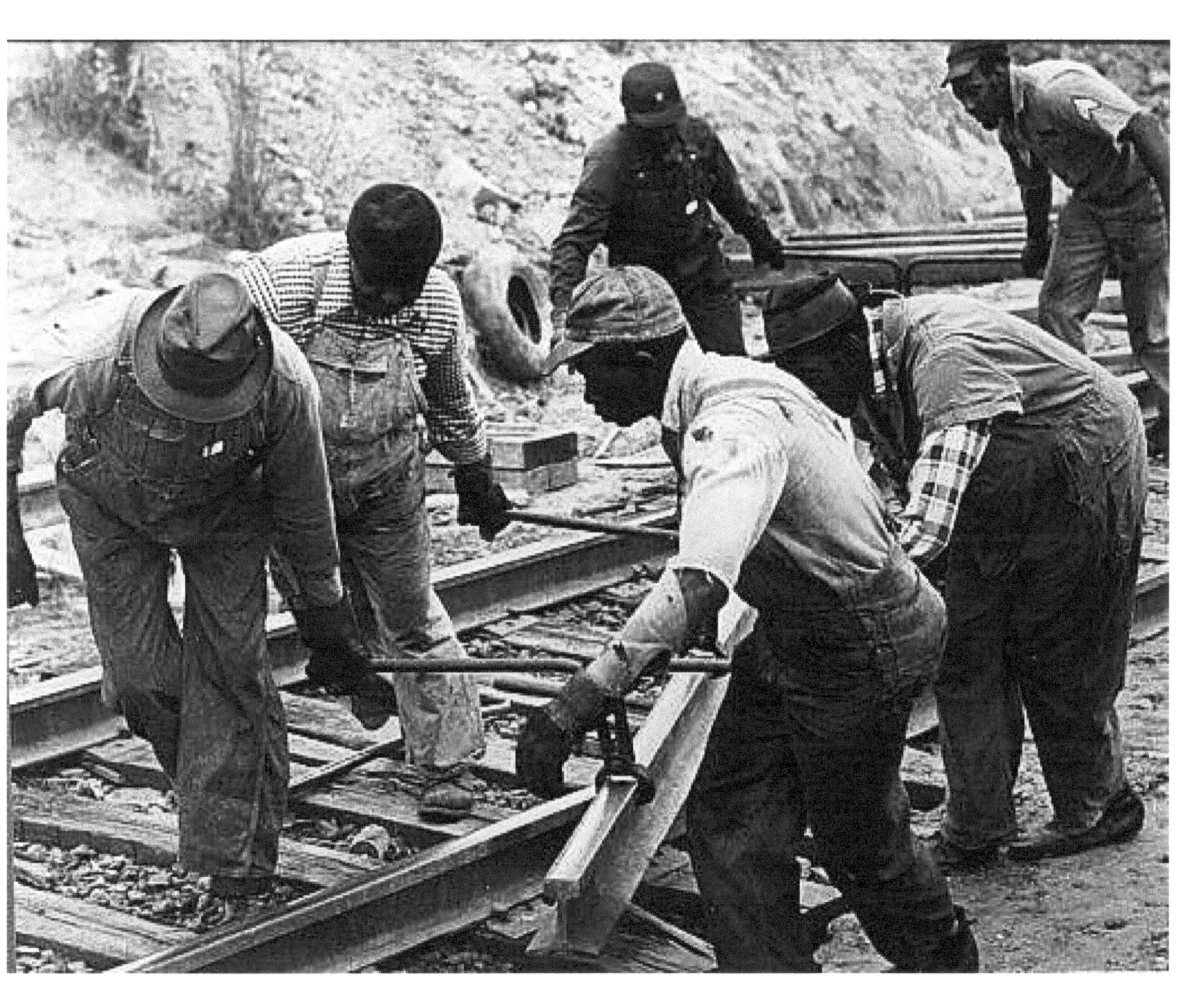

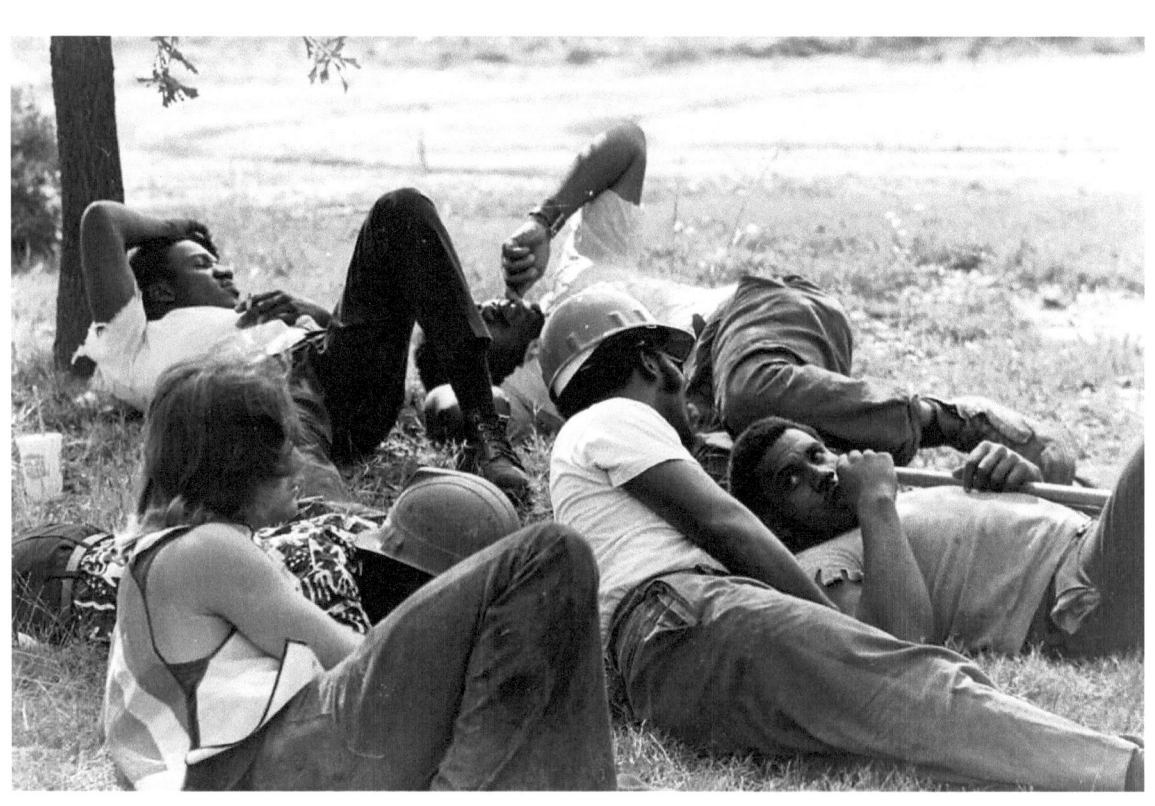

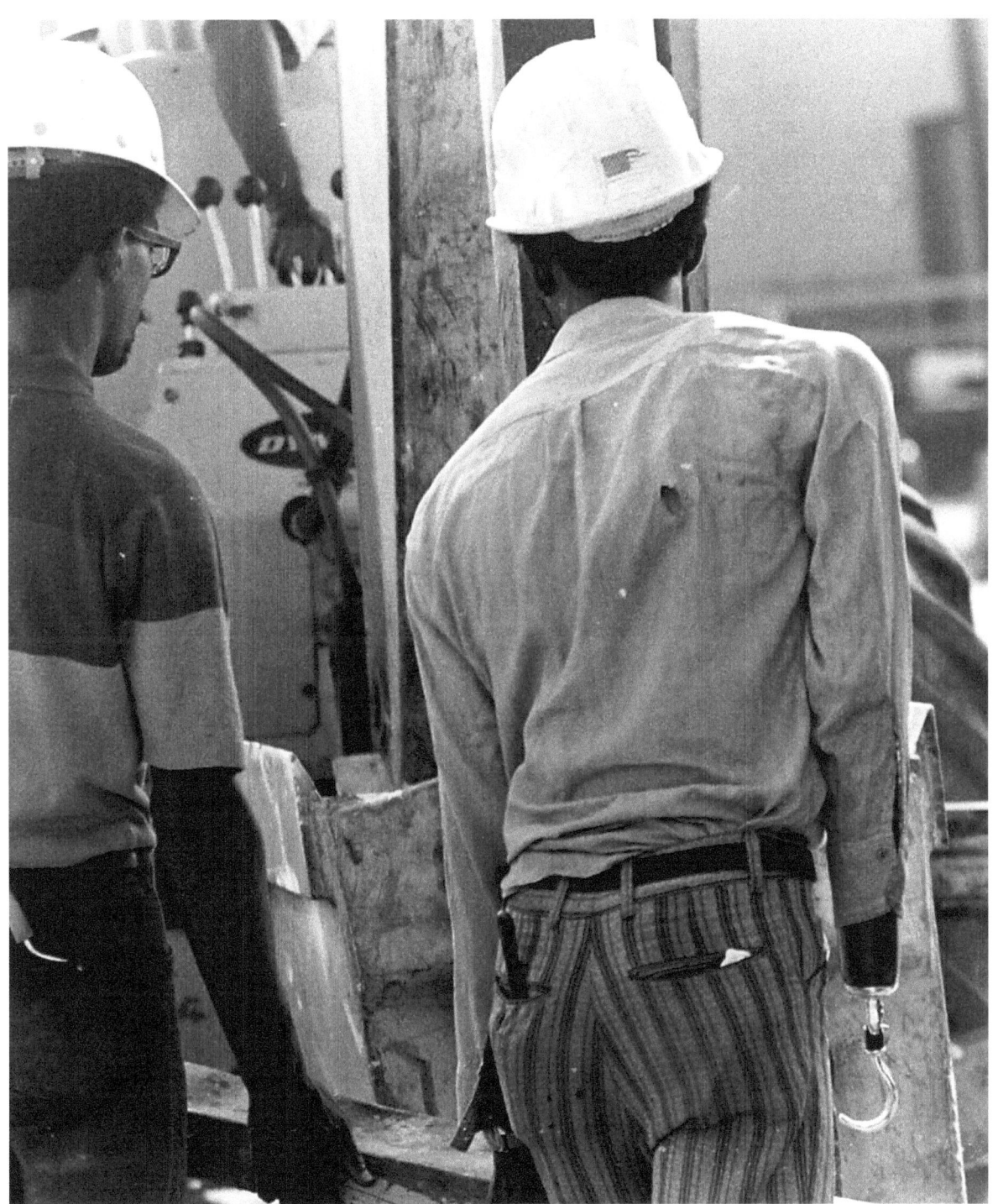

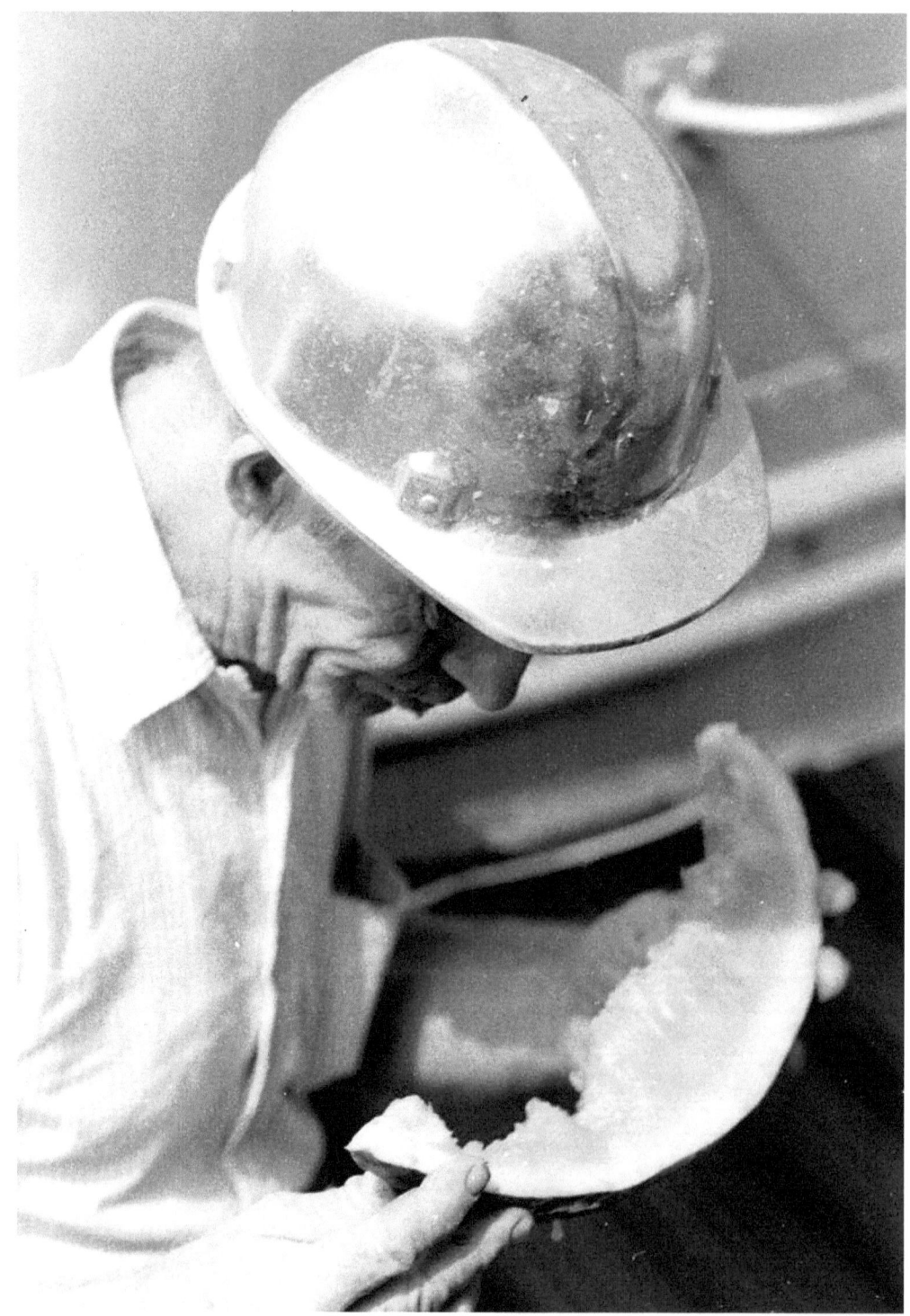

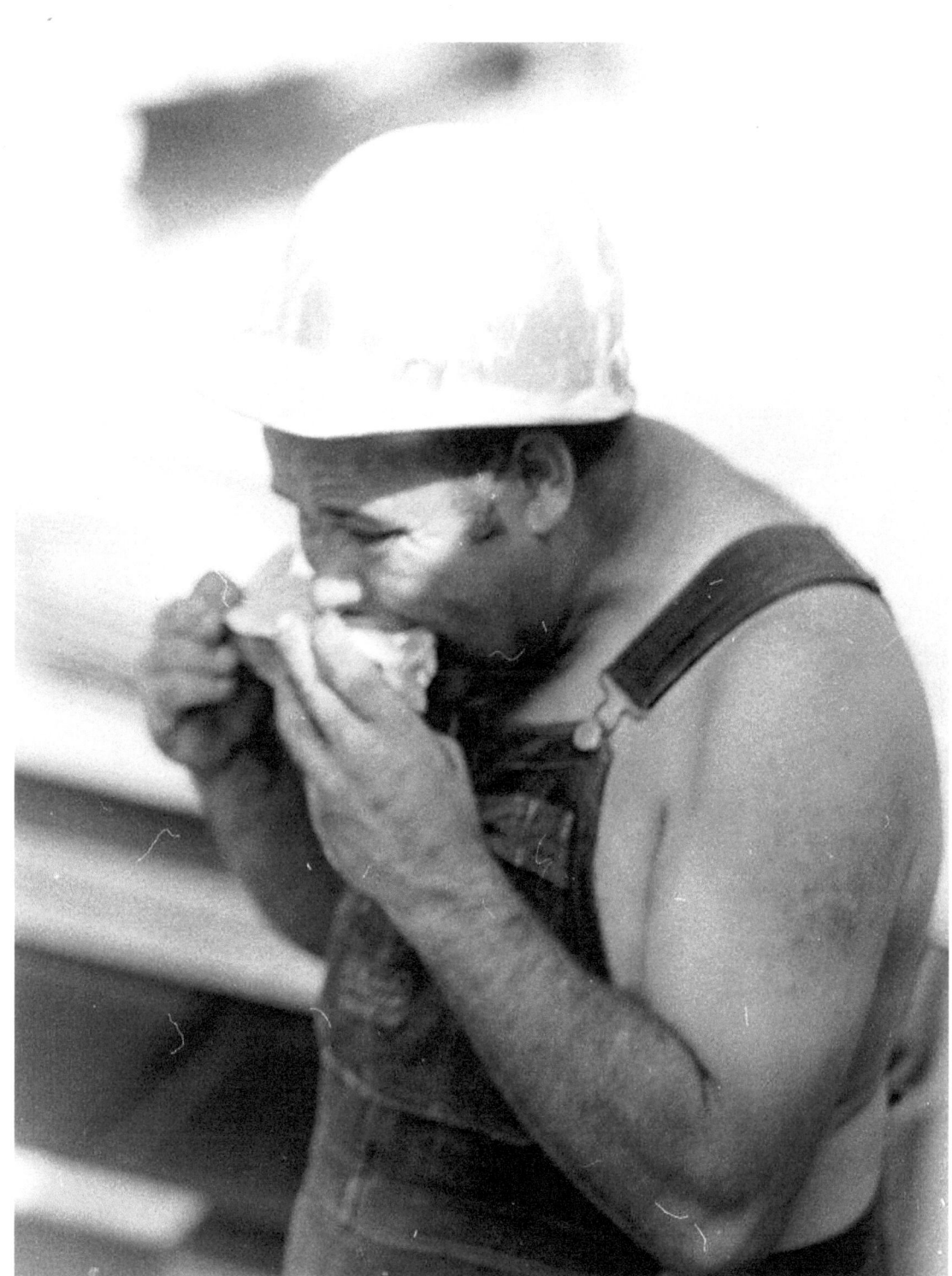

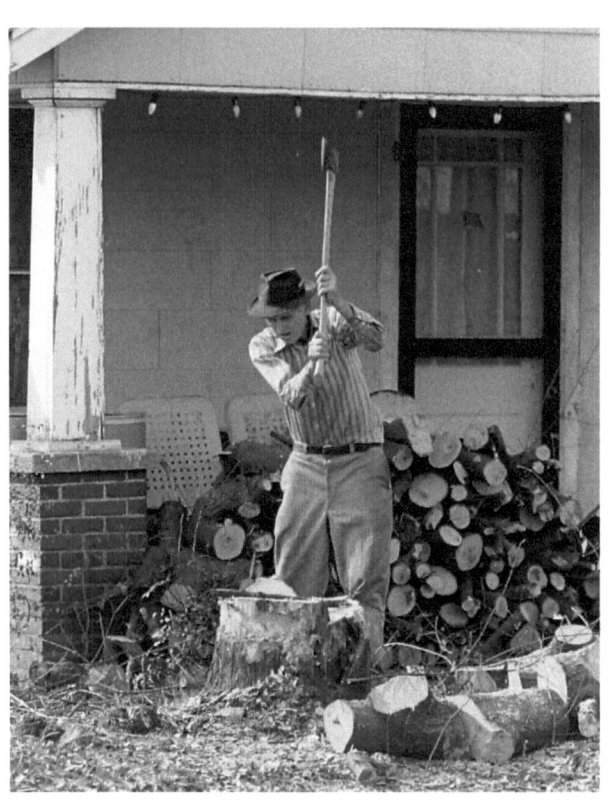

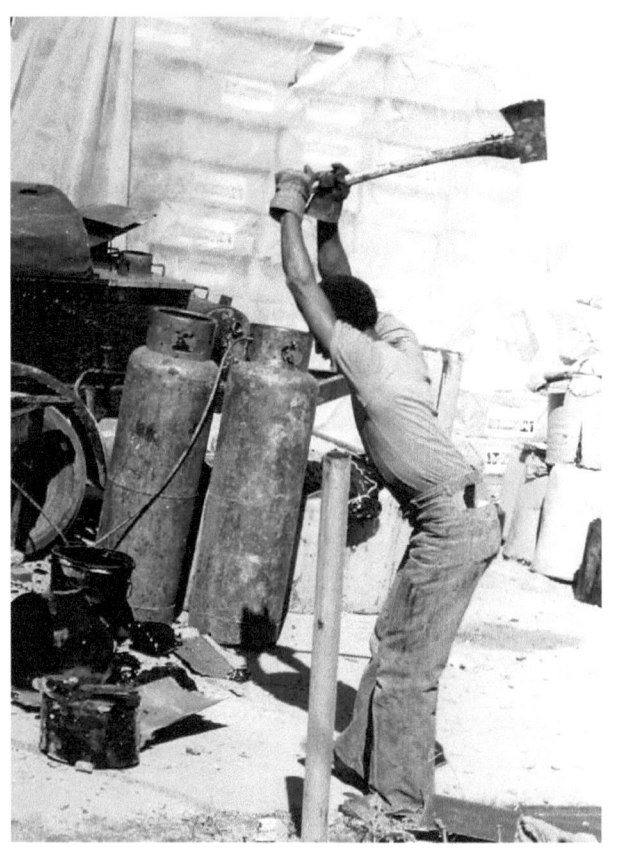

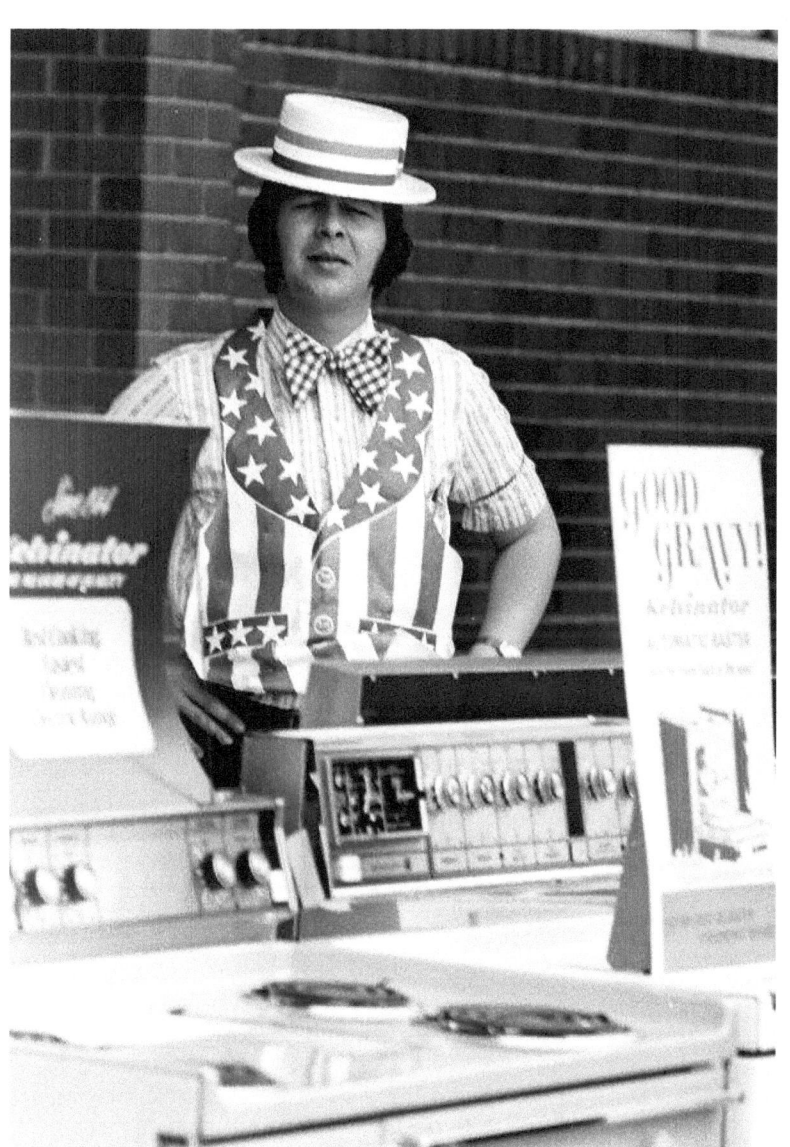

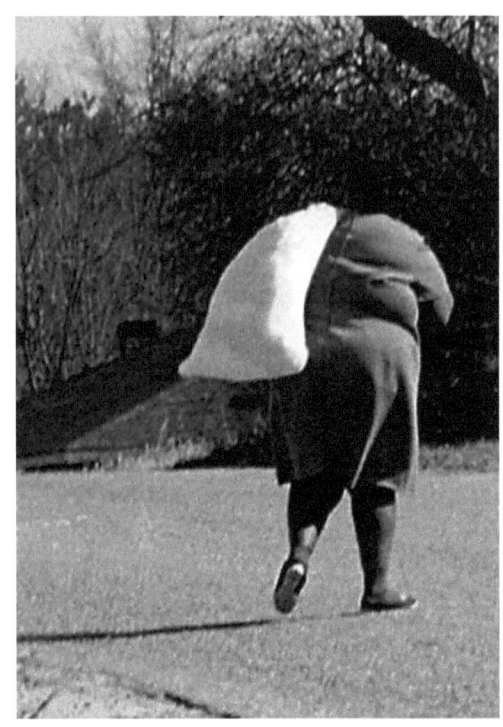

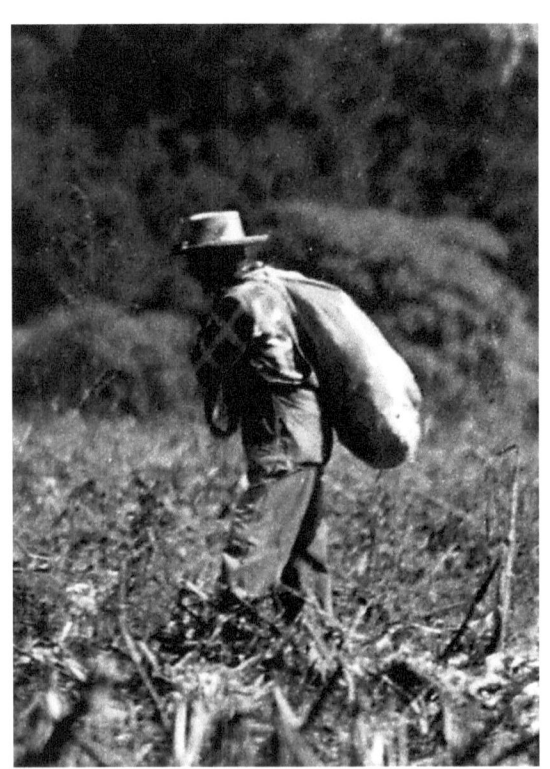

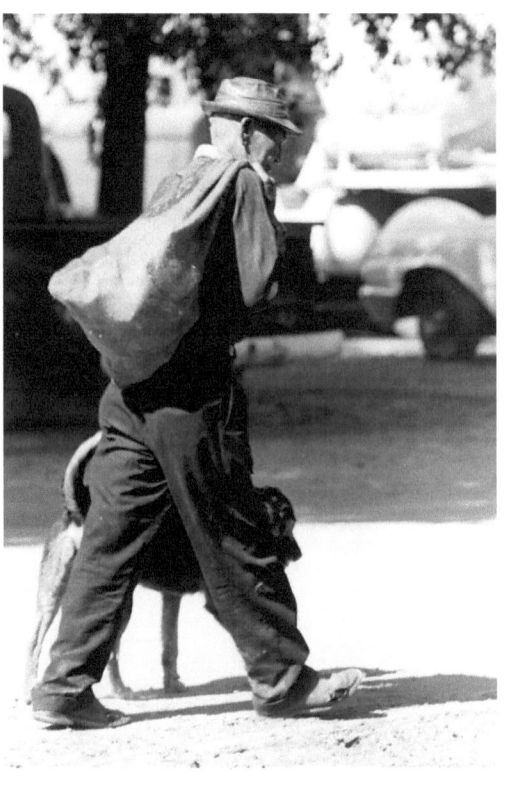

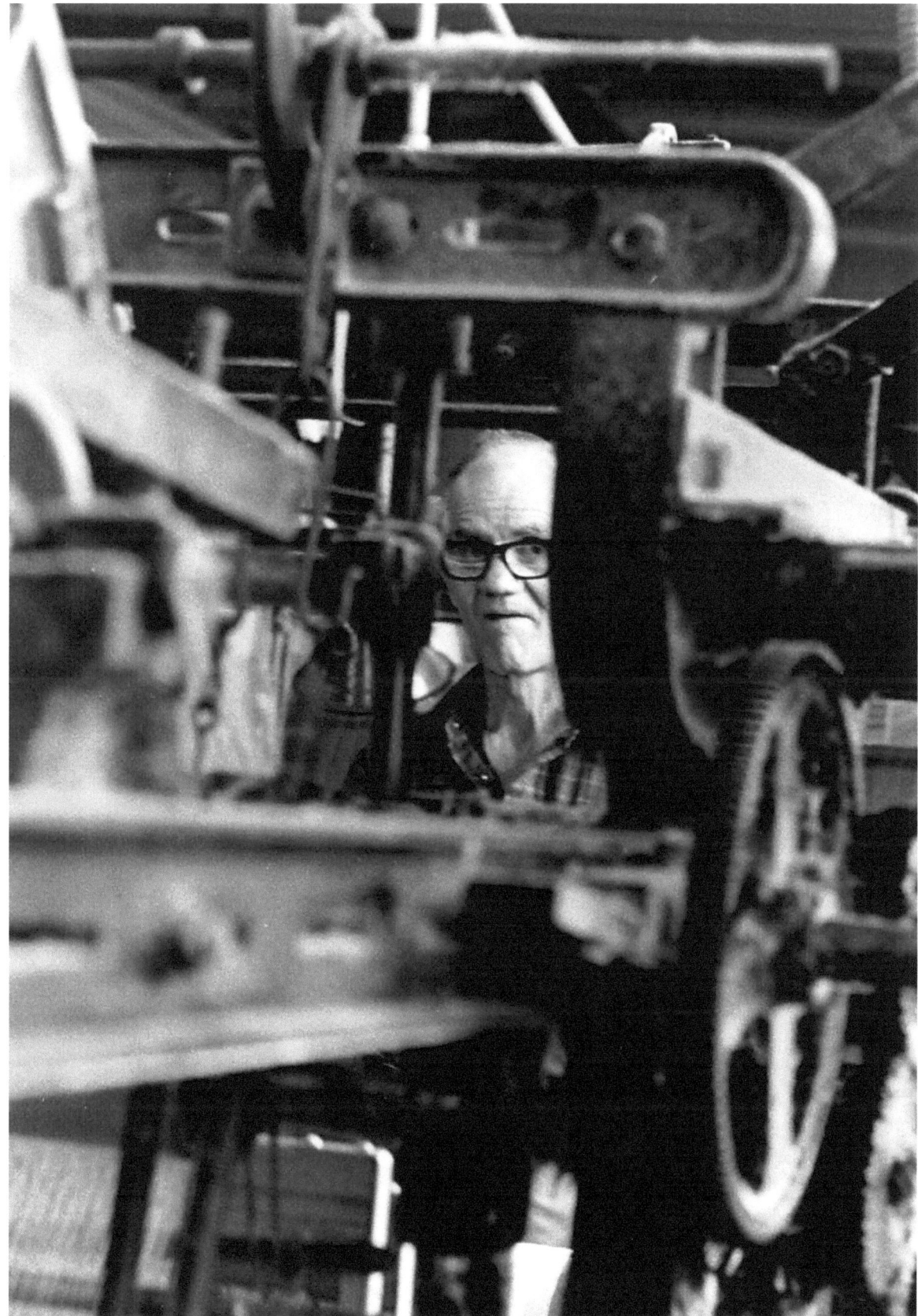

VI

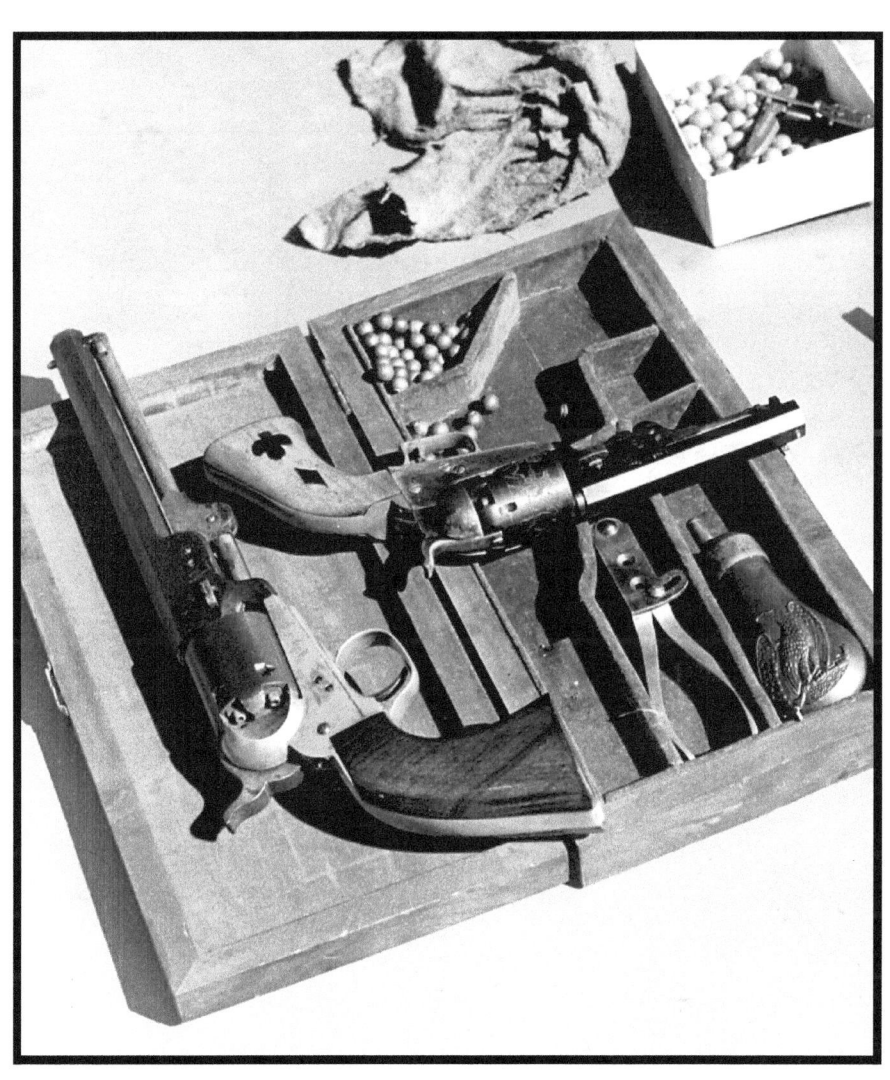

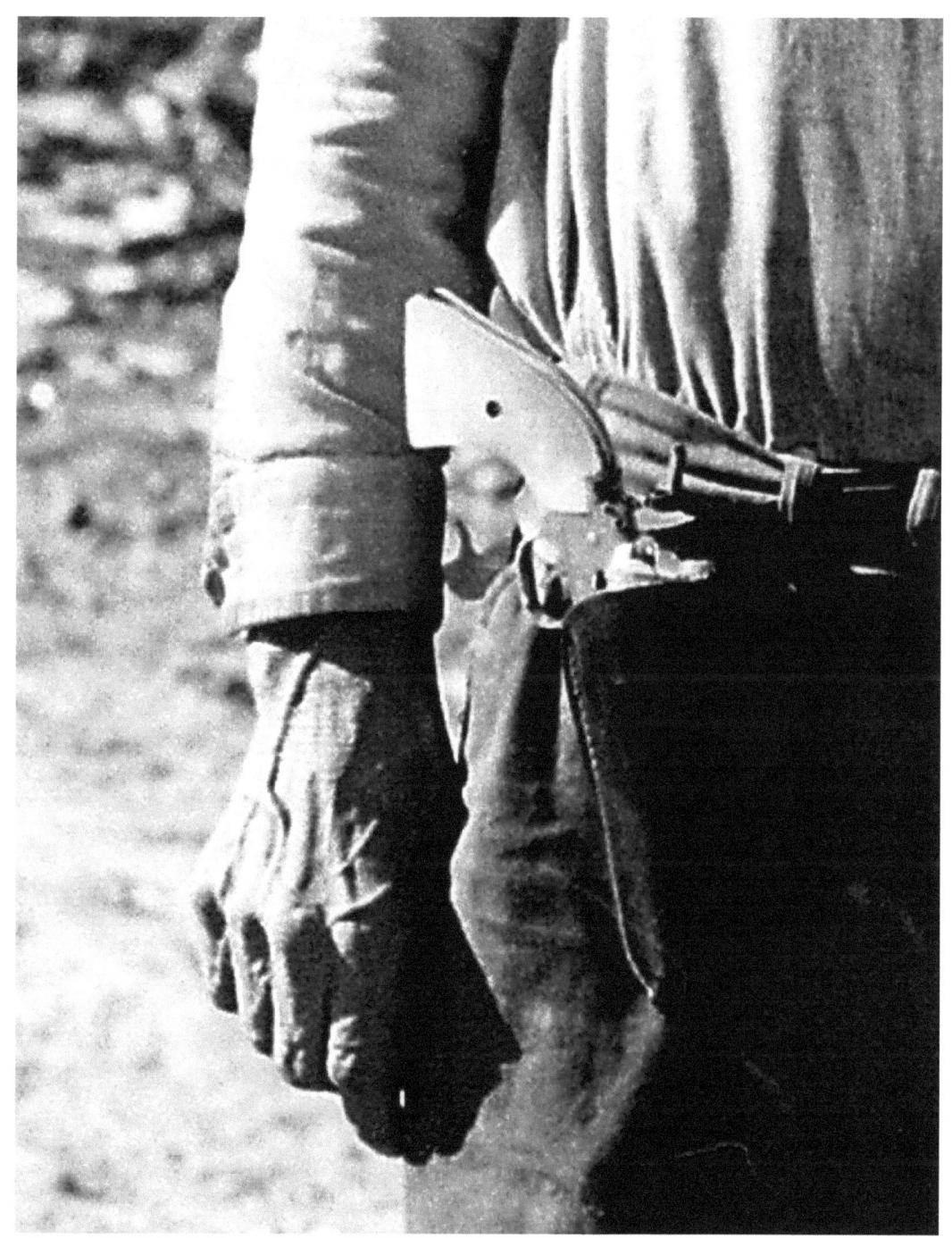

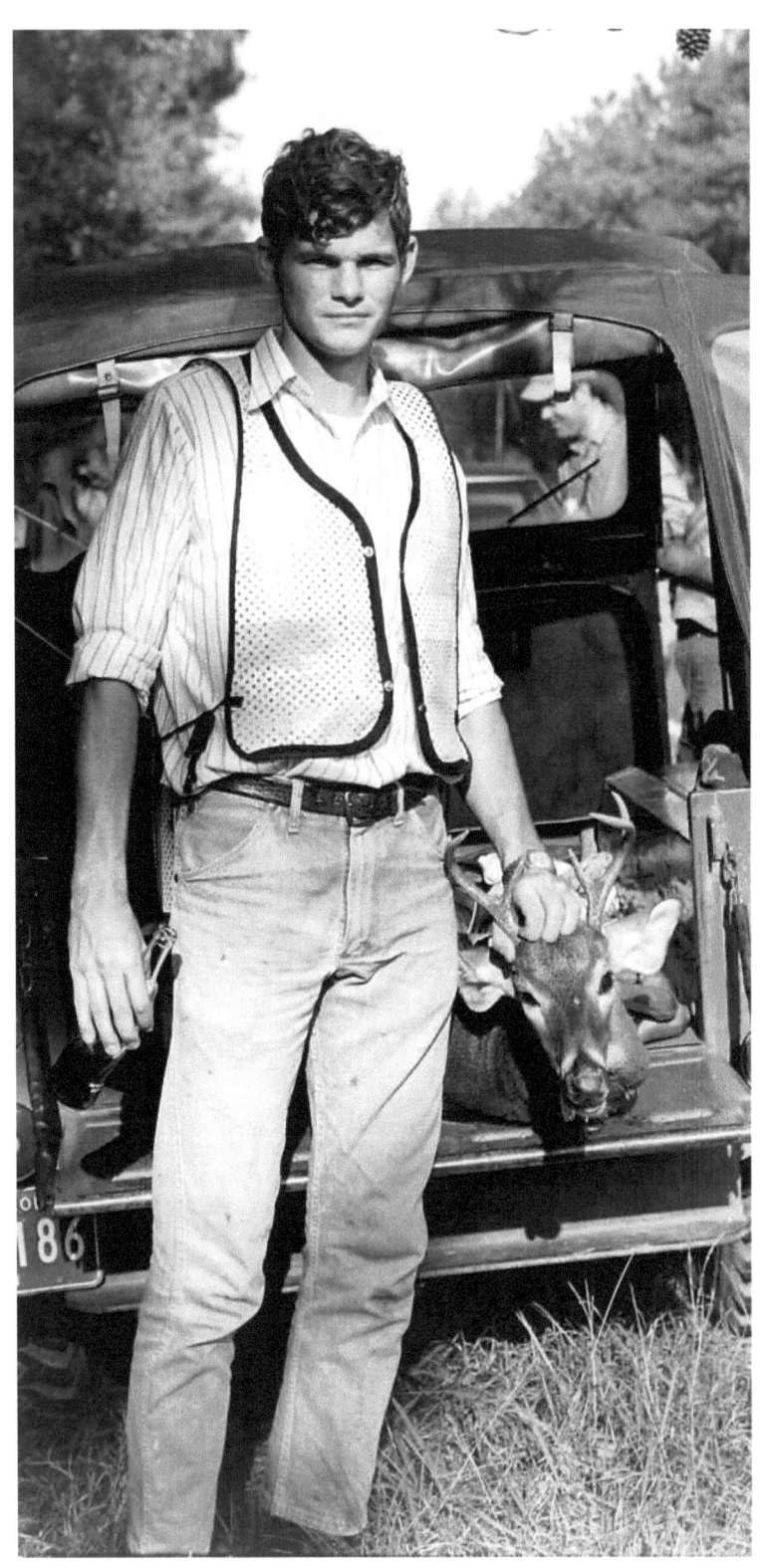

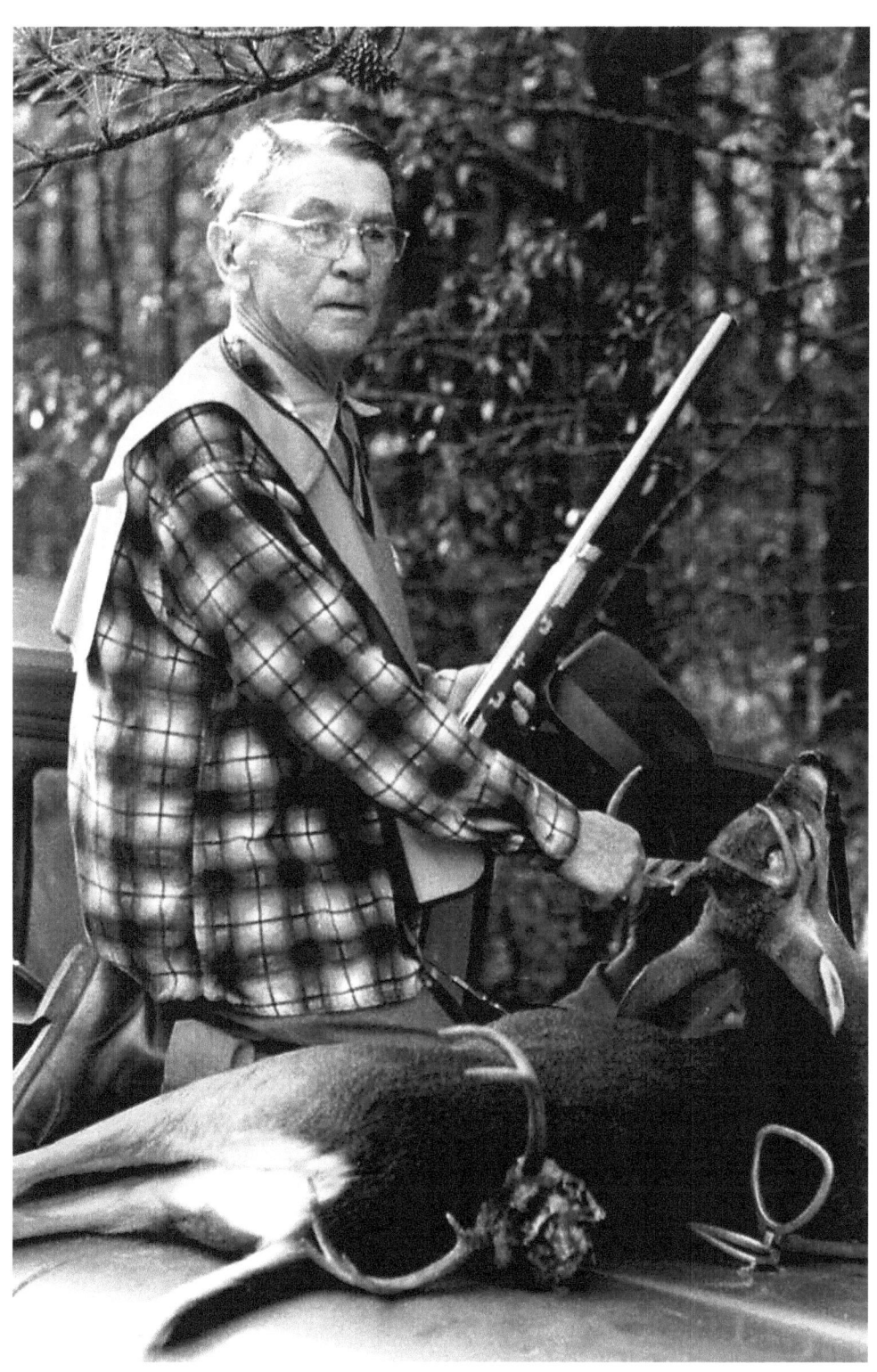

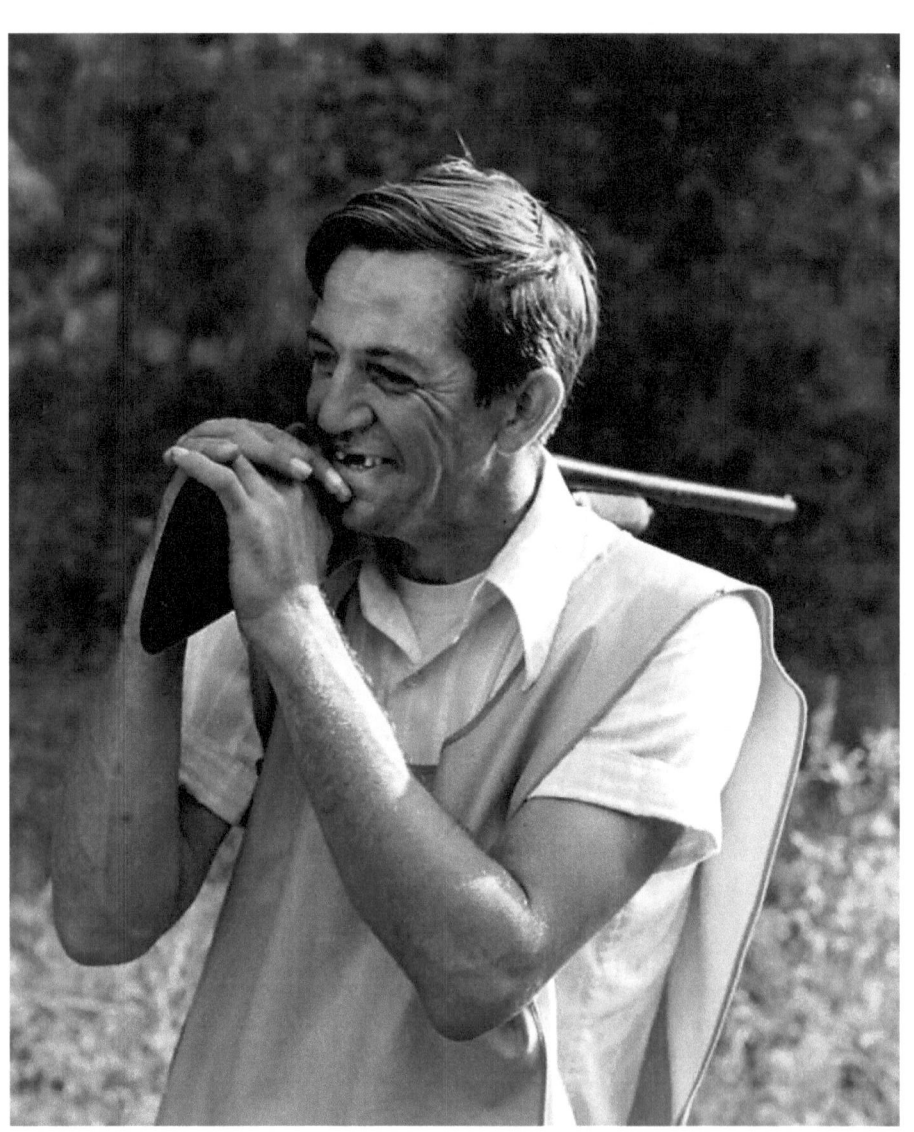

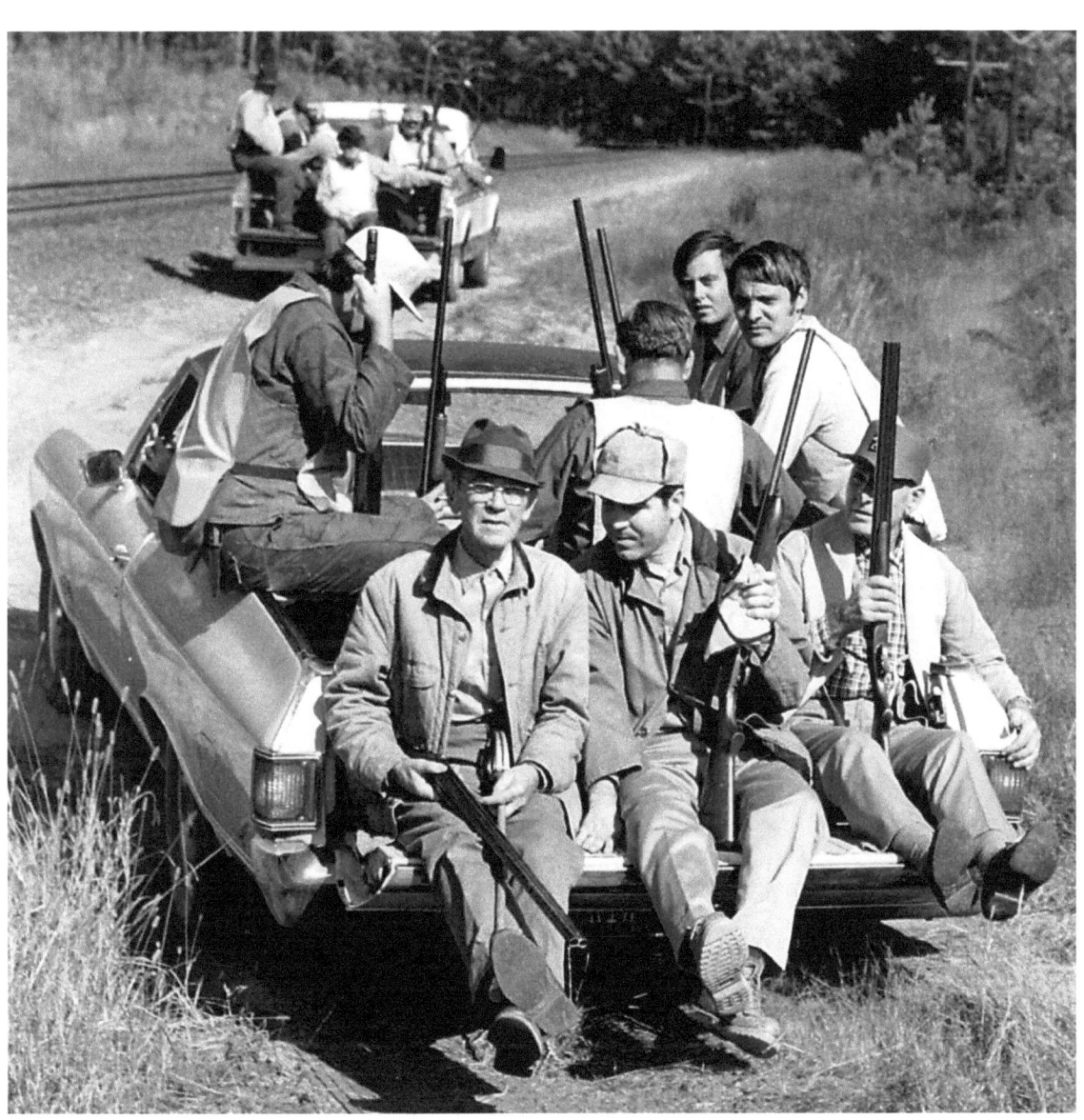

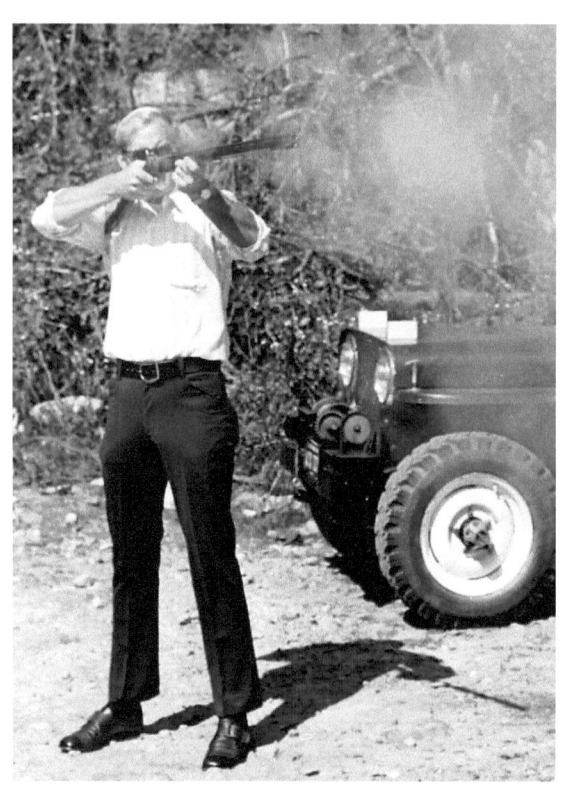

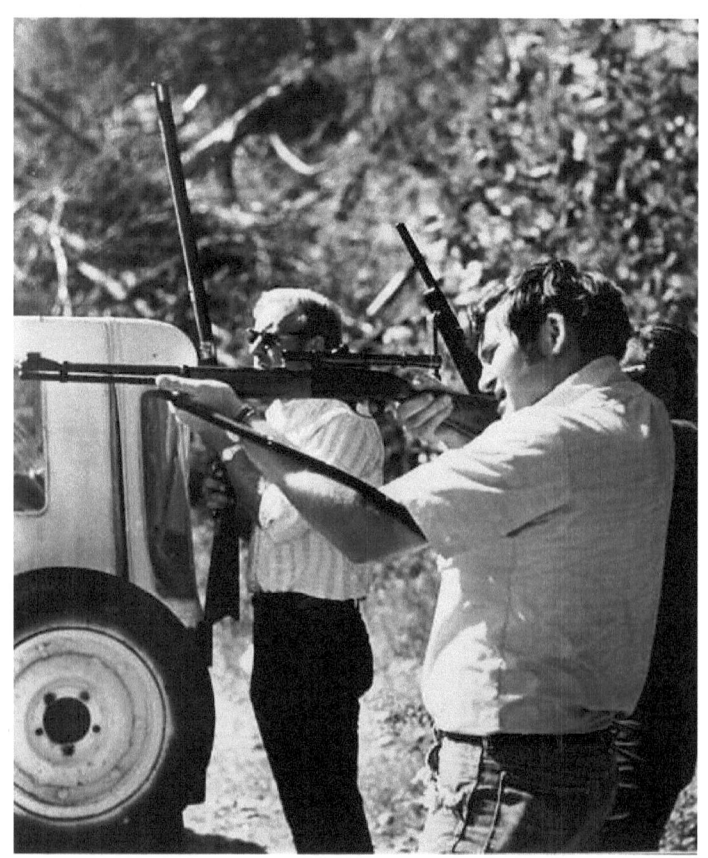

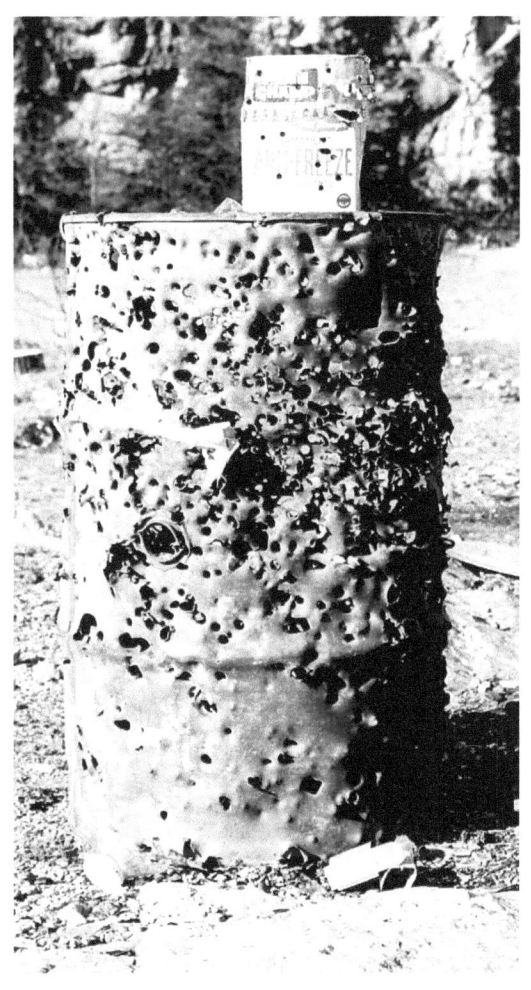

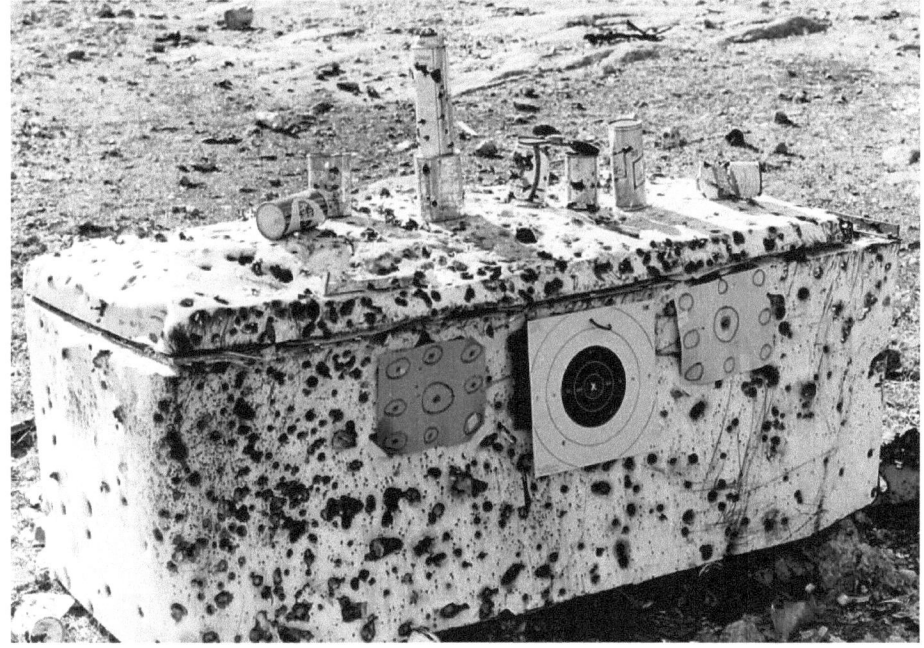

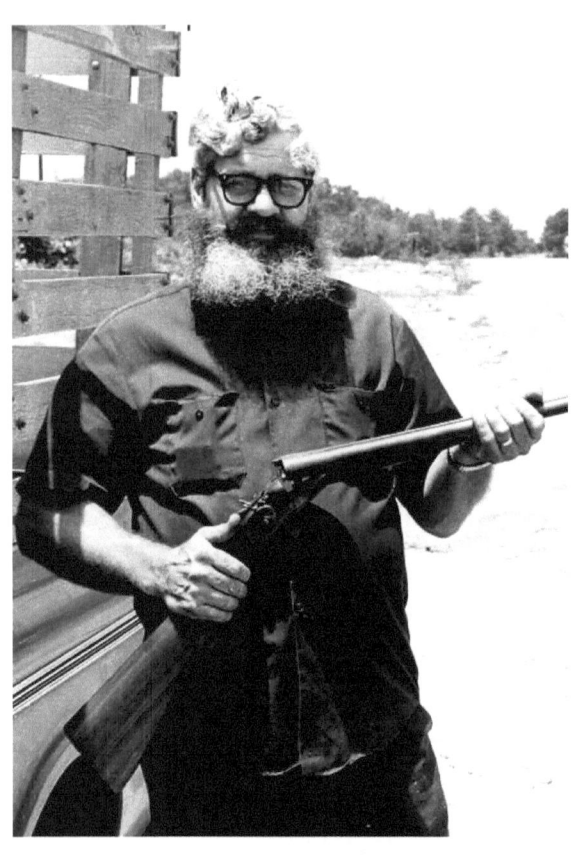

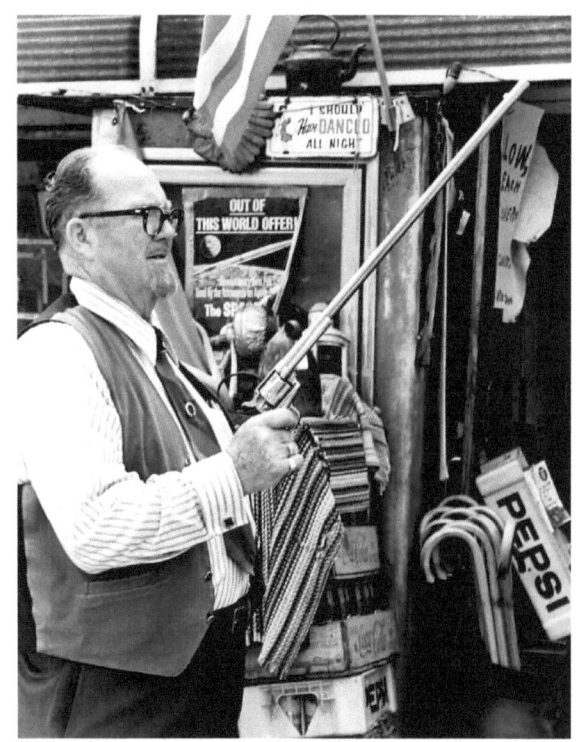

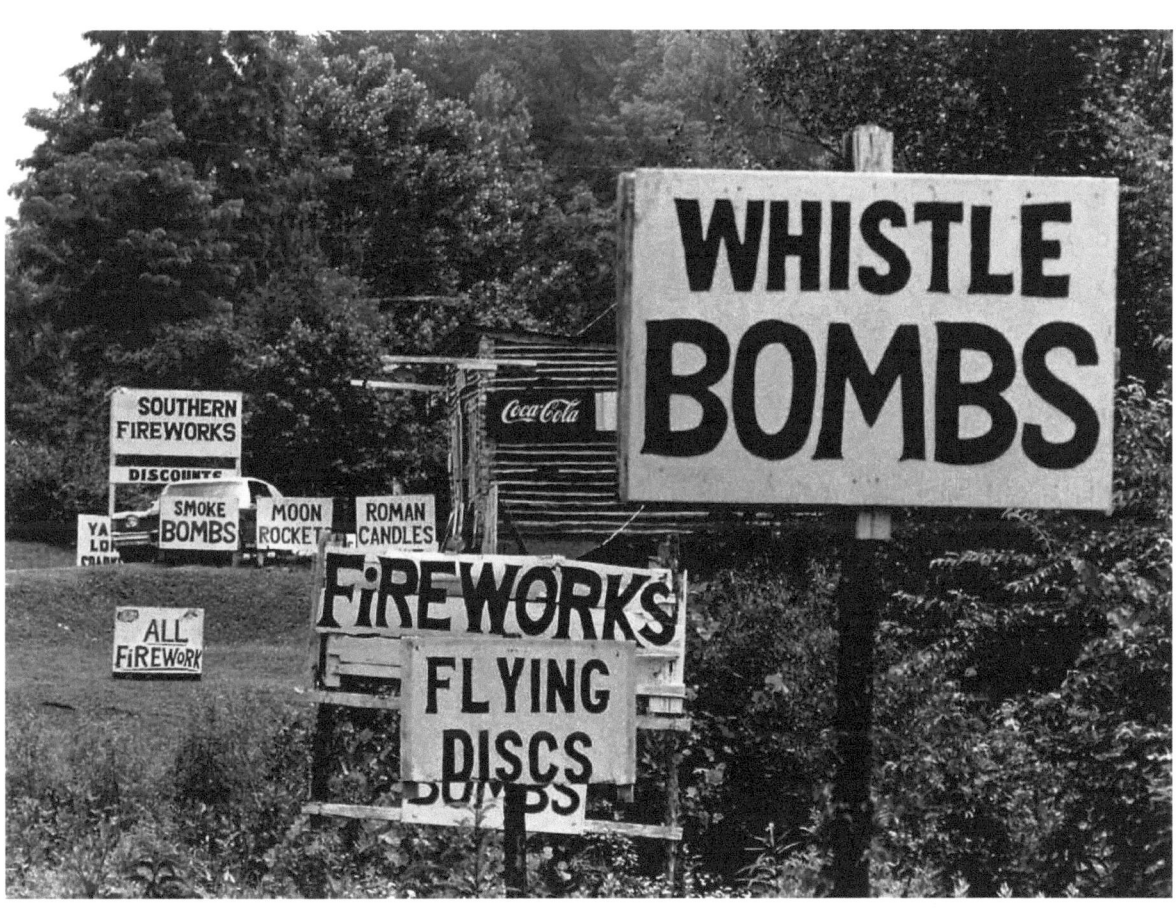

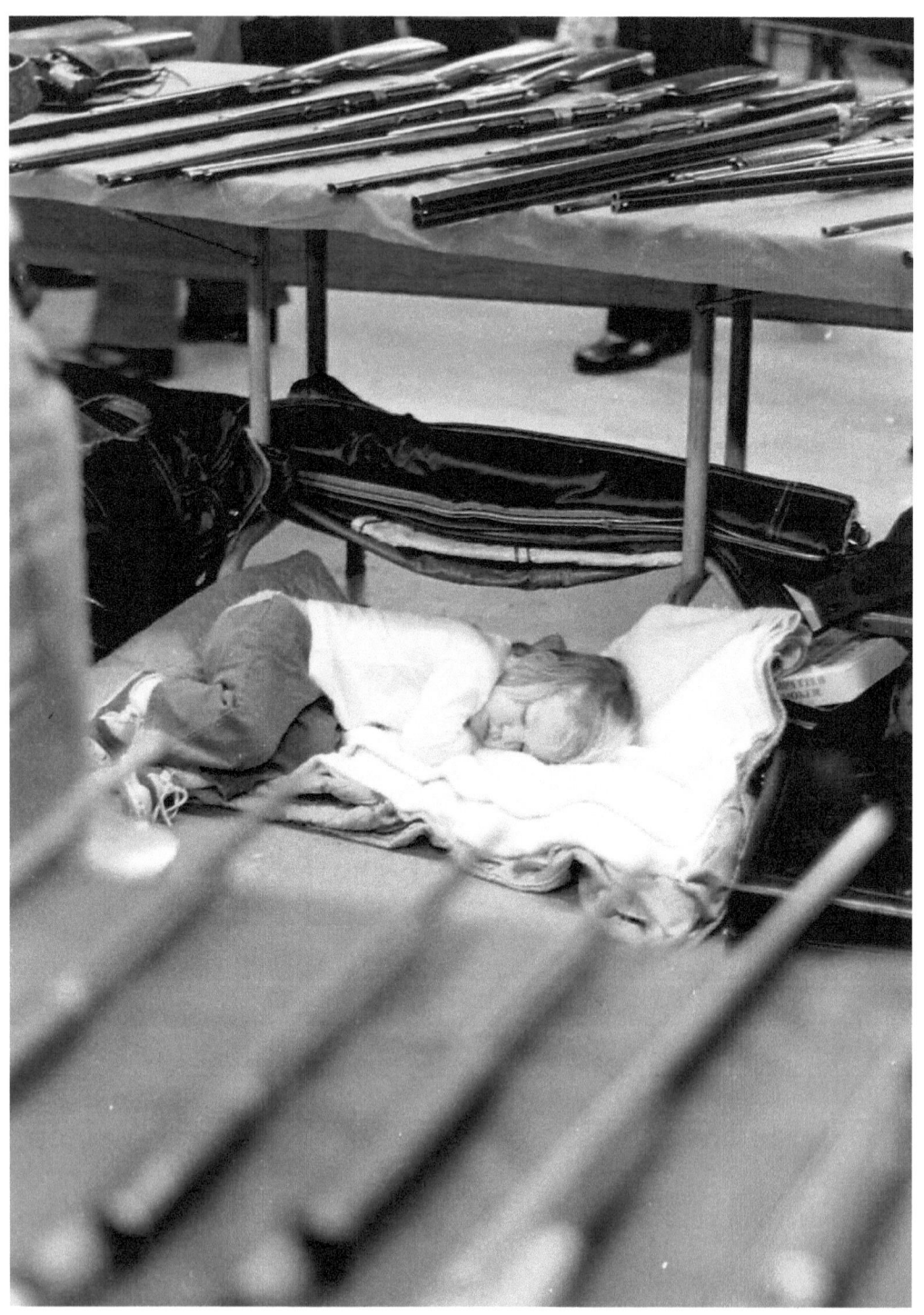

VII

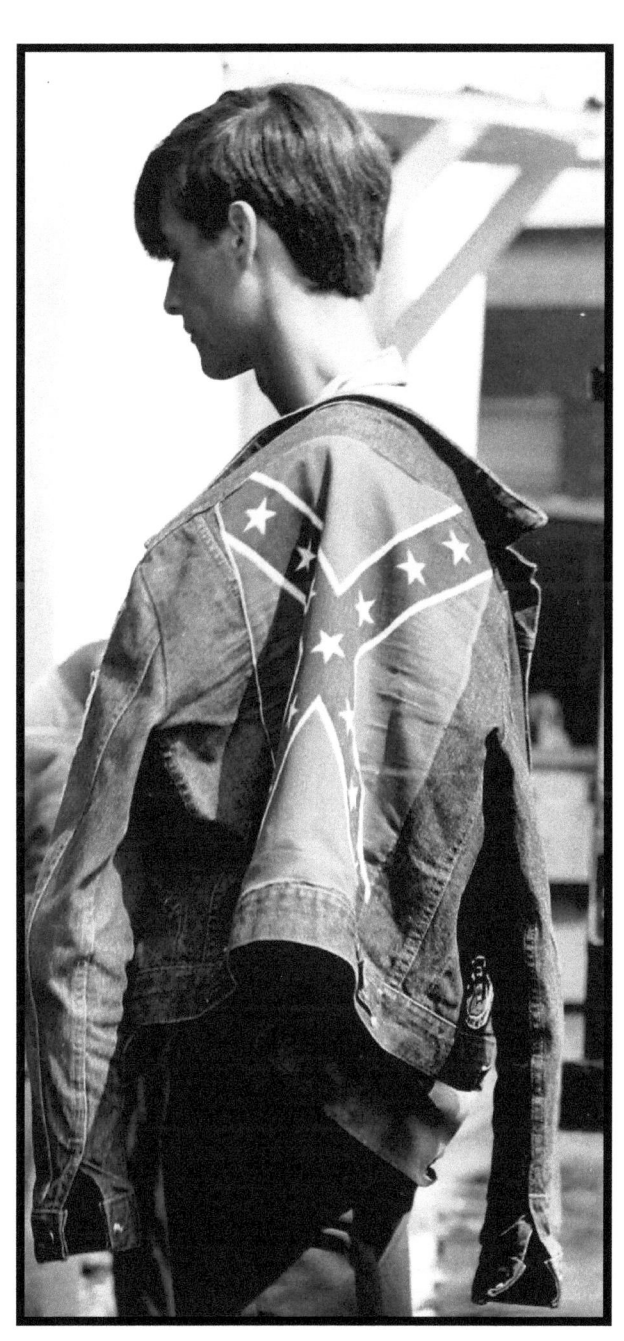

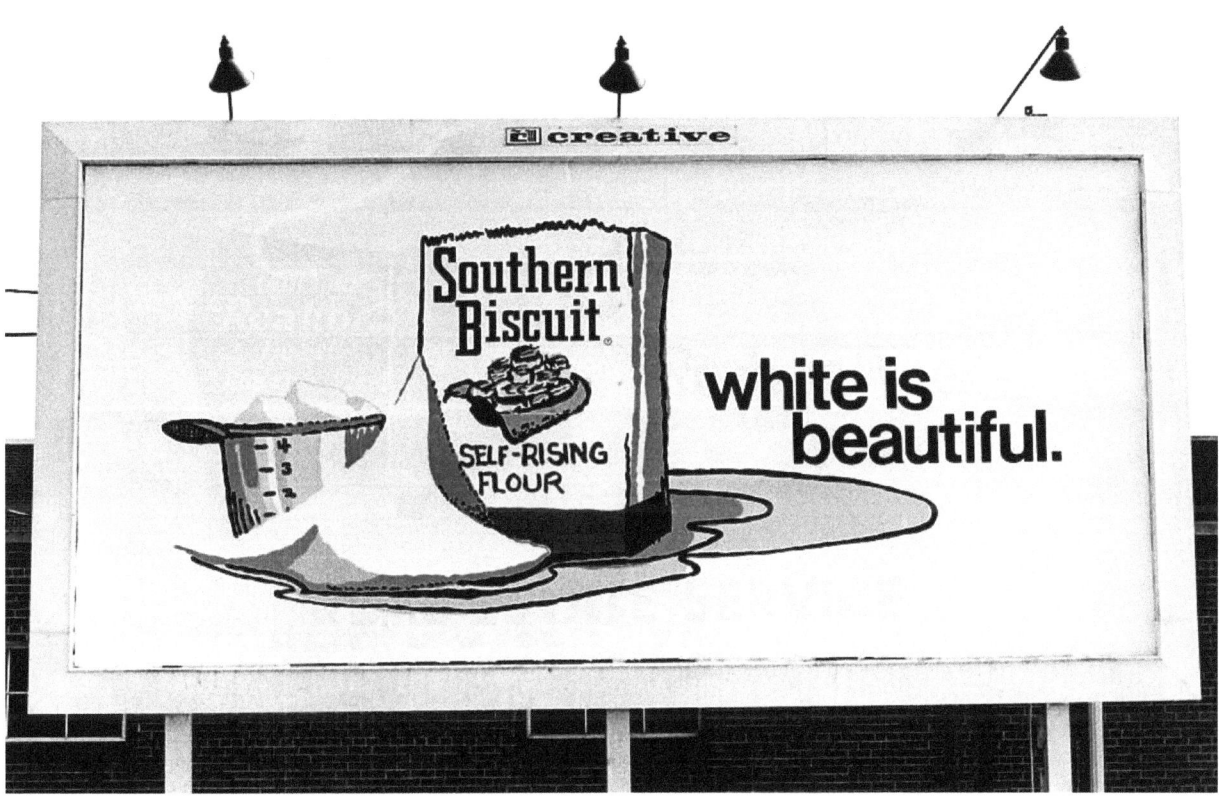

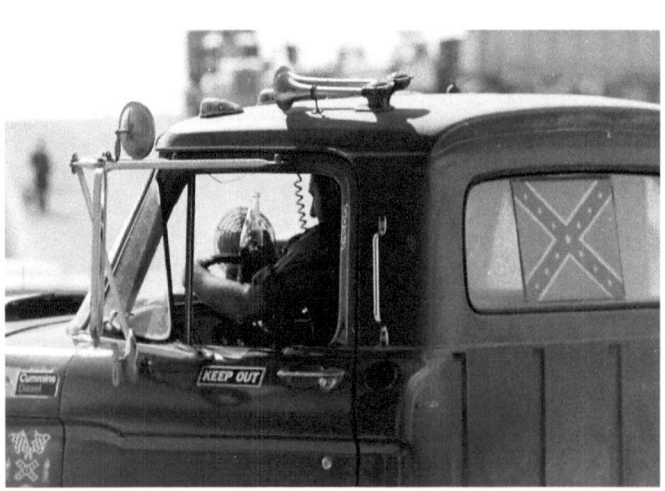

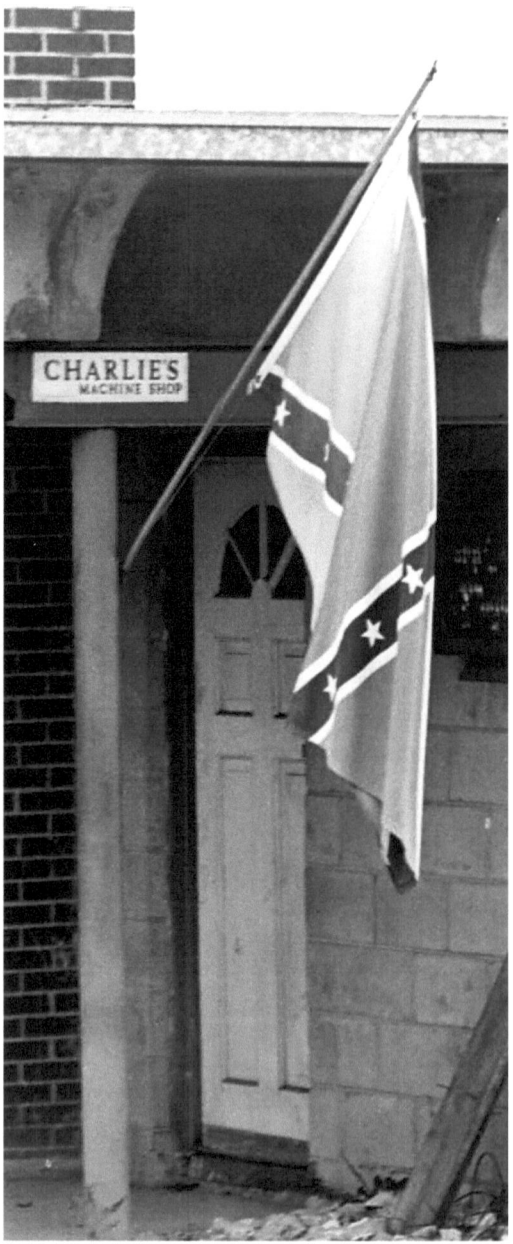

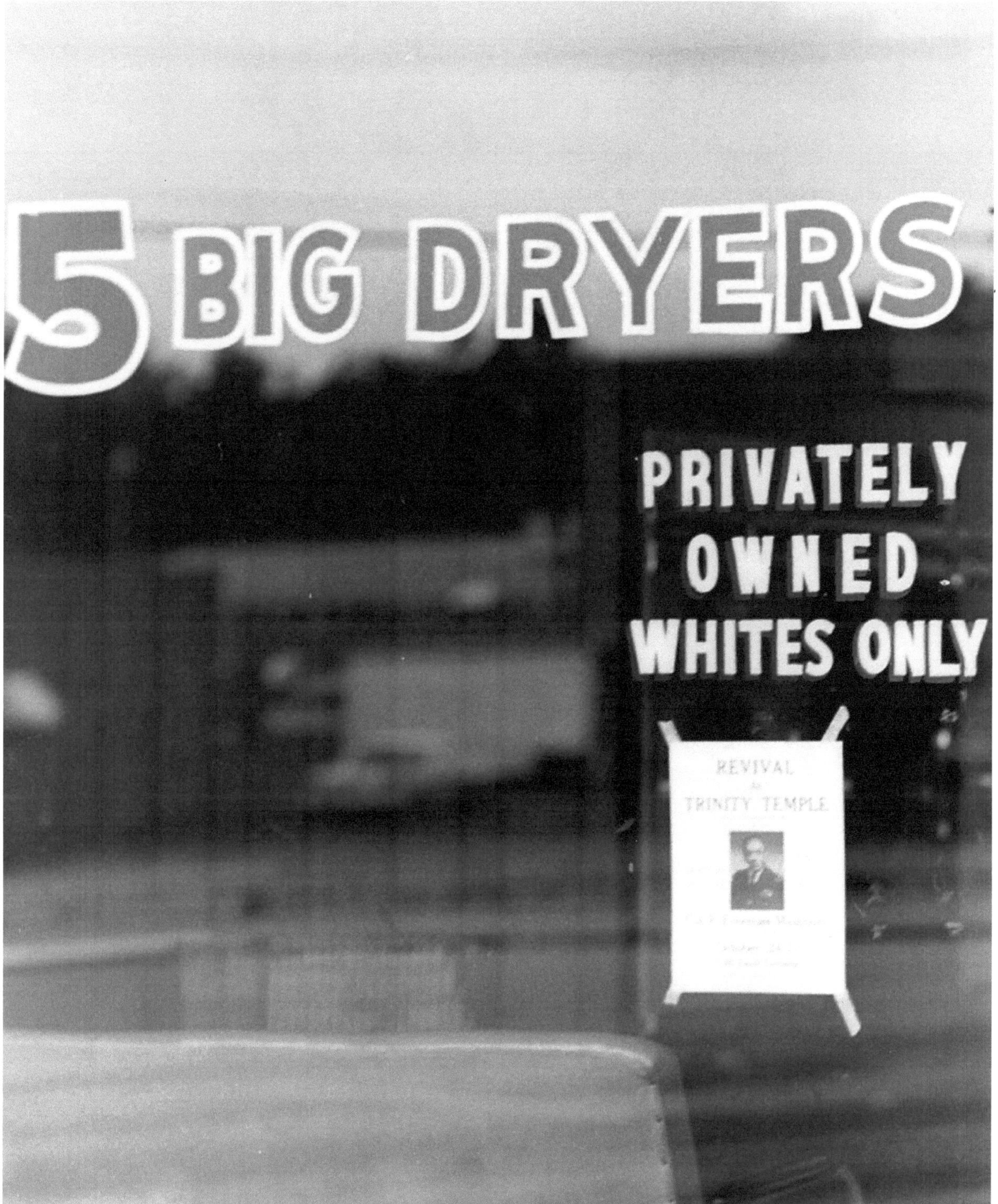
5 BIG DRYERS
PRIVATELY
OWNED
WHITES ONLY
REVIVAL
TRINITY TEMPLE

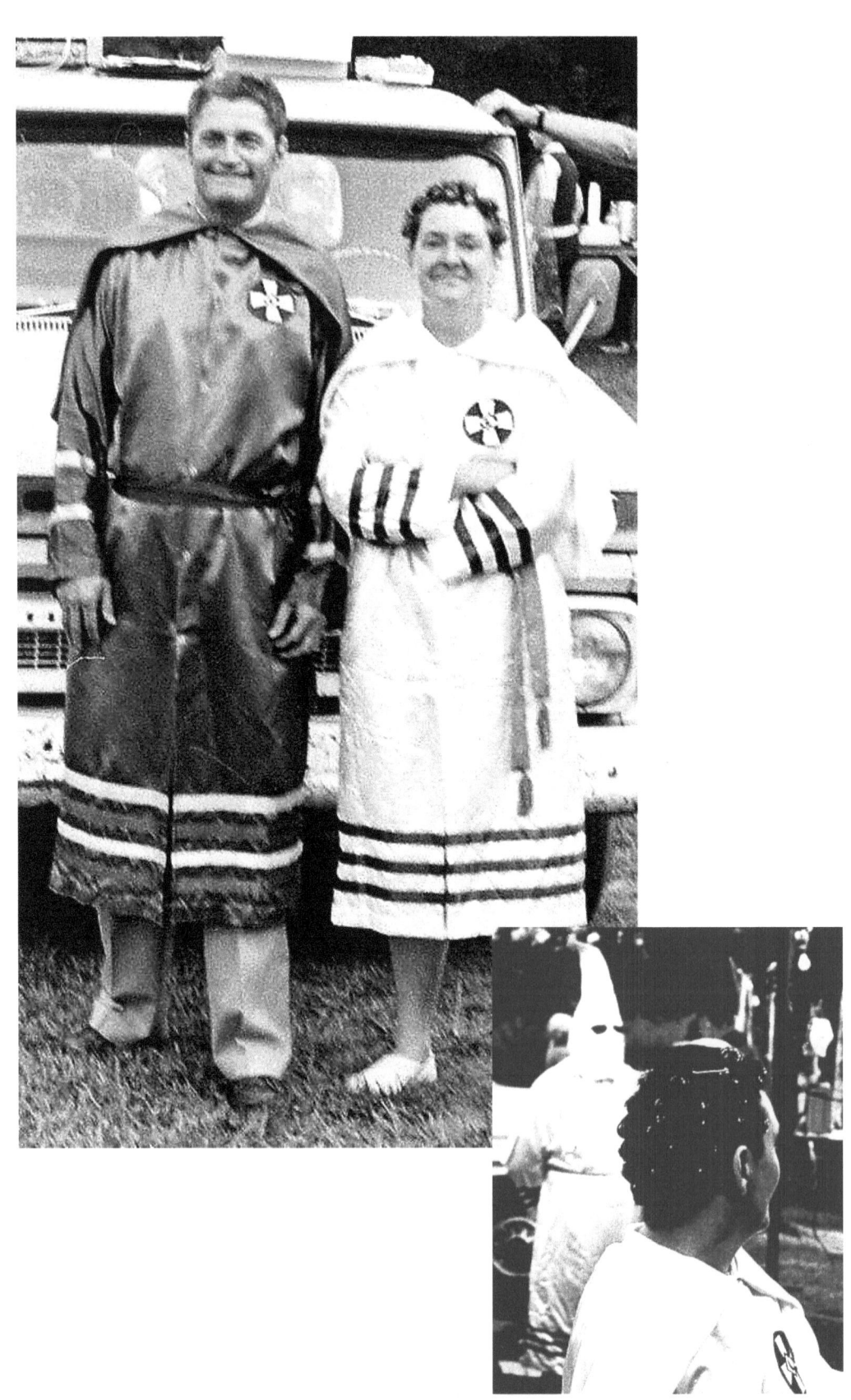

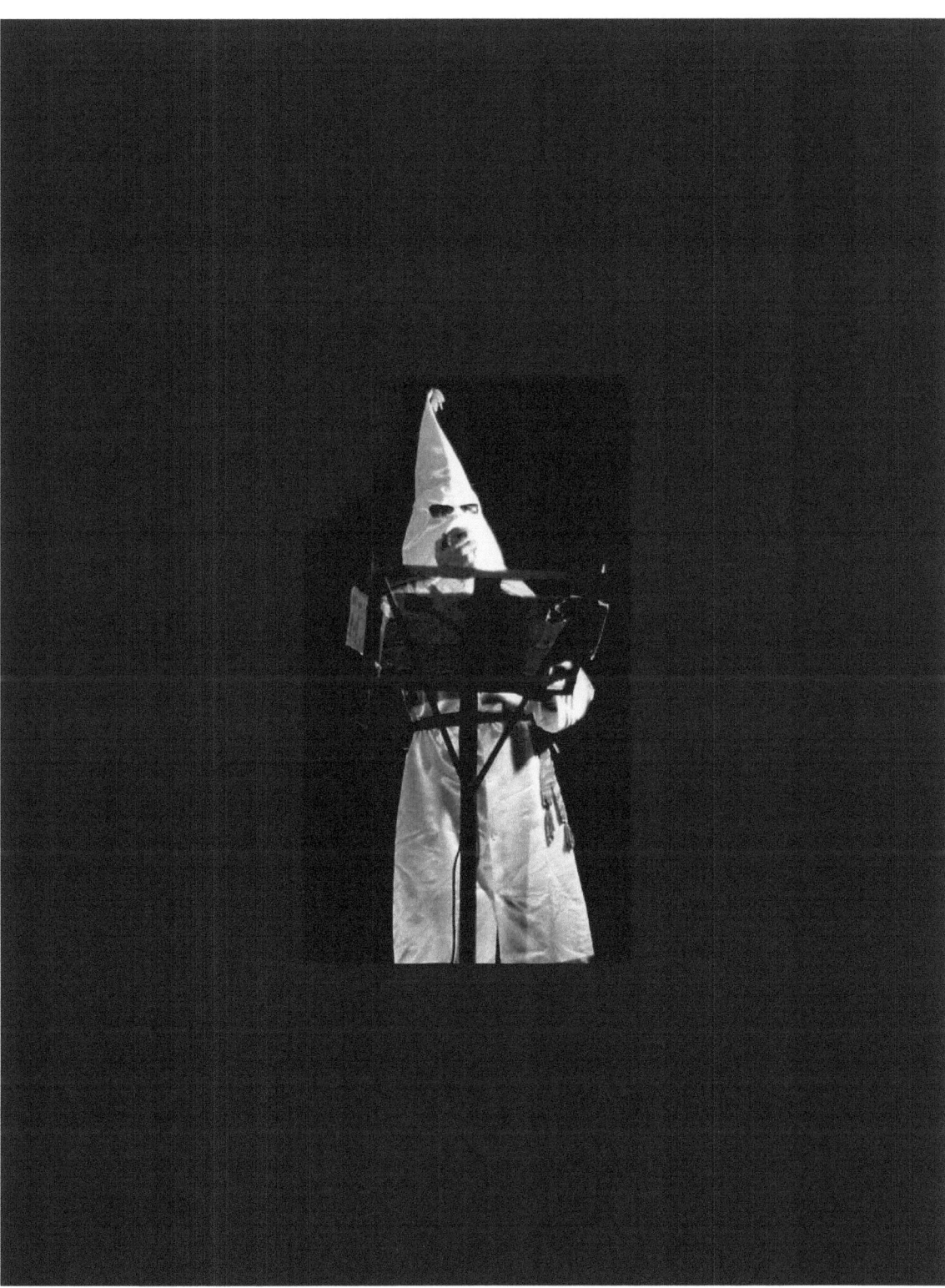

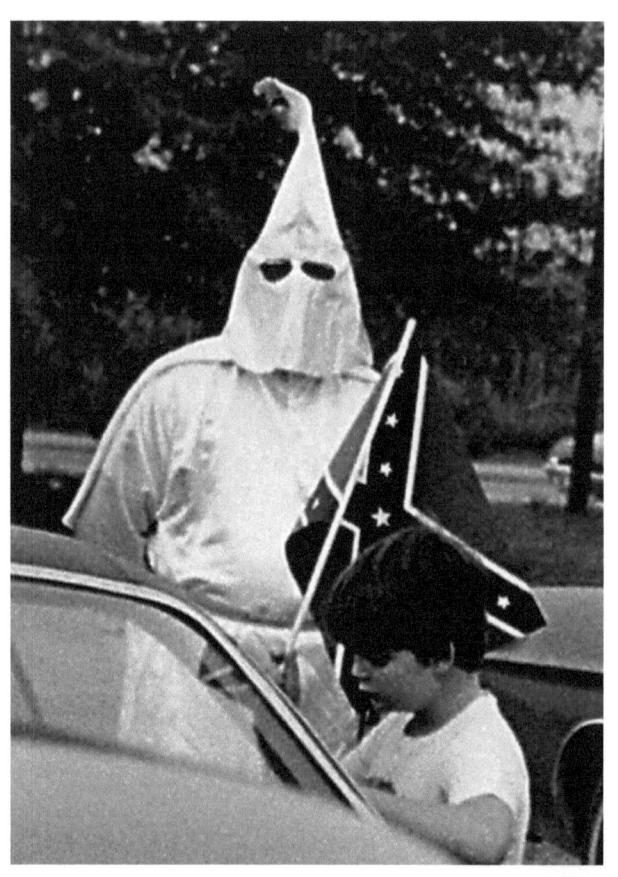

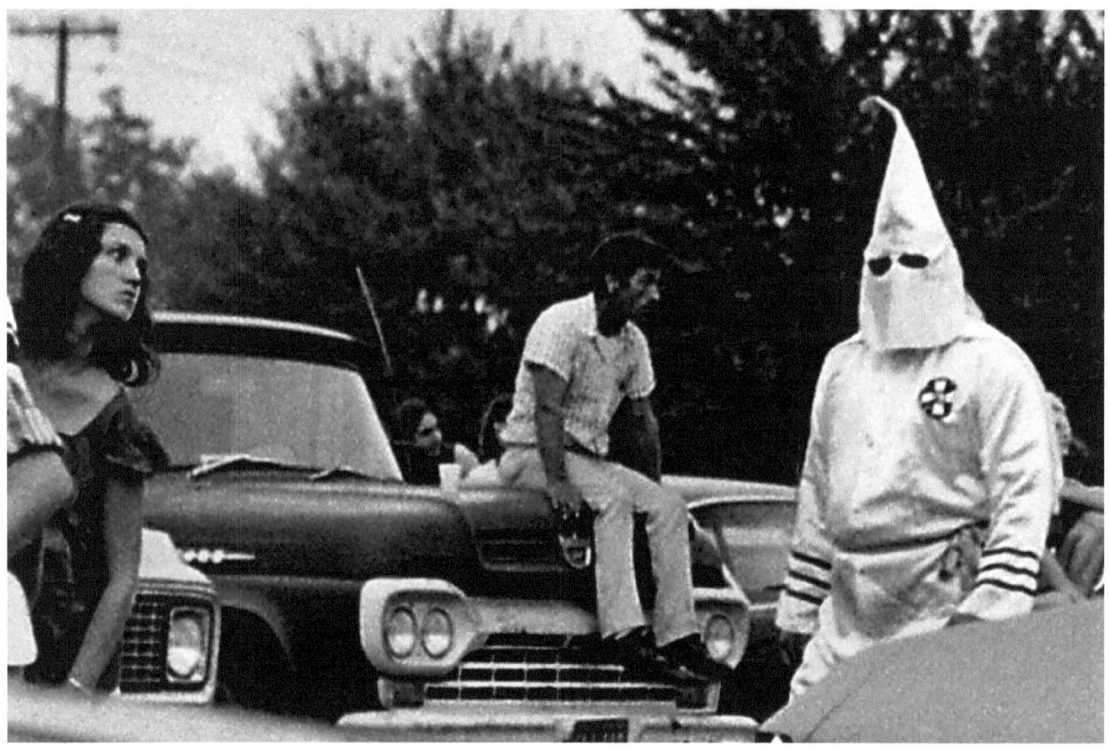

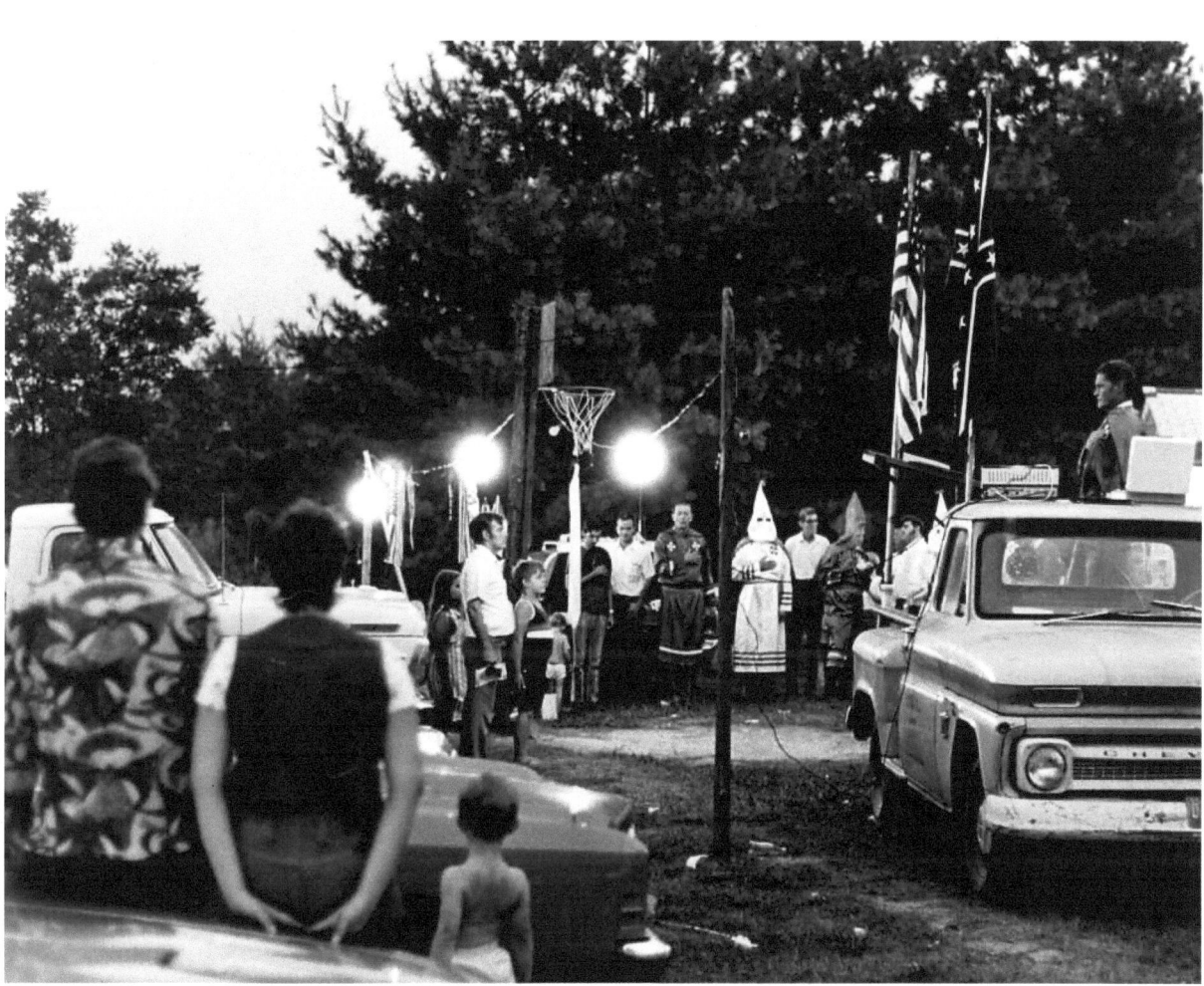

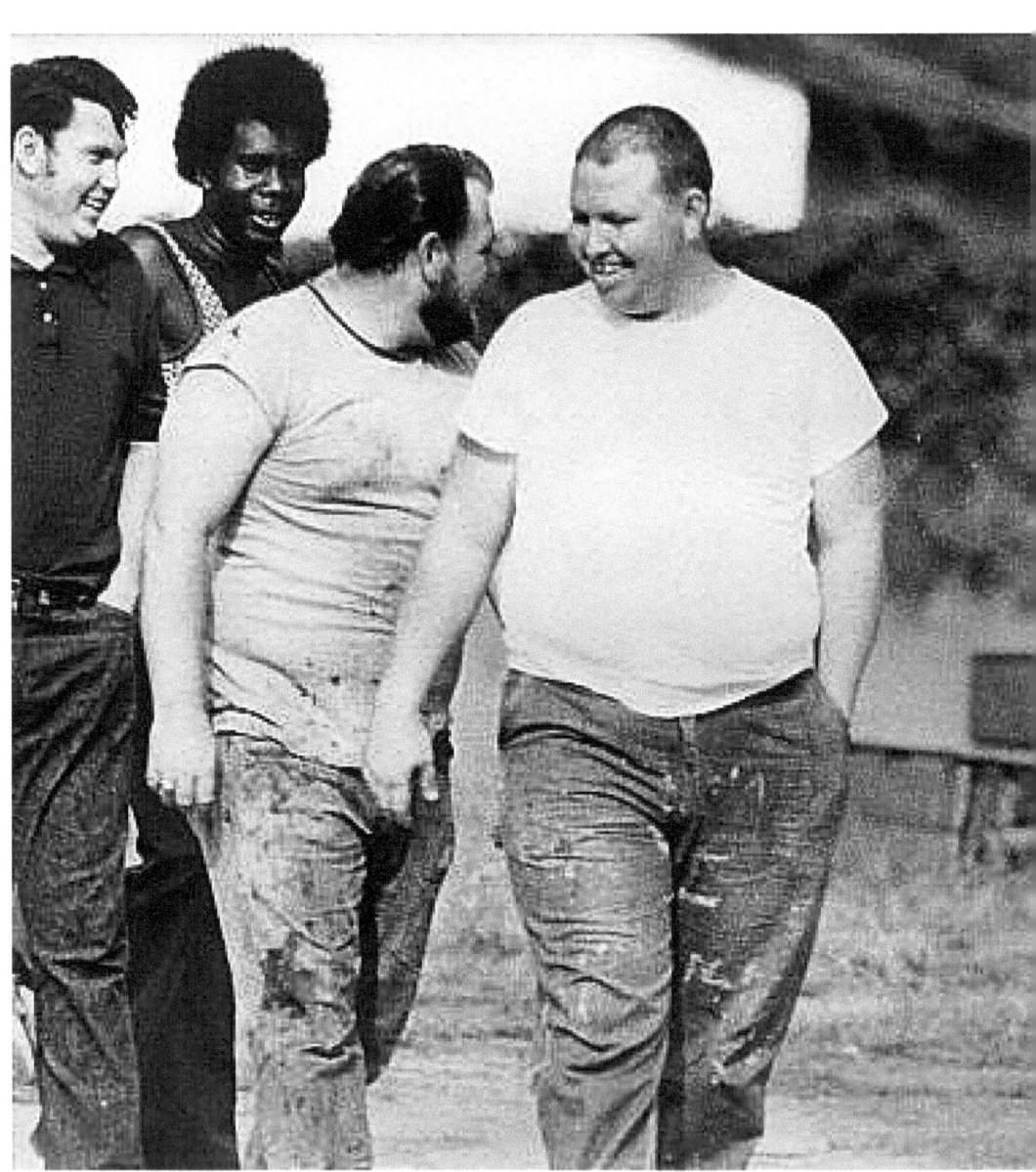

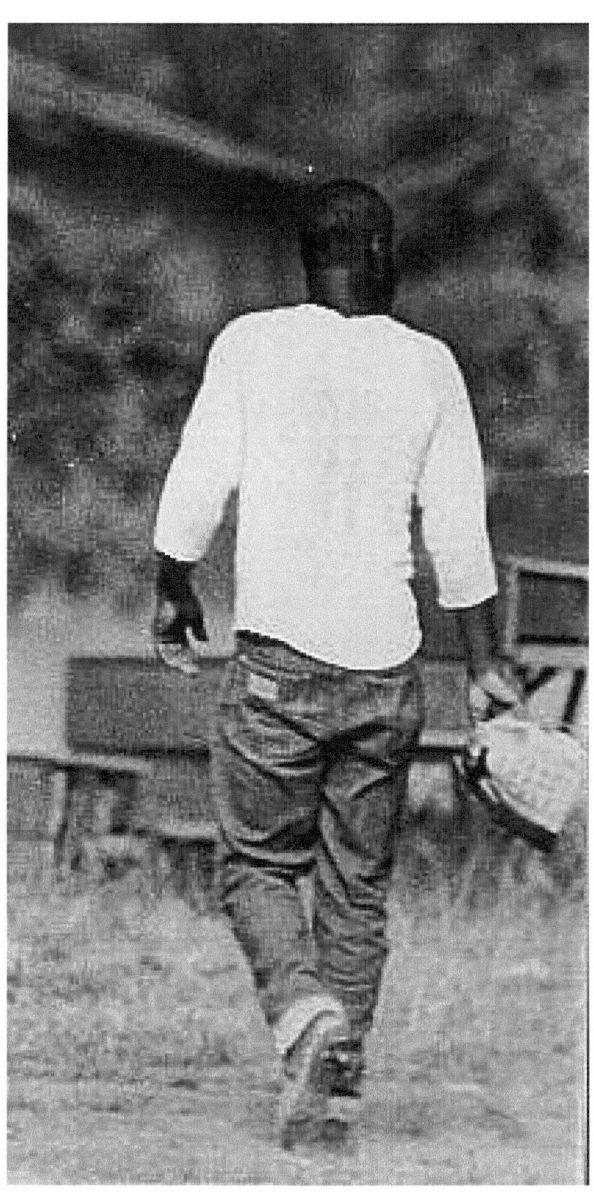

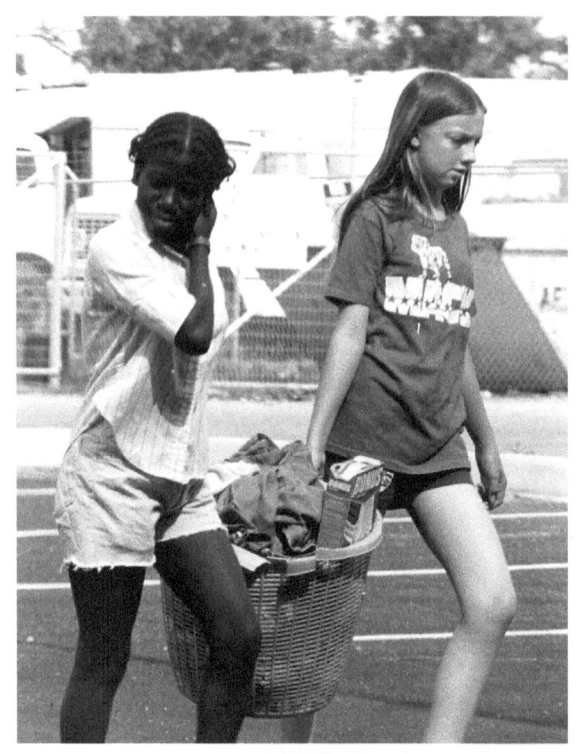

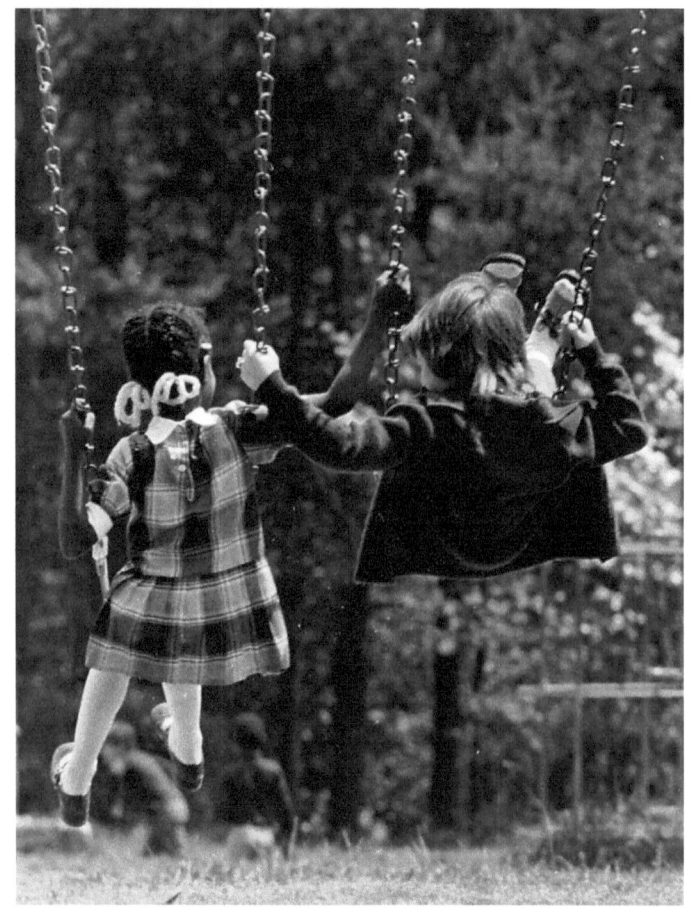

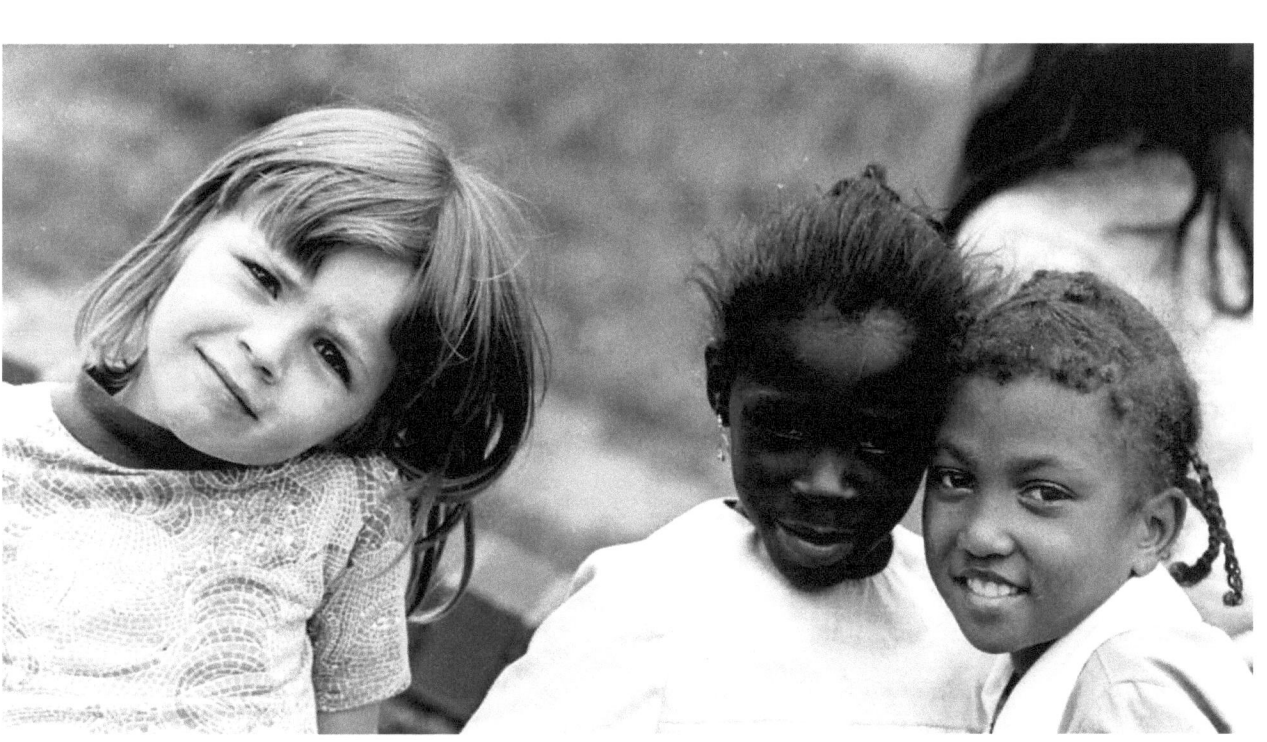

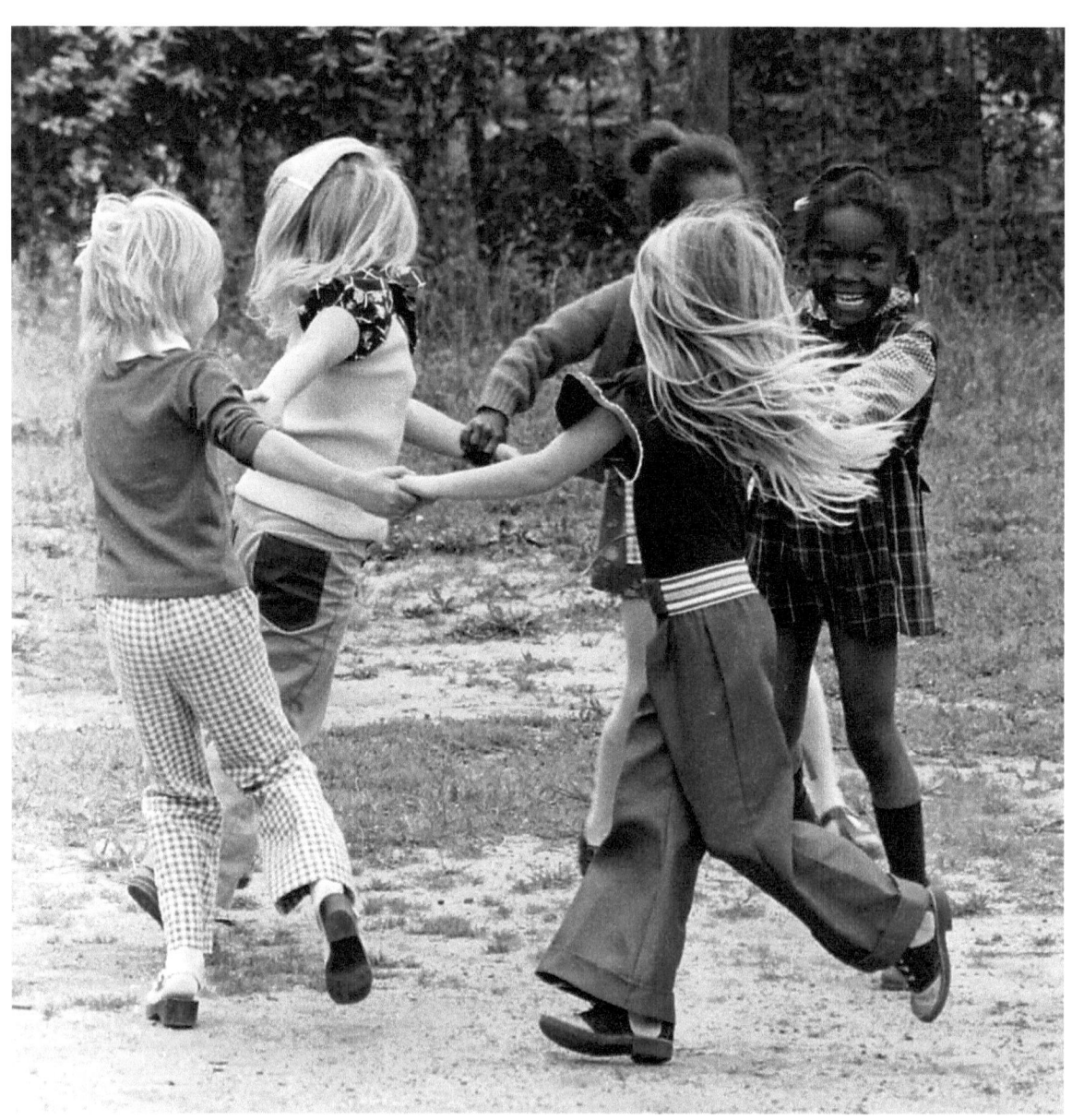

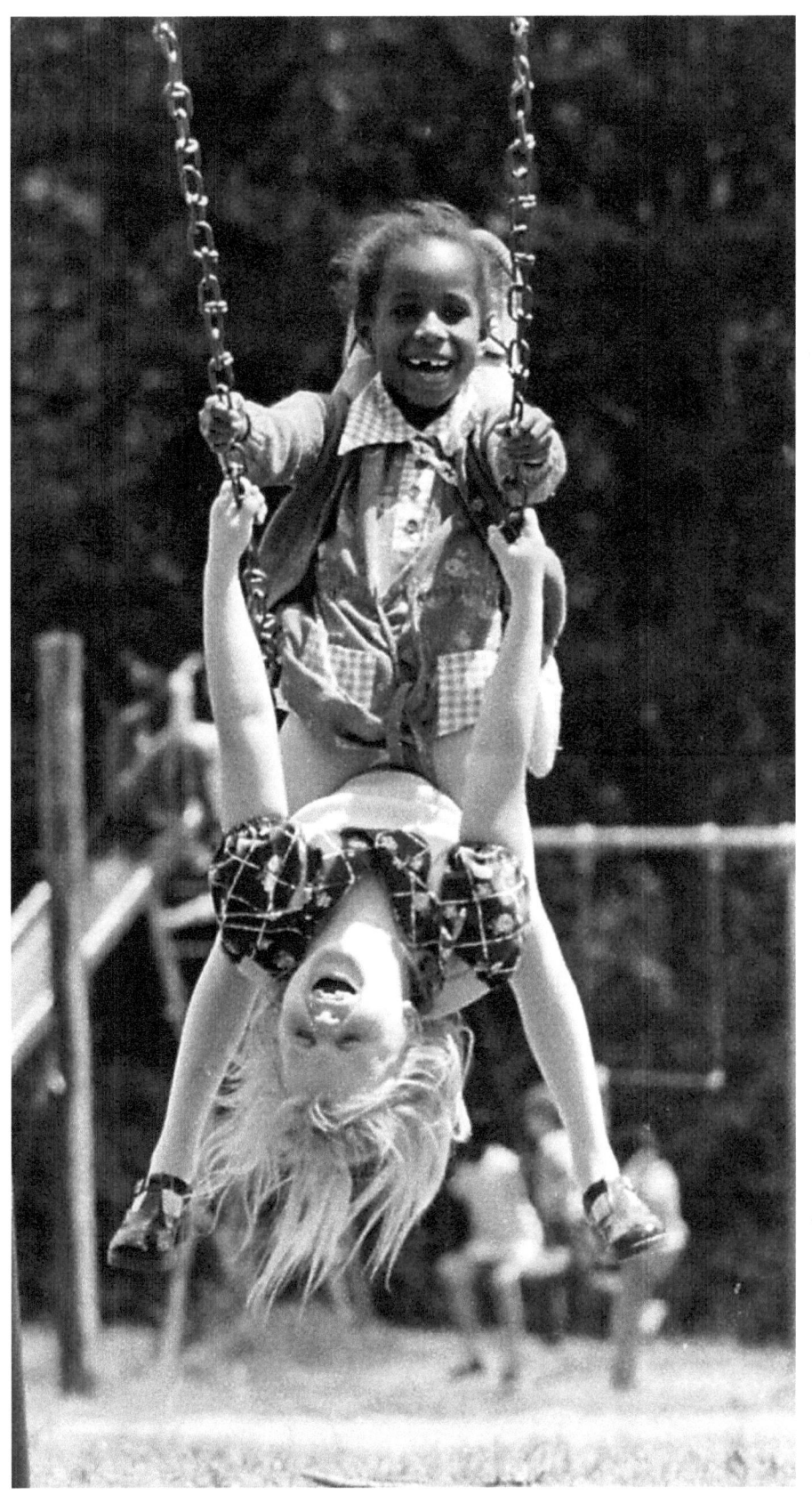

VIII

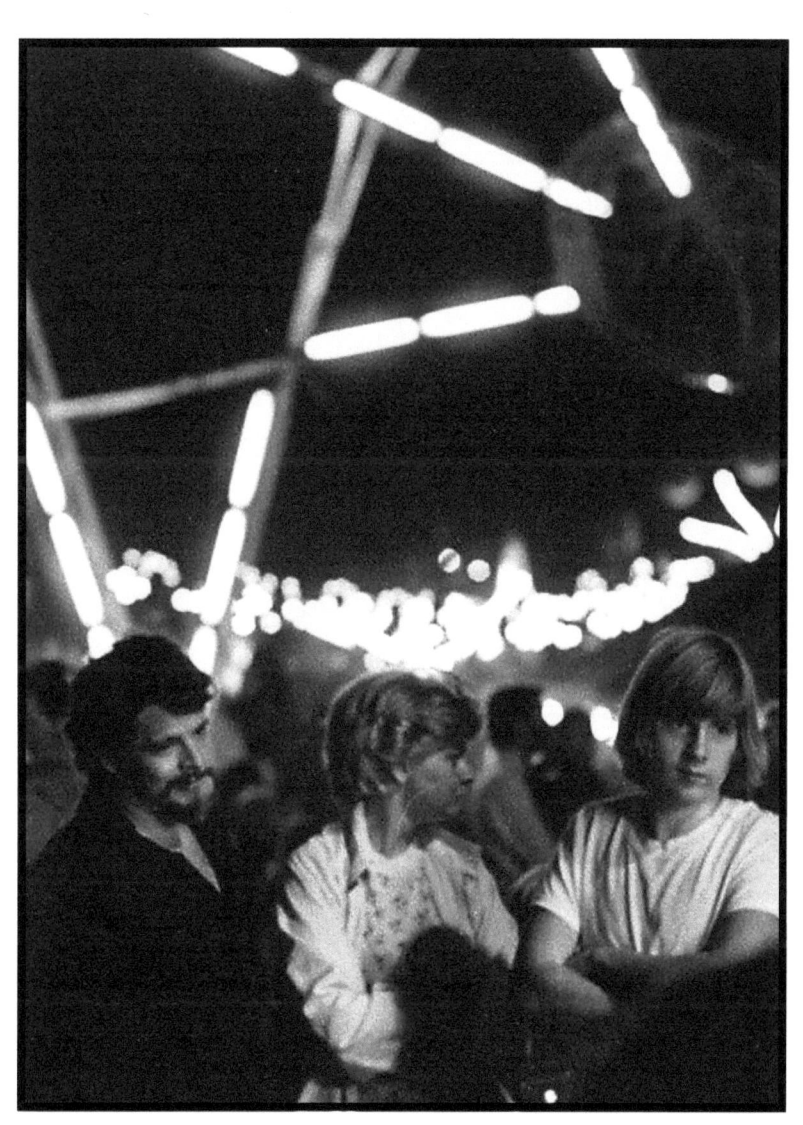

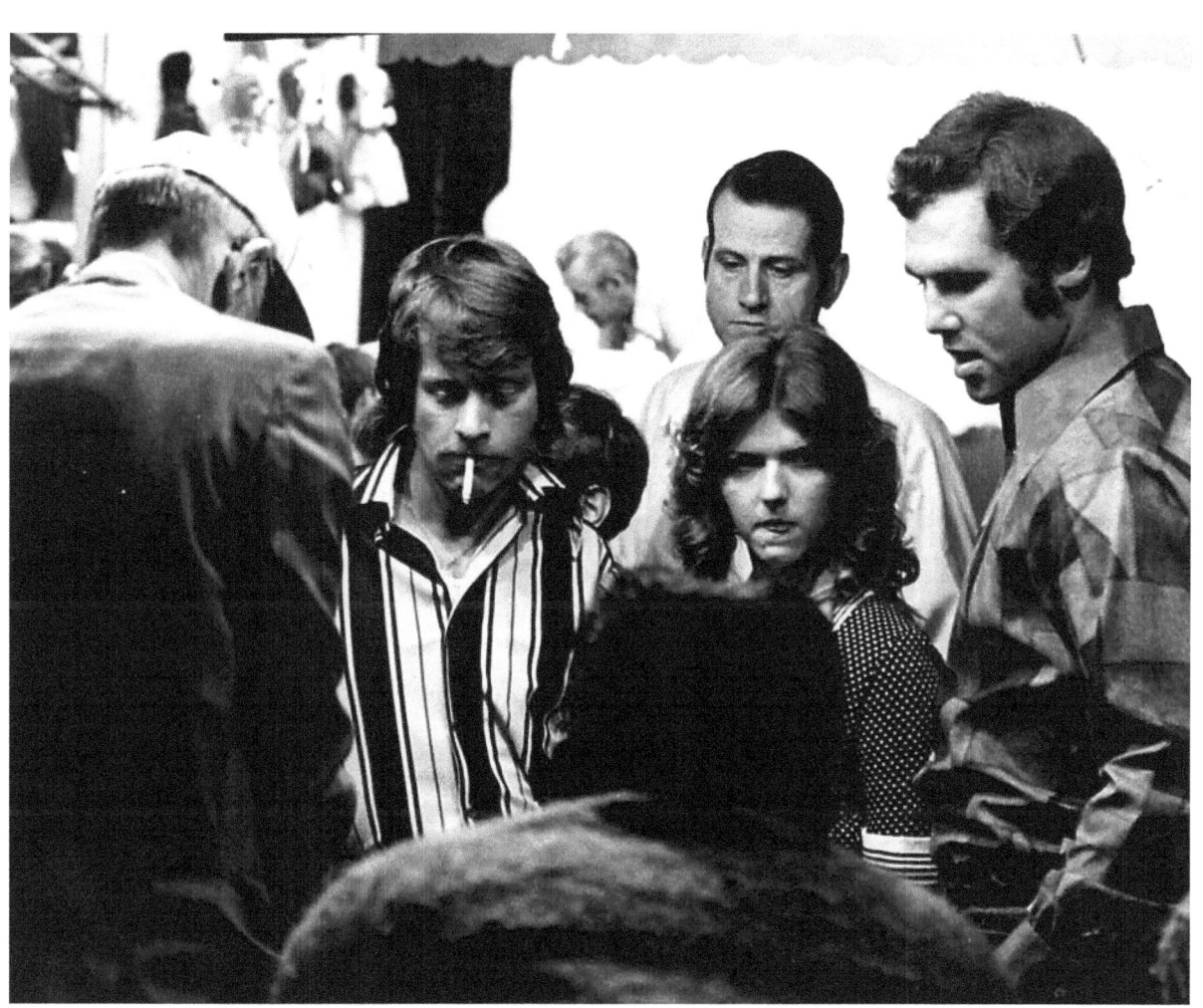

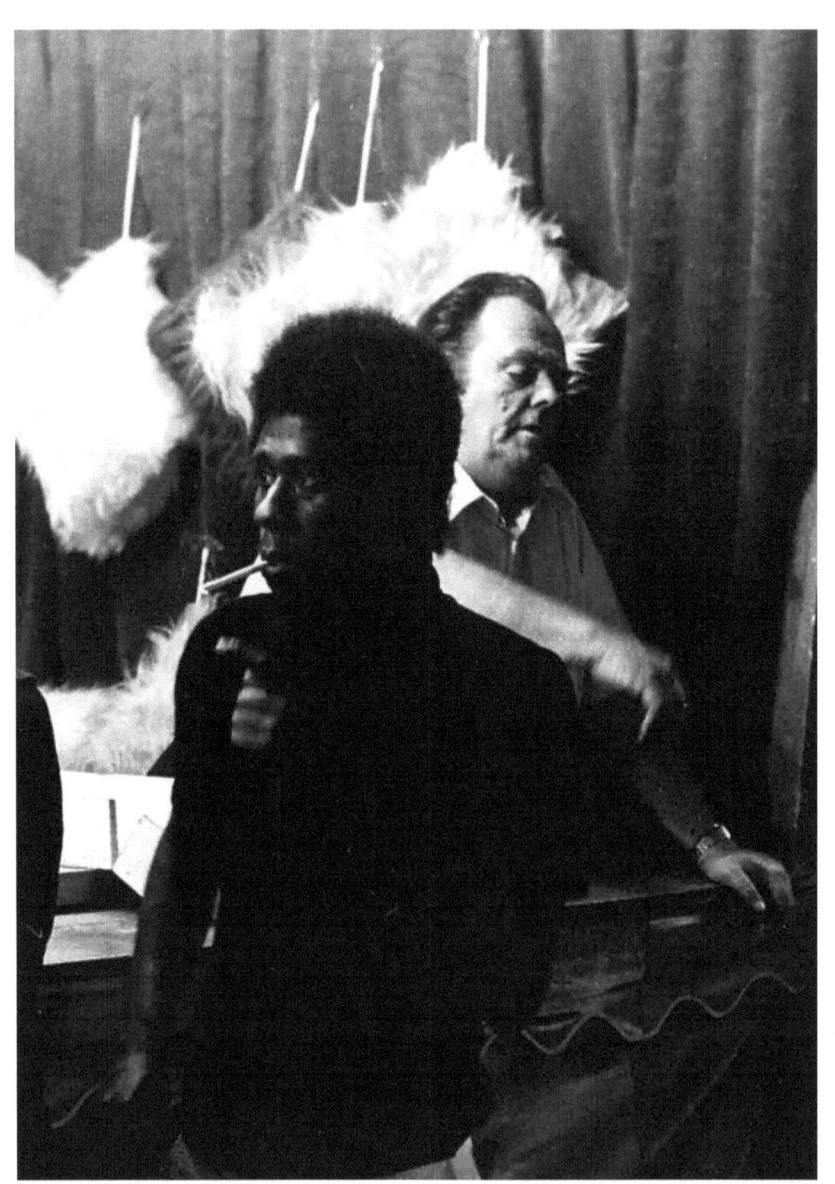

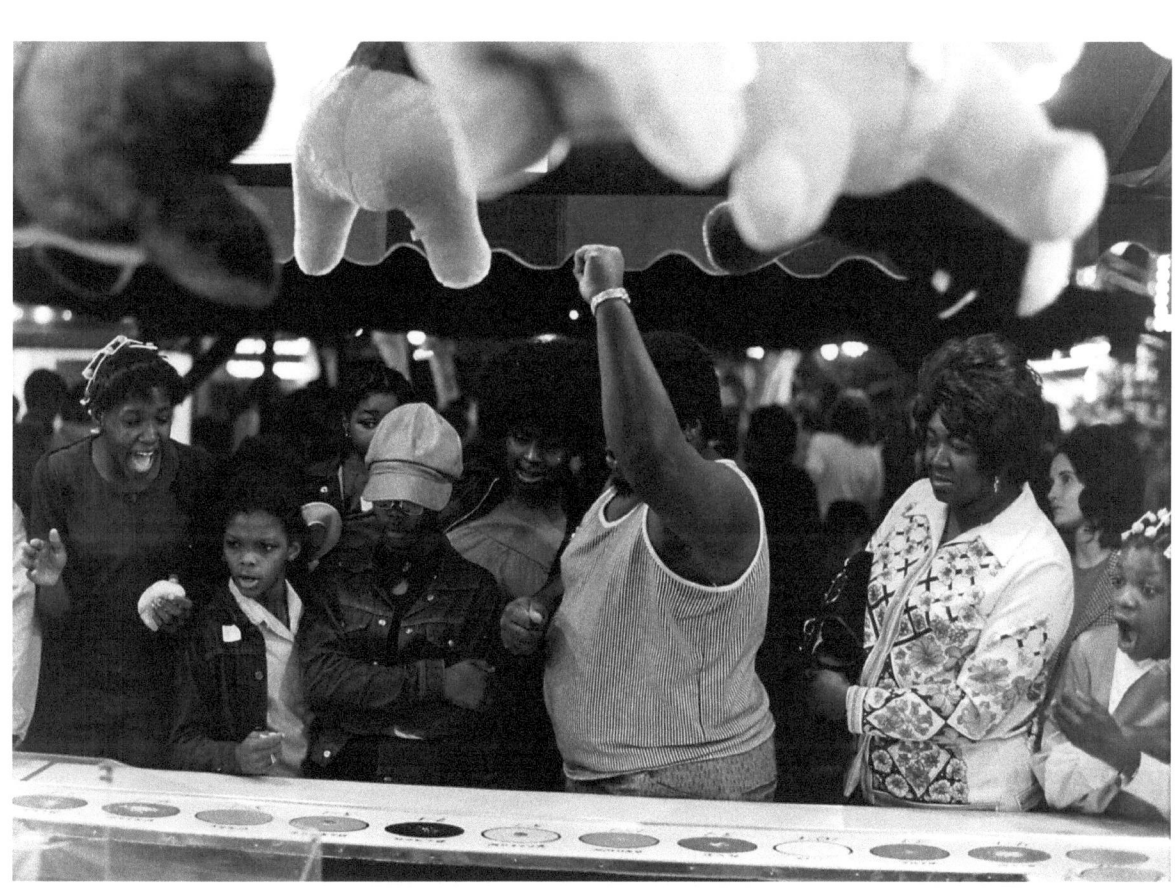

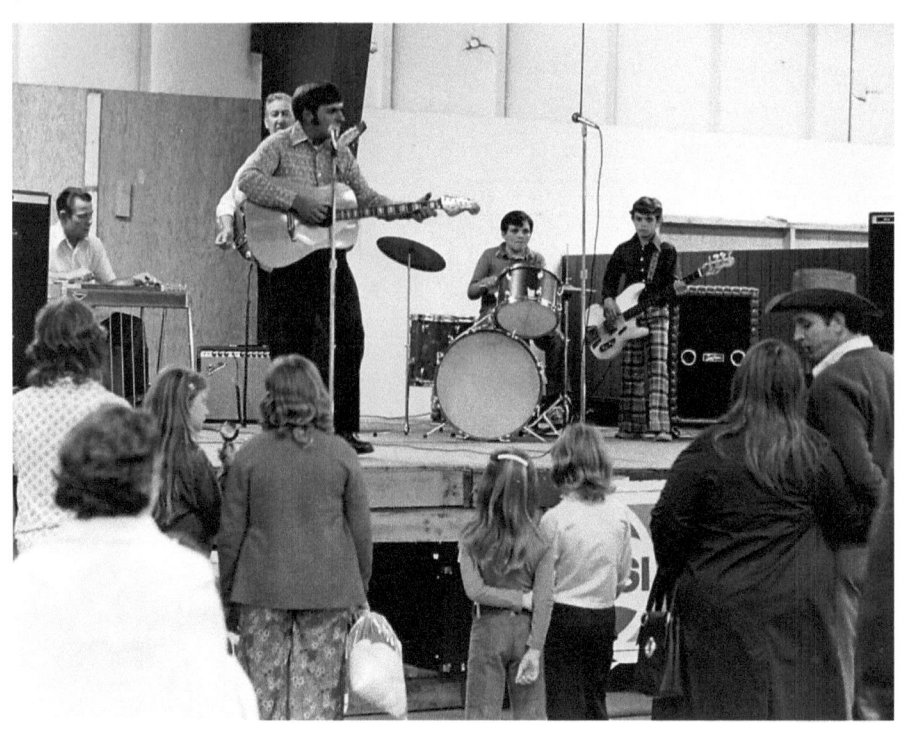

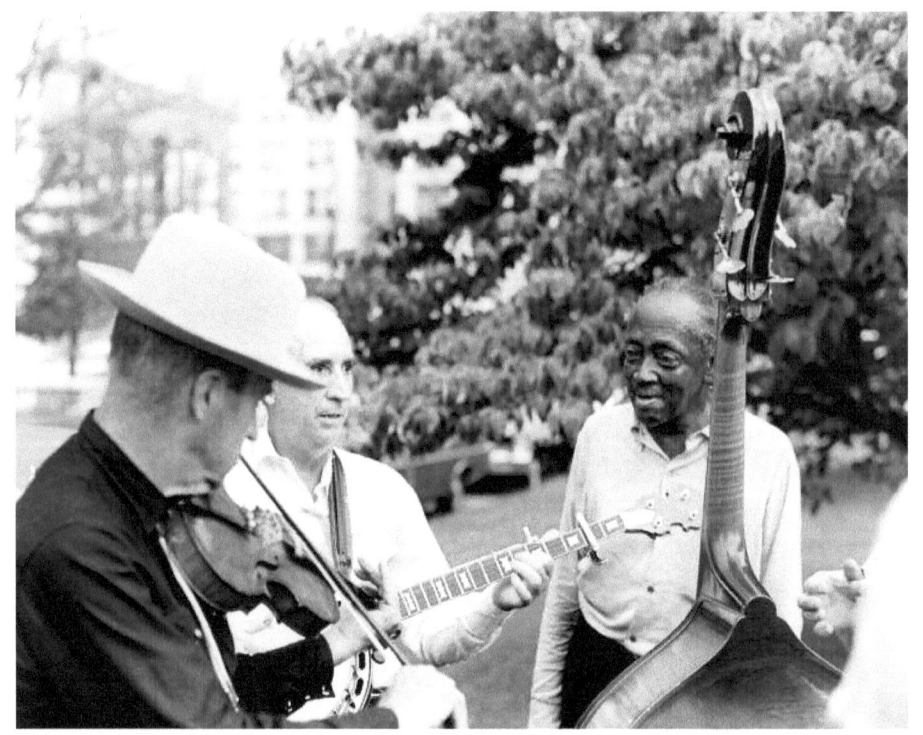

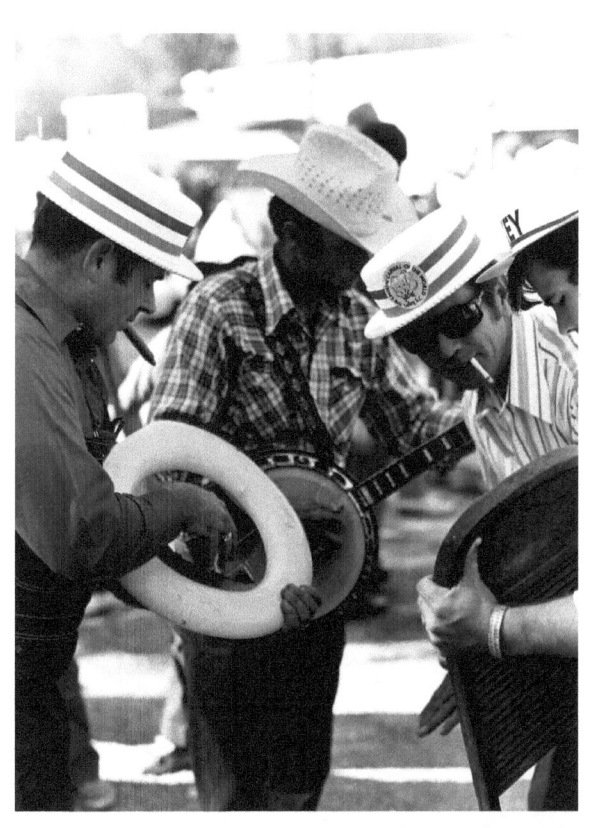

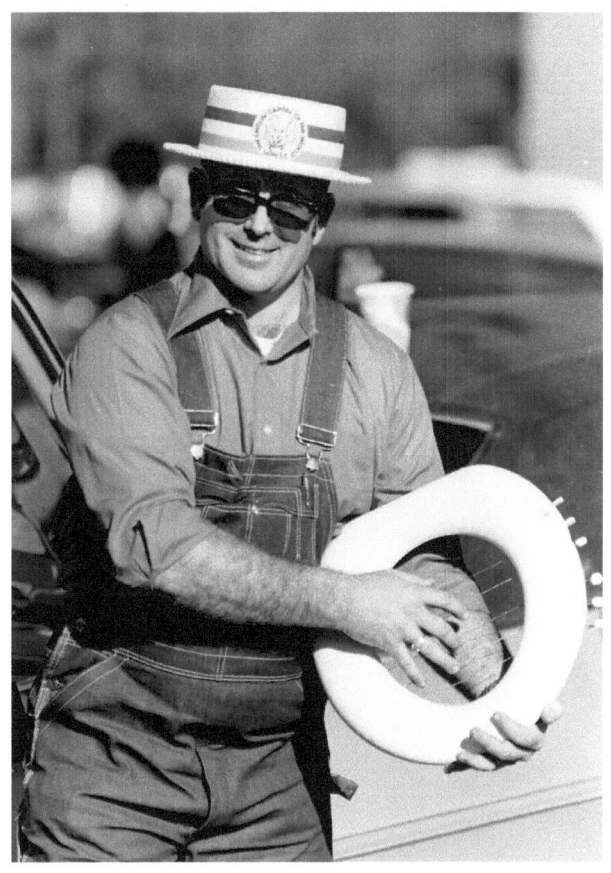

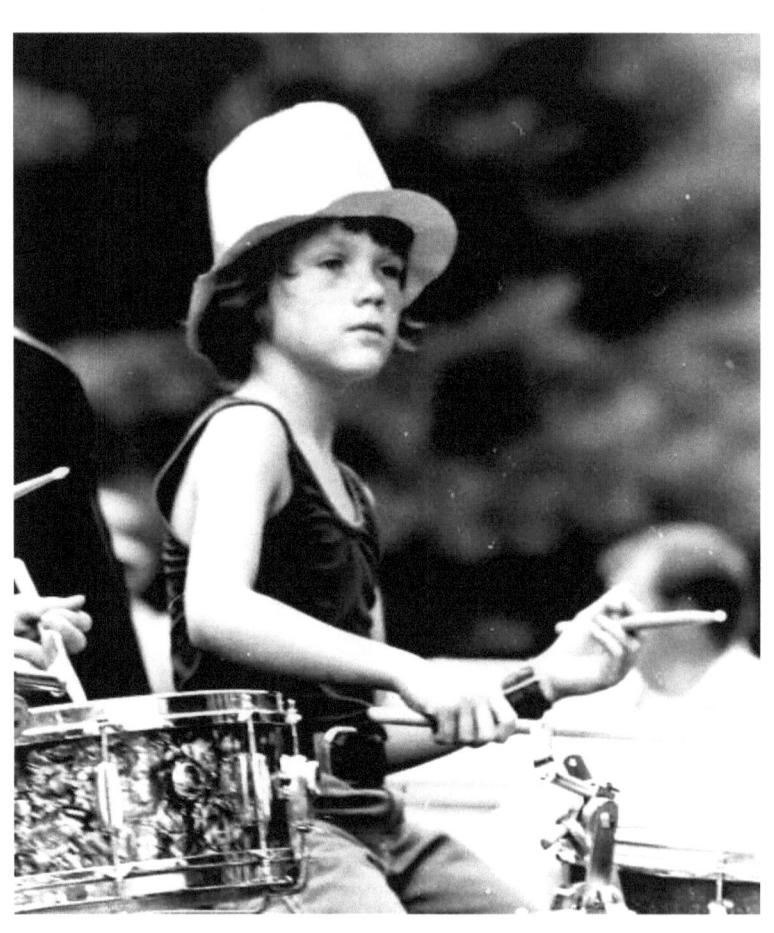

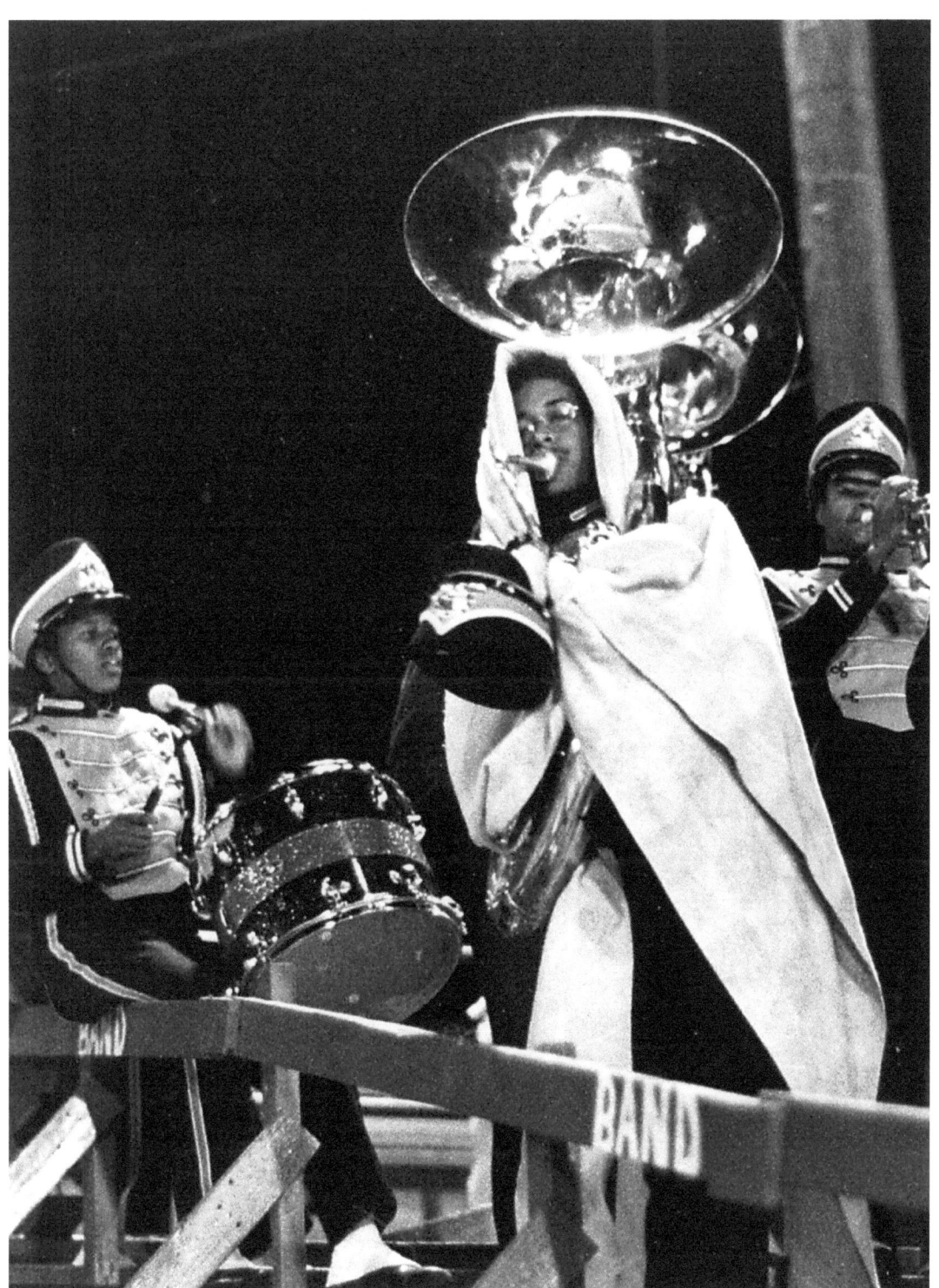

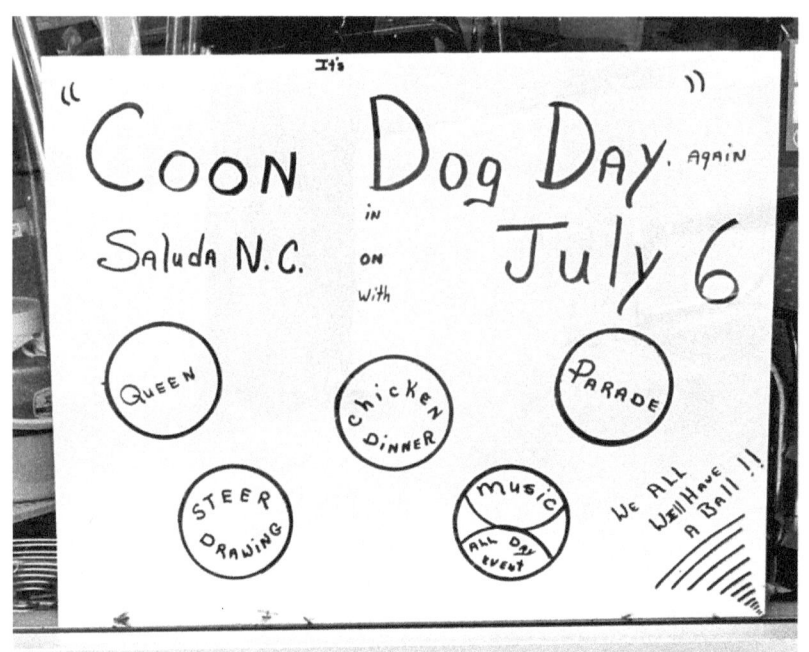

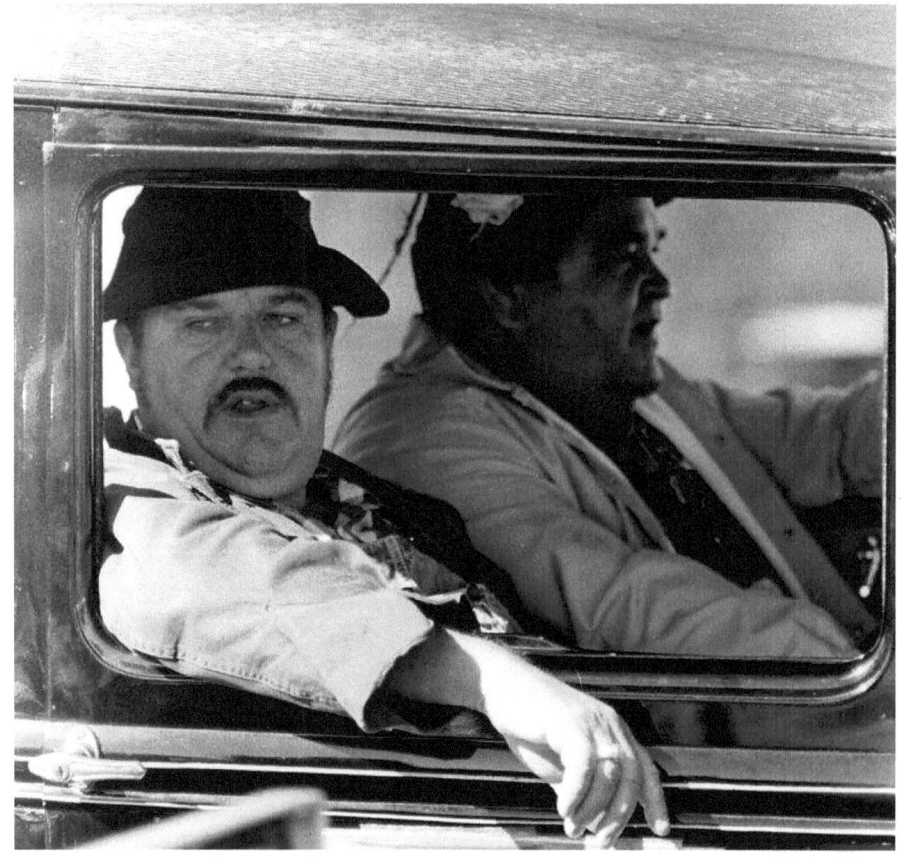

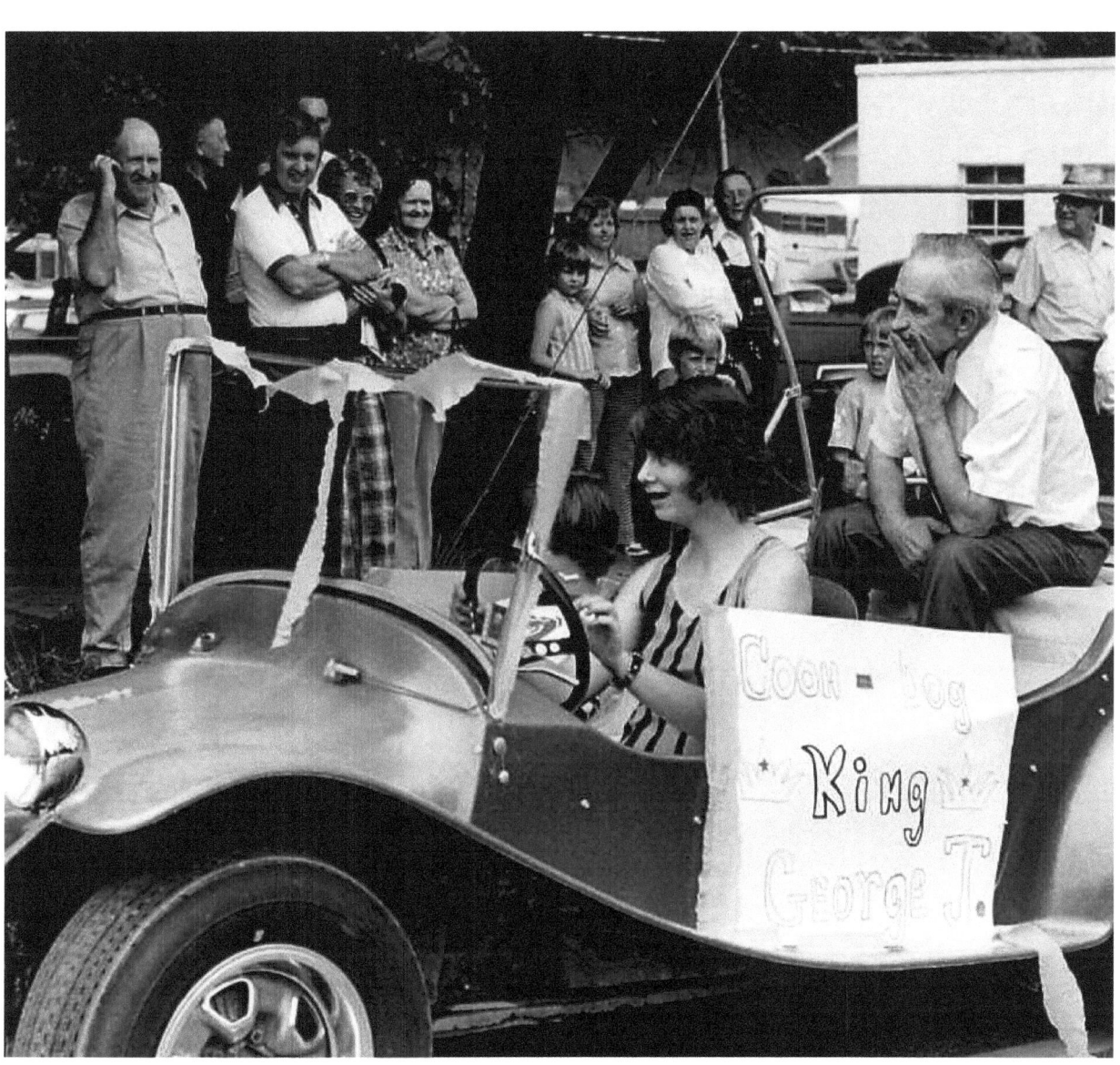

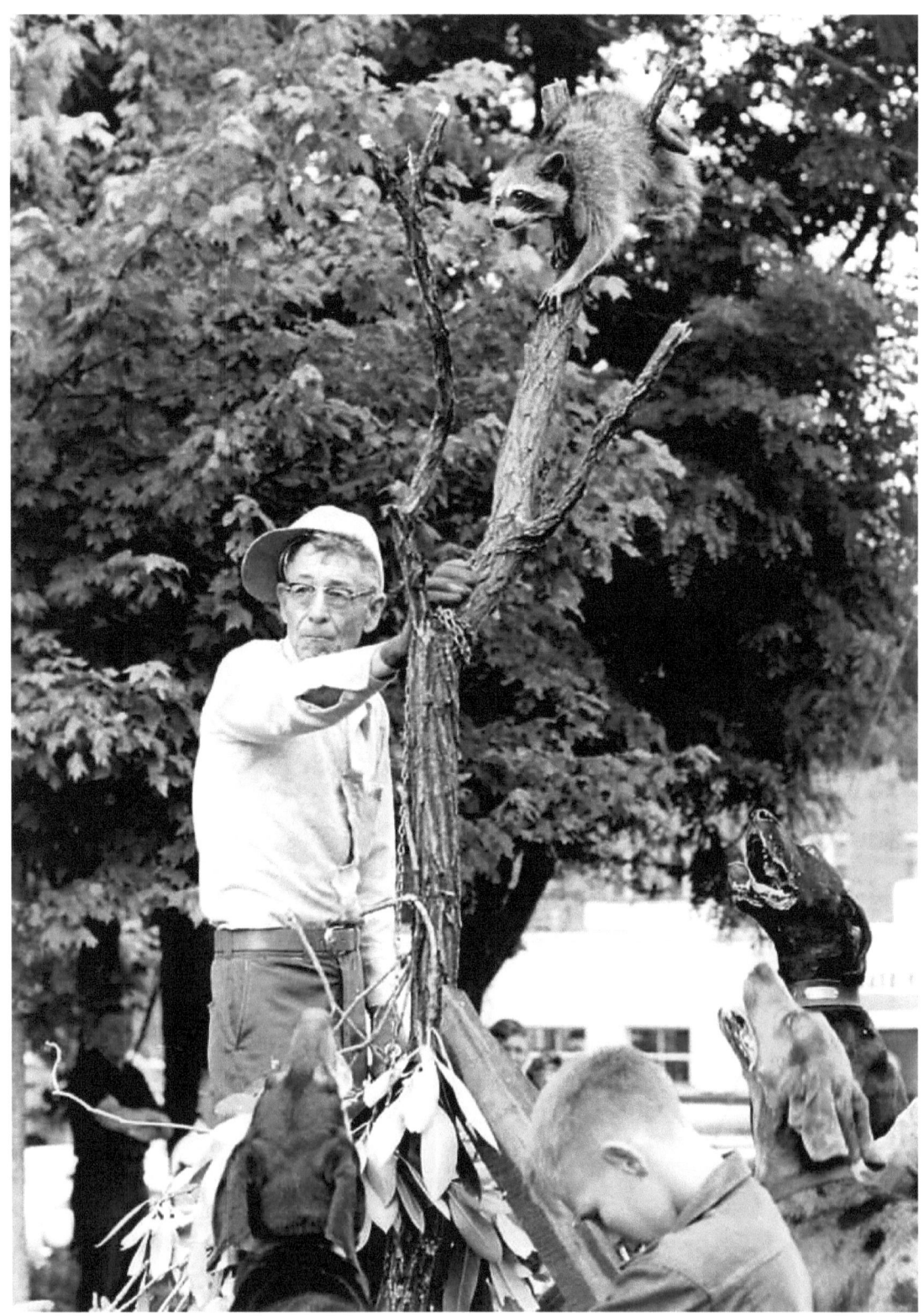

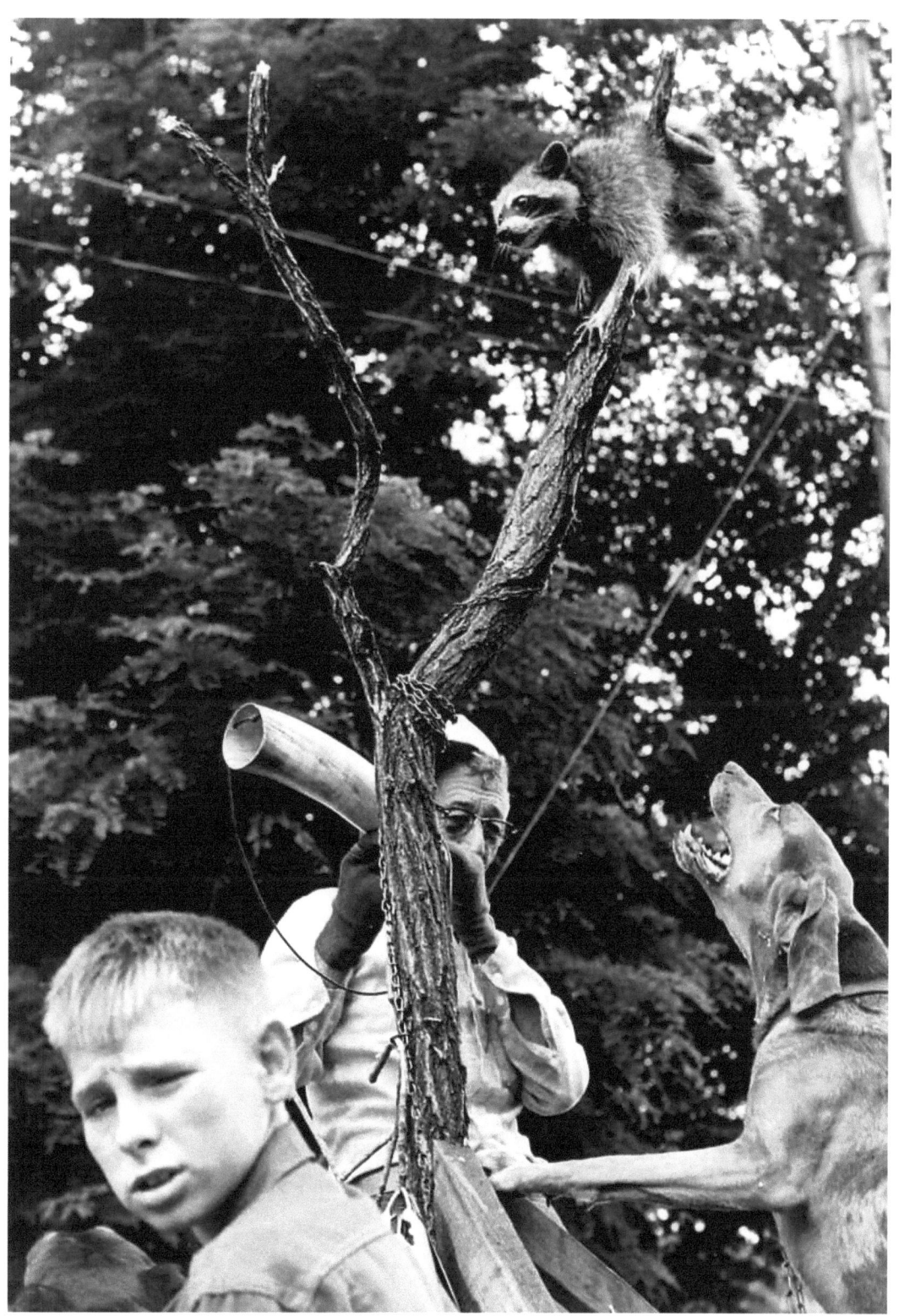

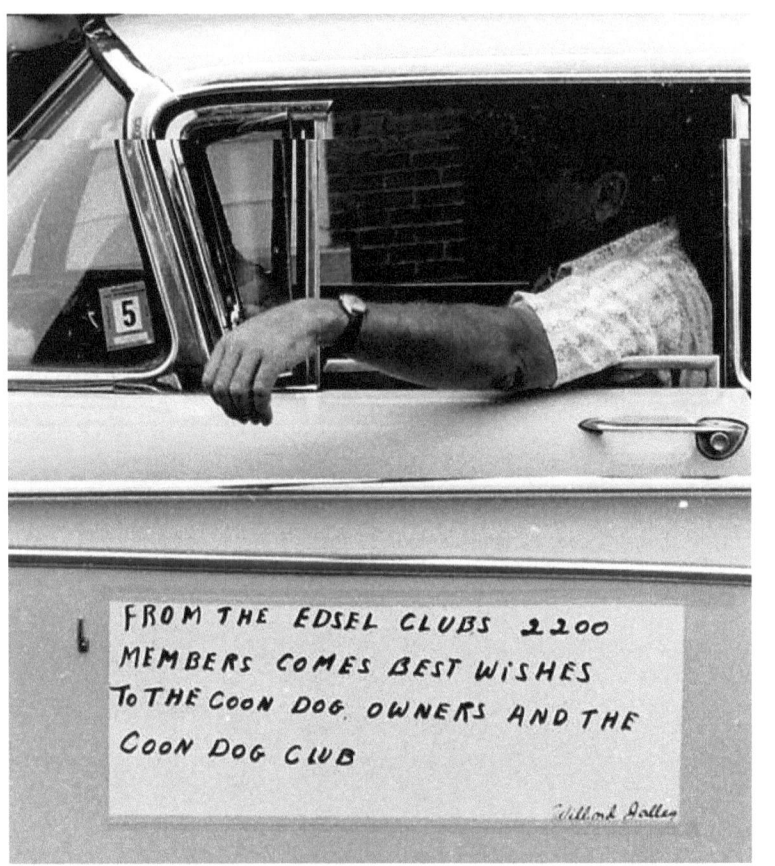

FROM THE EDSEL CLUBS 2200
MEMBERS COMES BEST WISHES
TO THE COON DOG. OWNERS AND THE
COON DOG CLUB

Willard Dalley

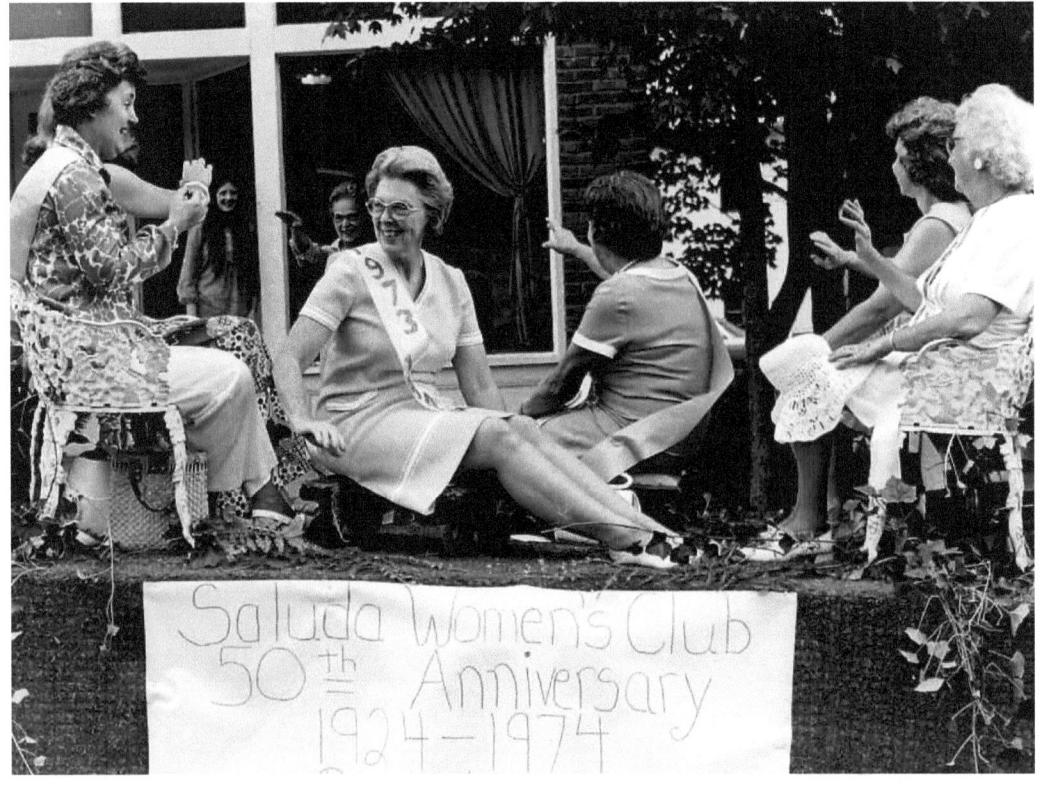

Saluda Women's Club
50th Anniversary
1924-1974

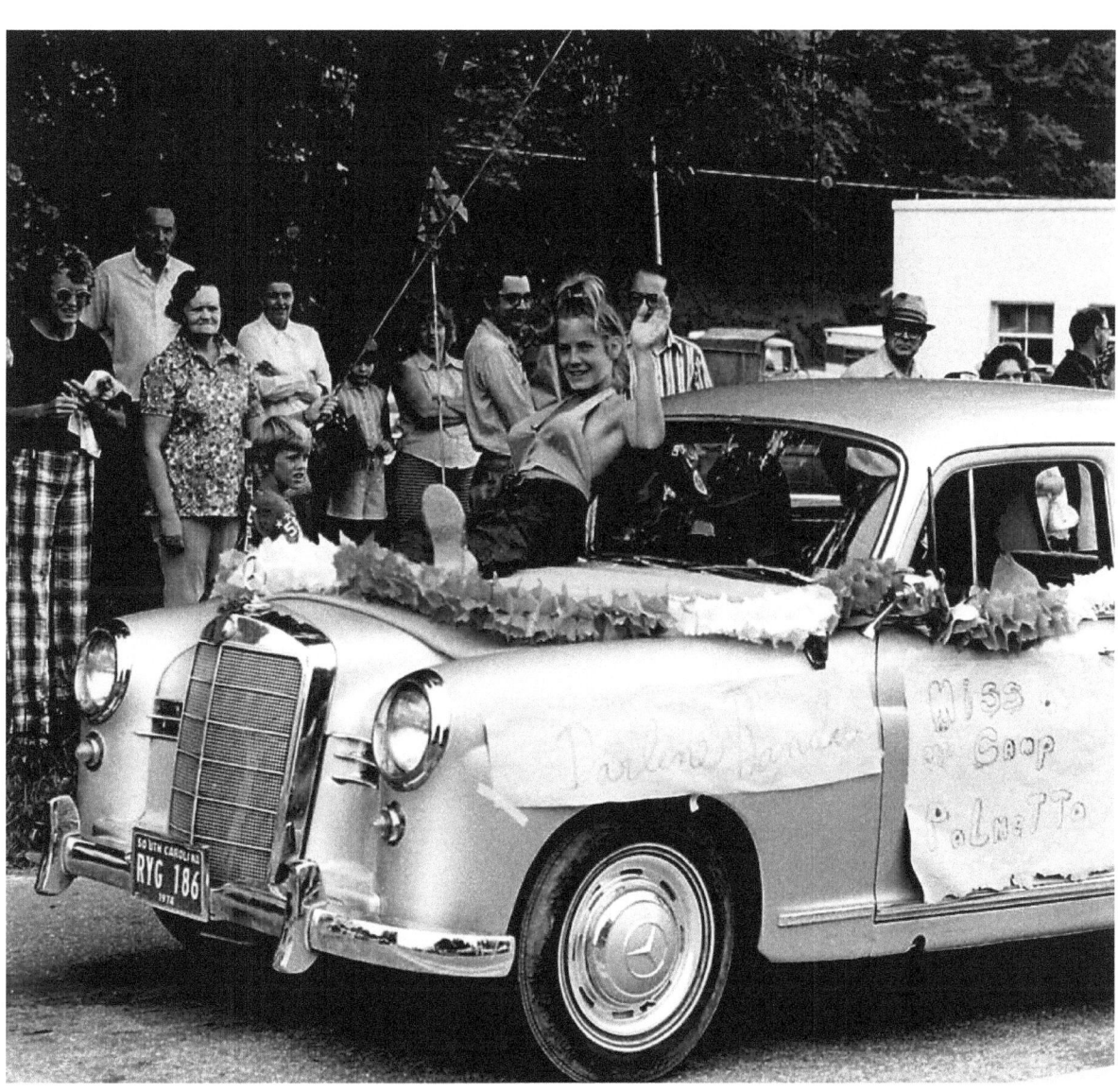

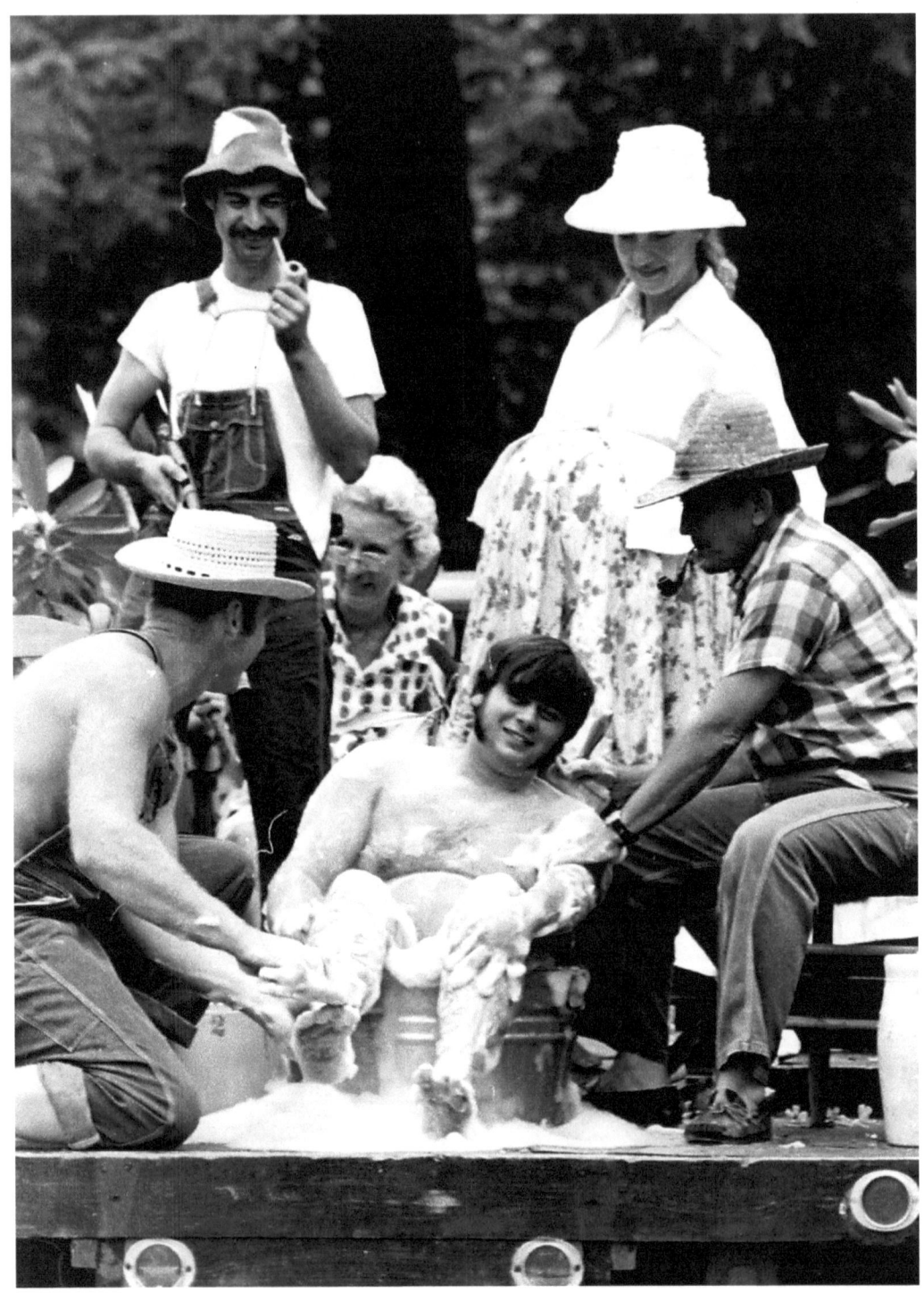

IX

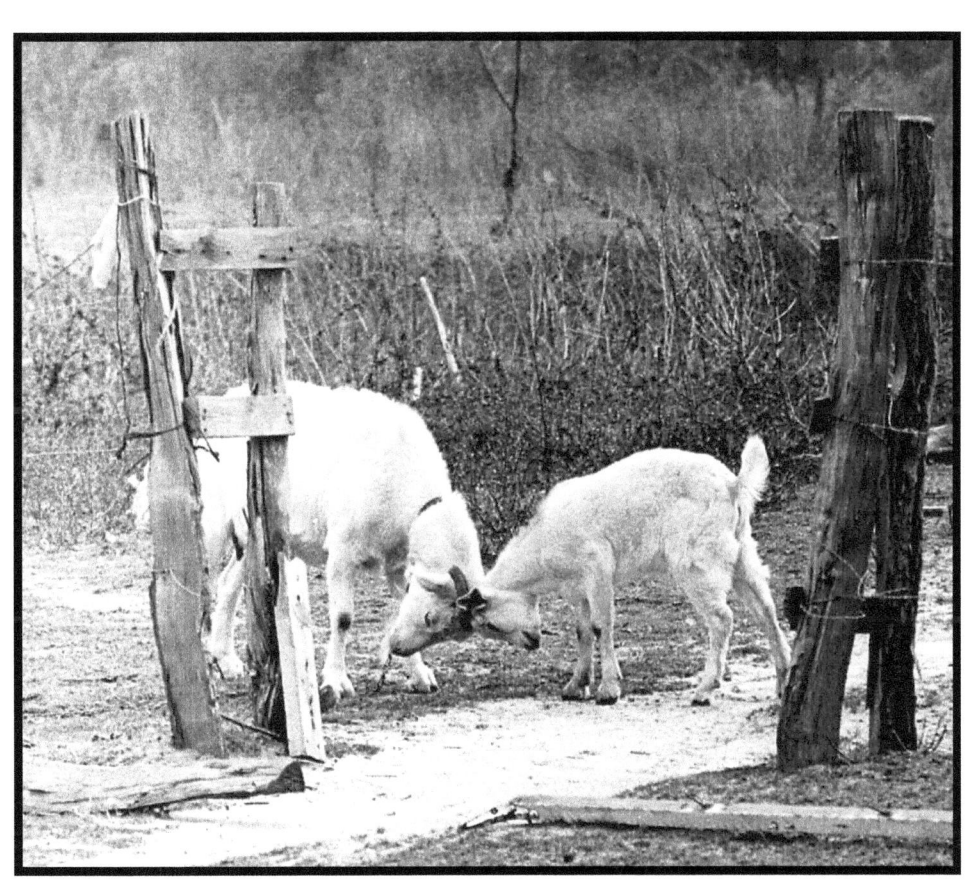

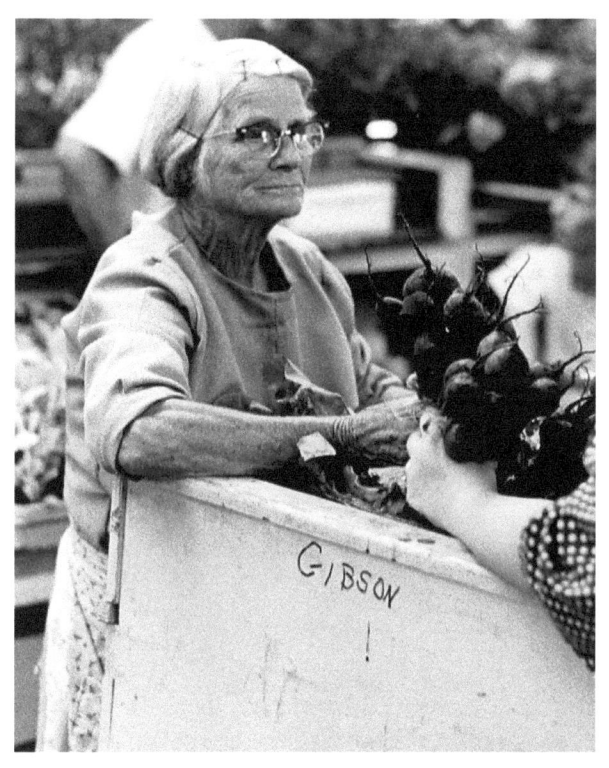

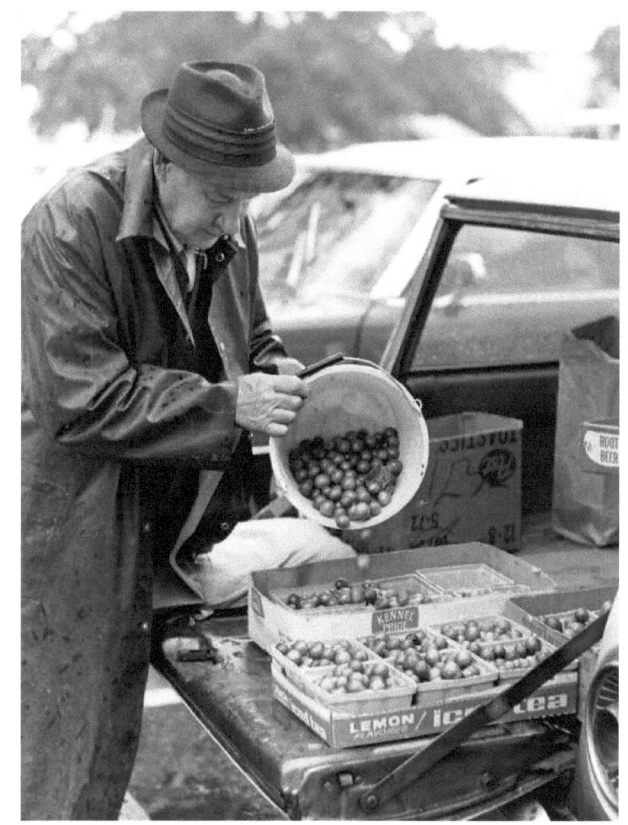

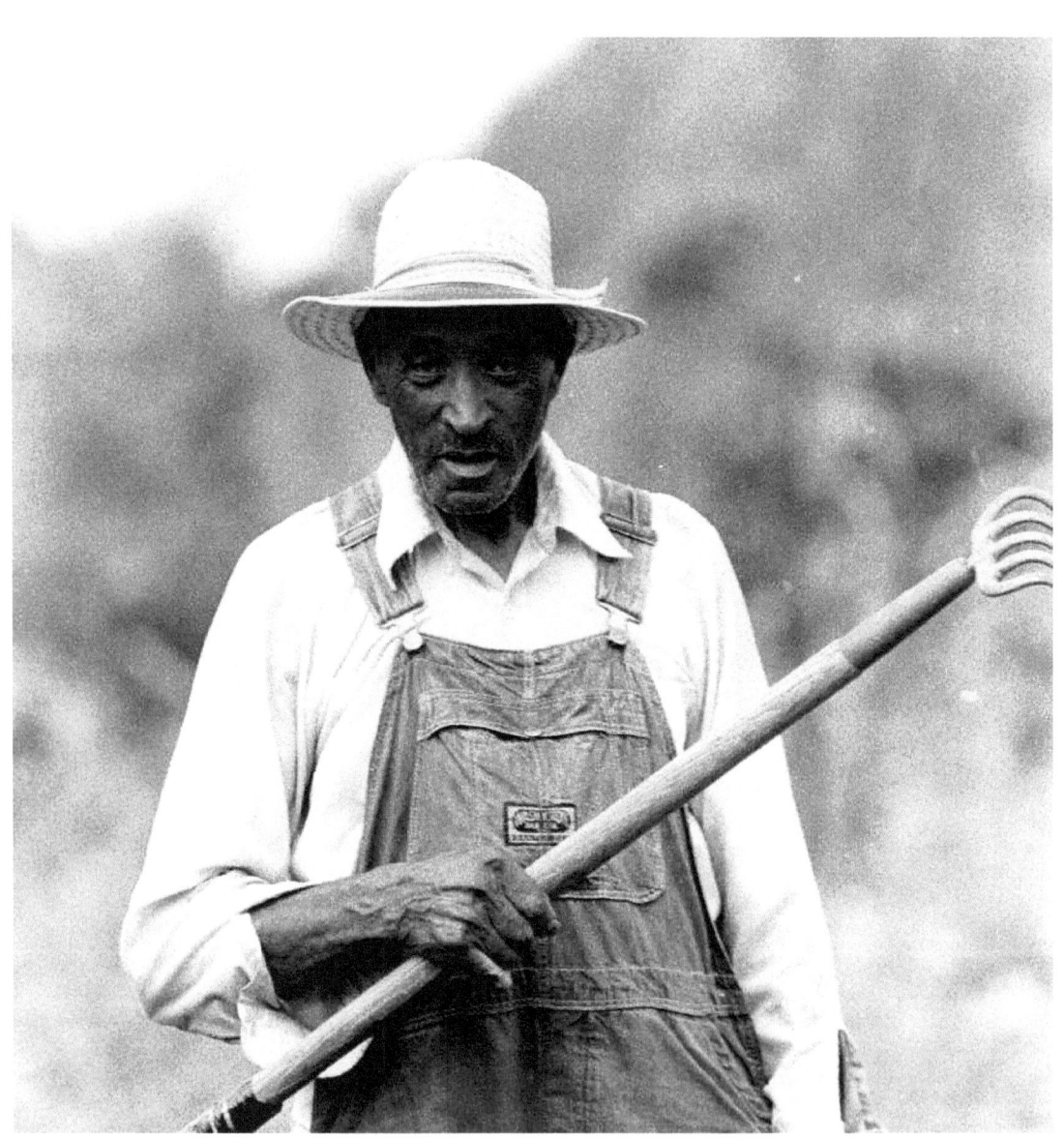

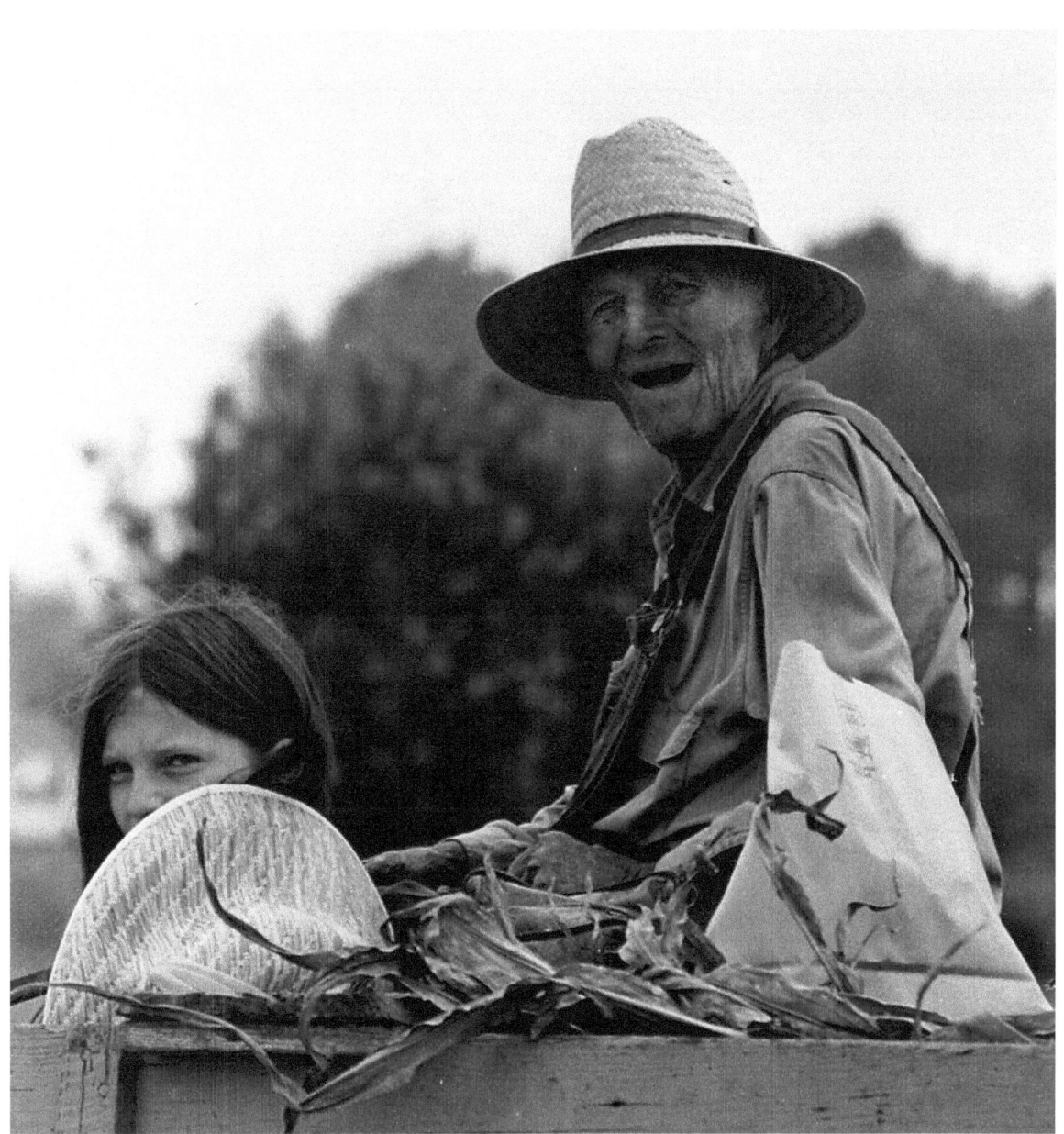

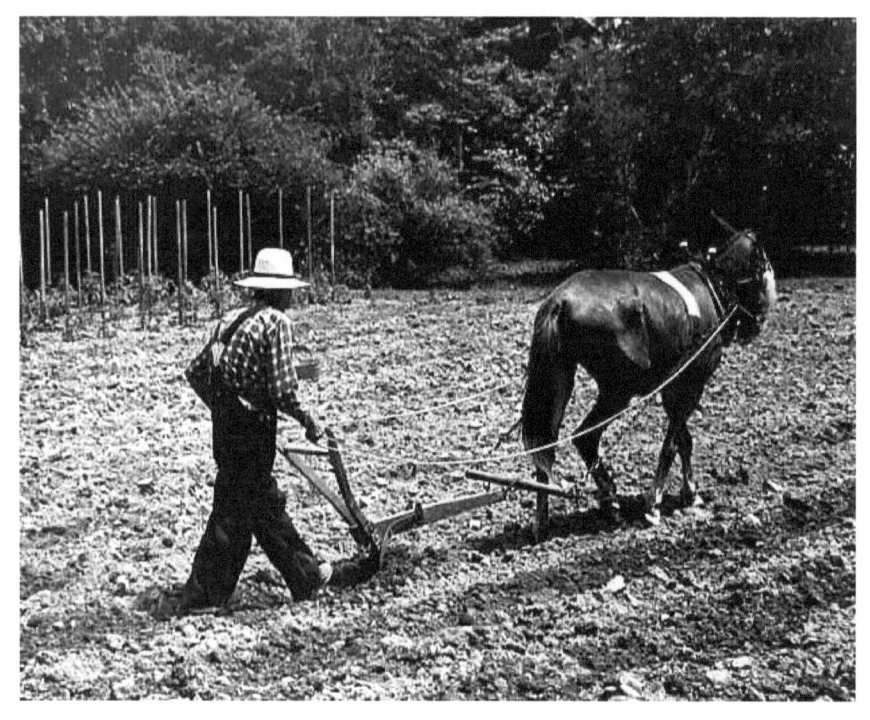

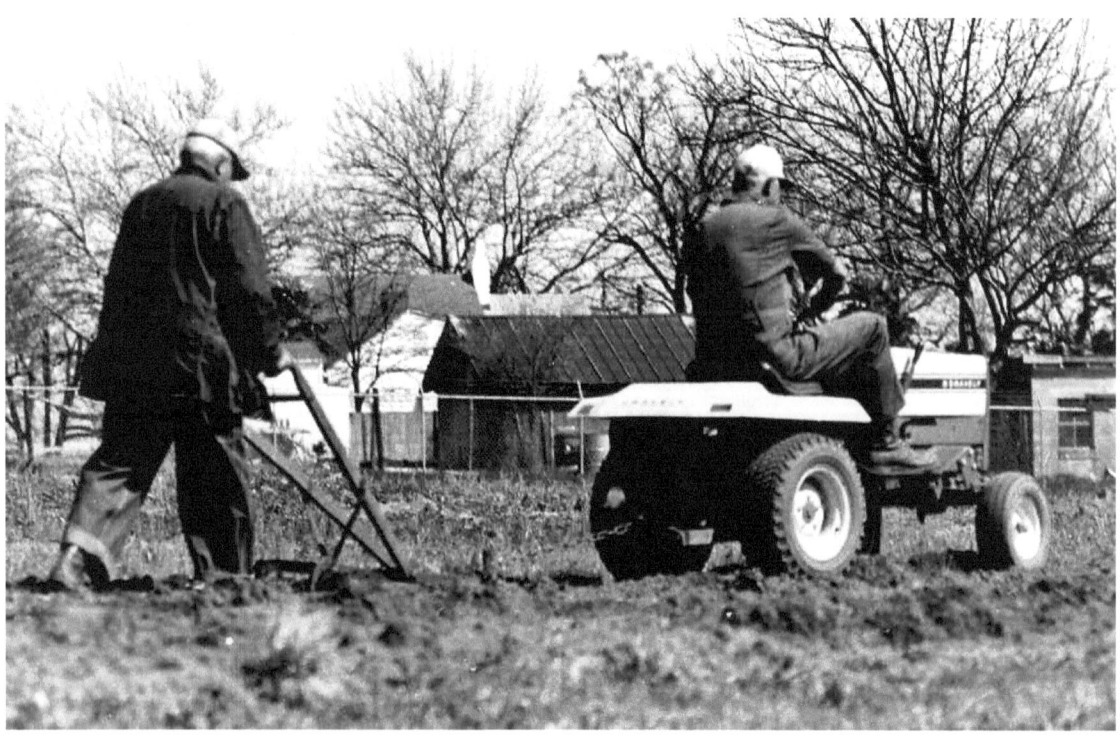

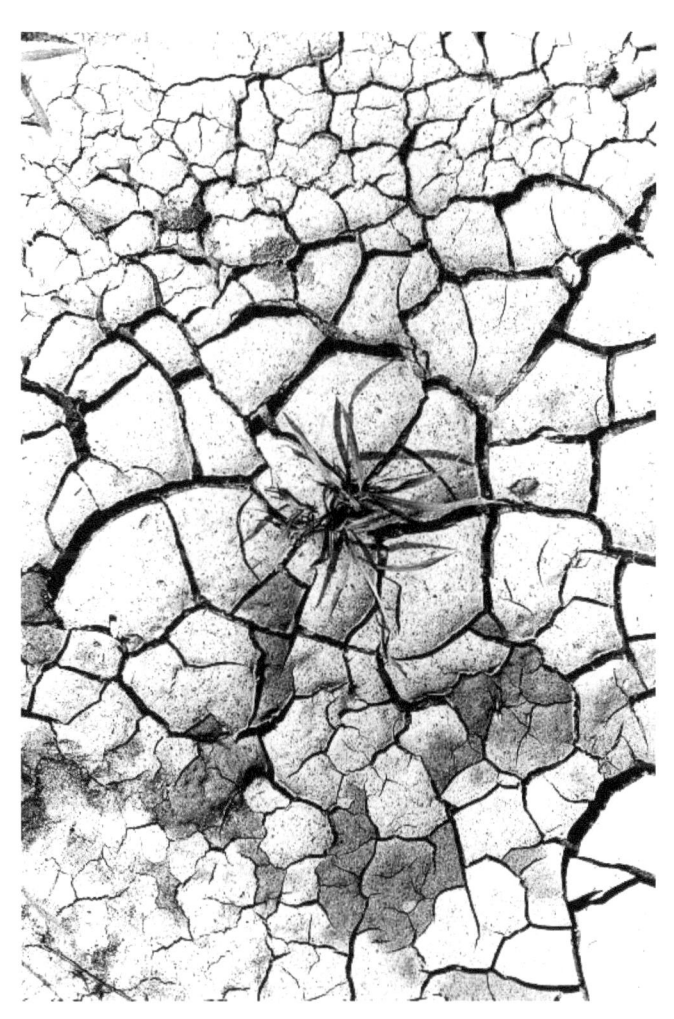

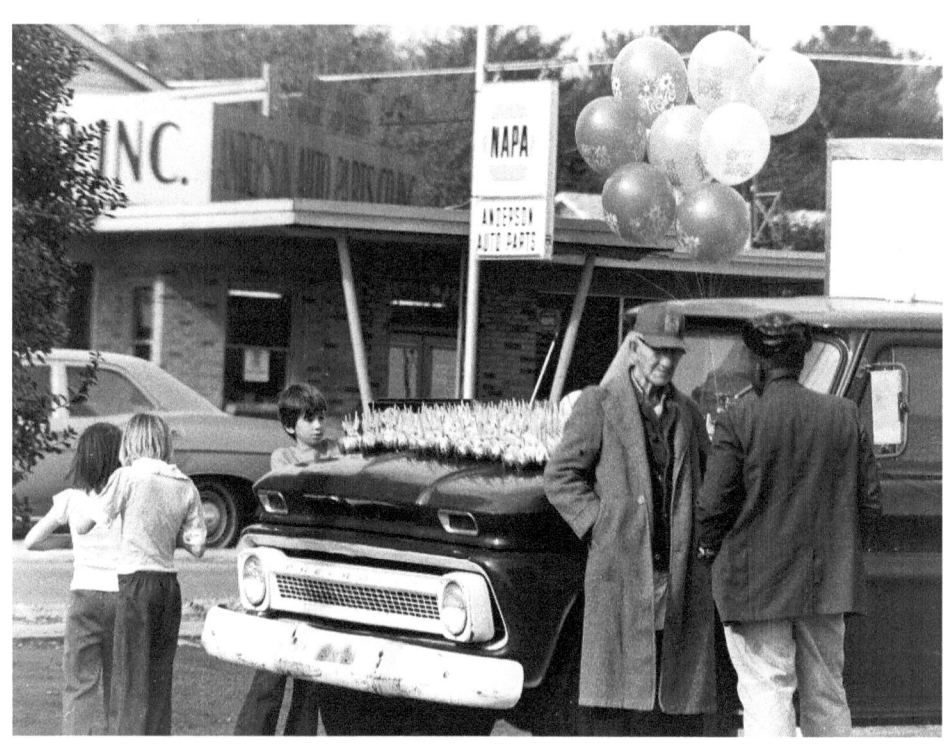

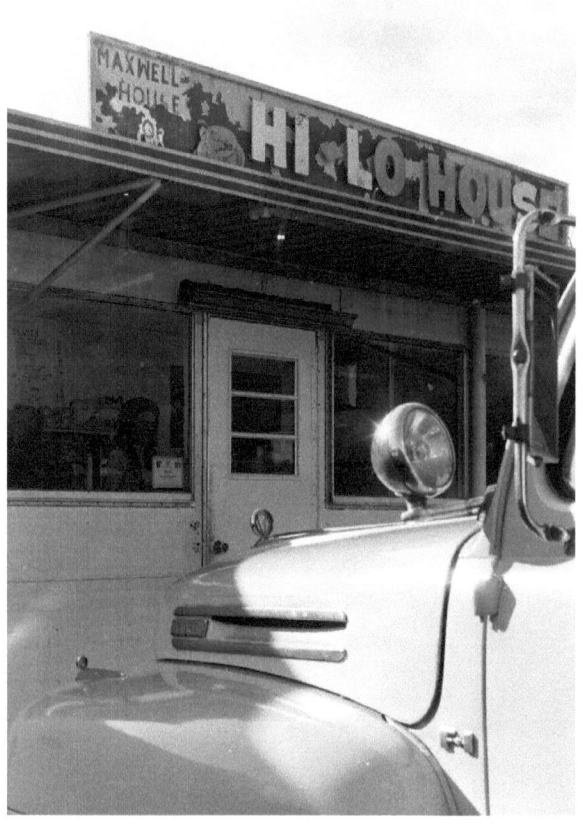

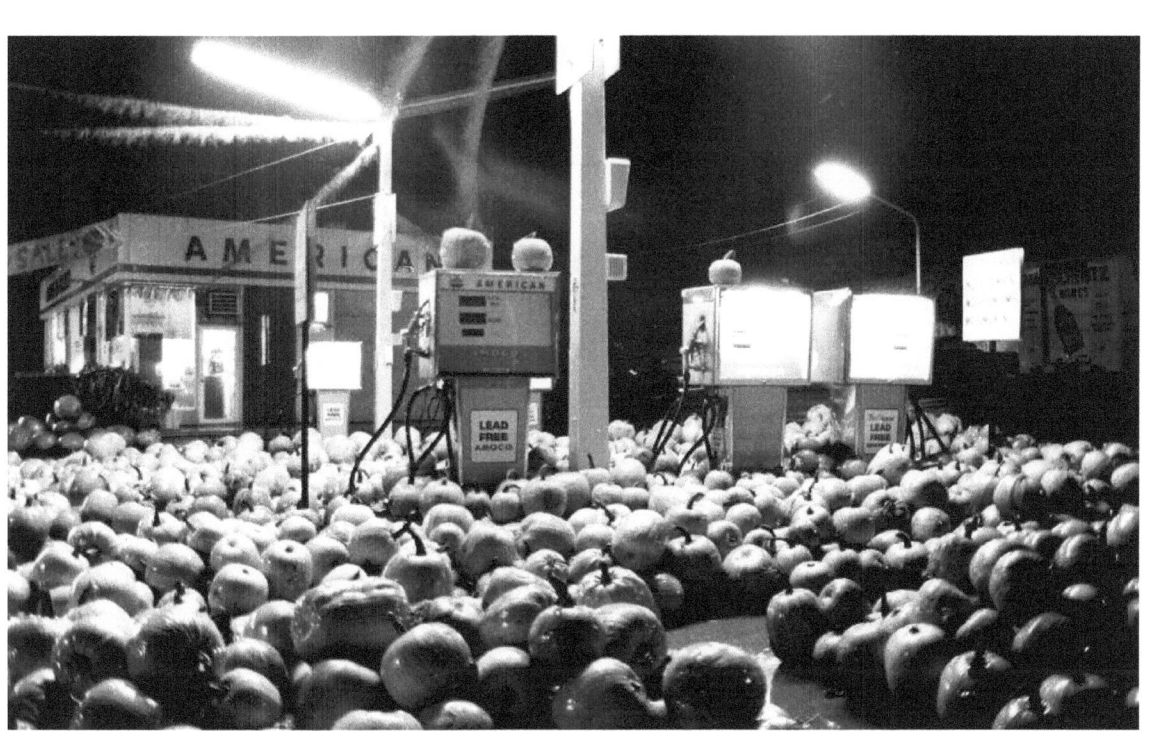

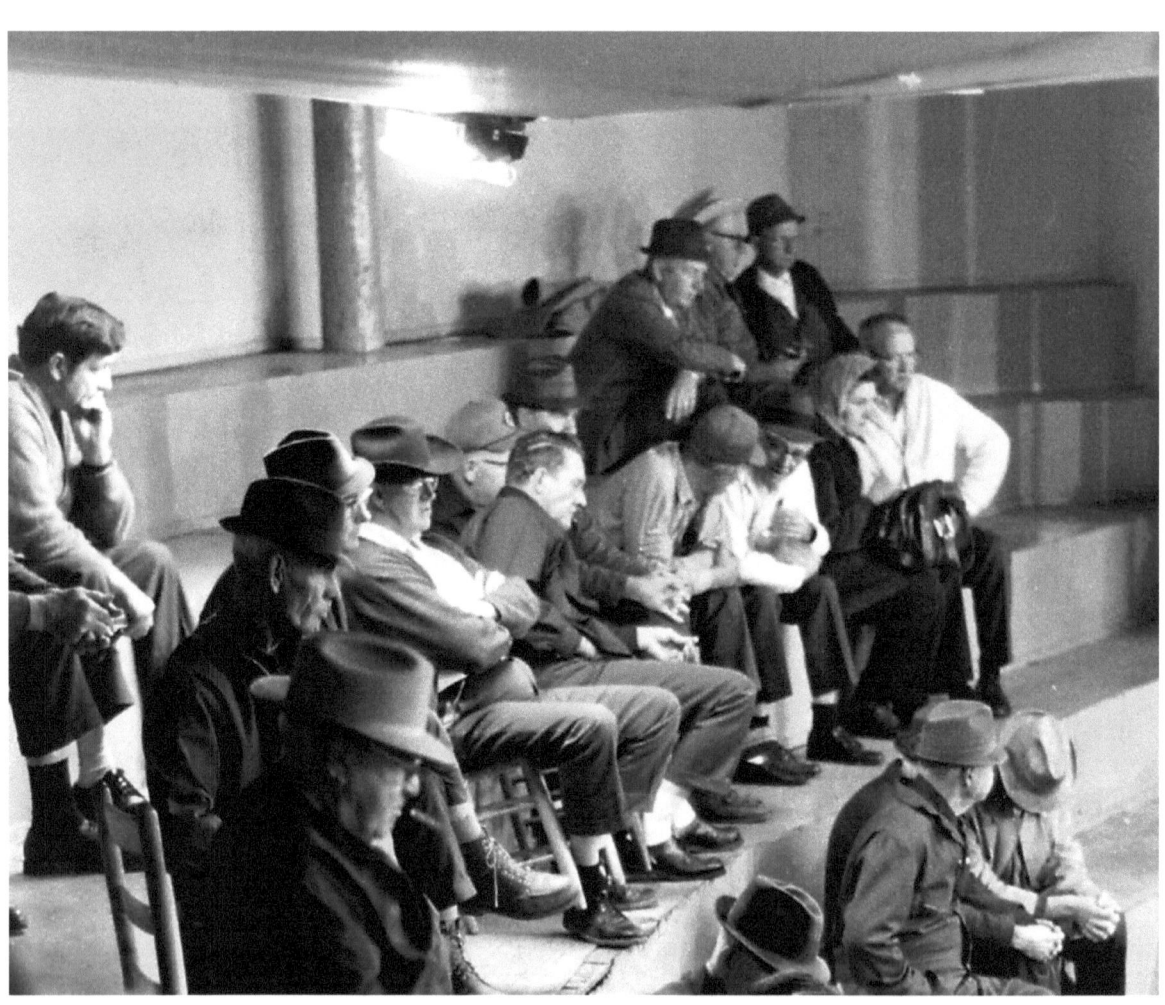

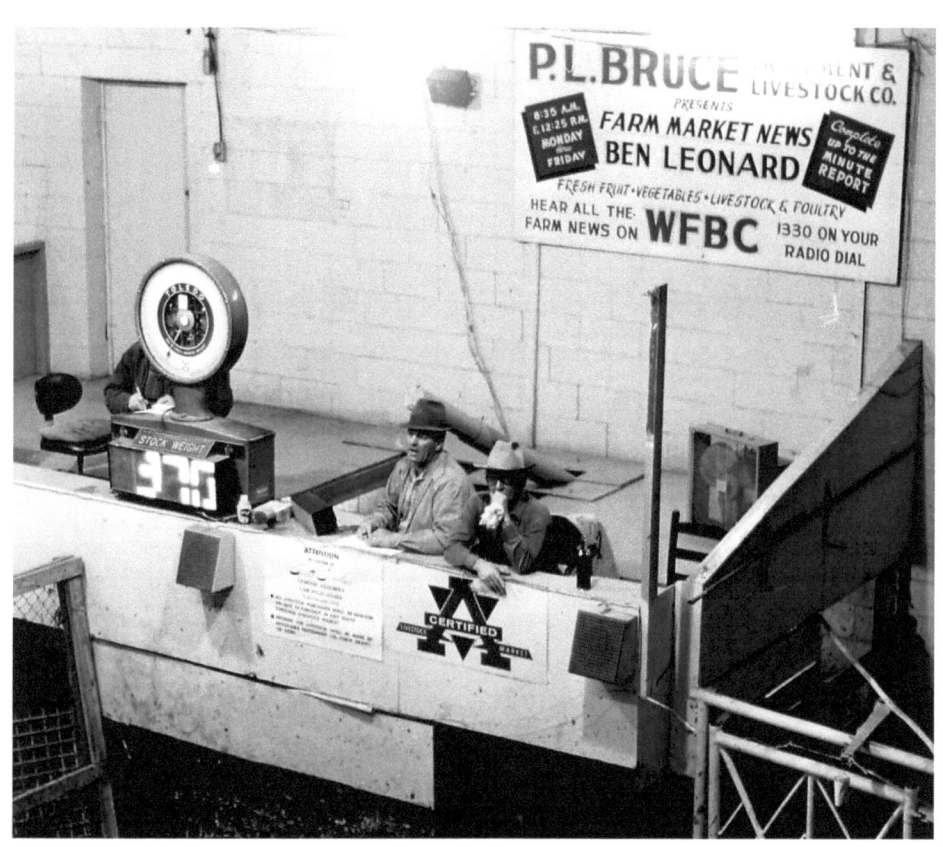

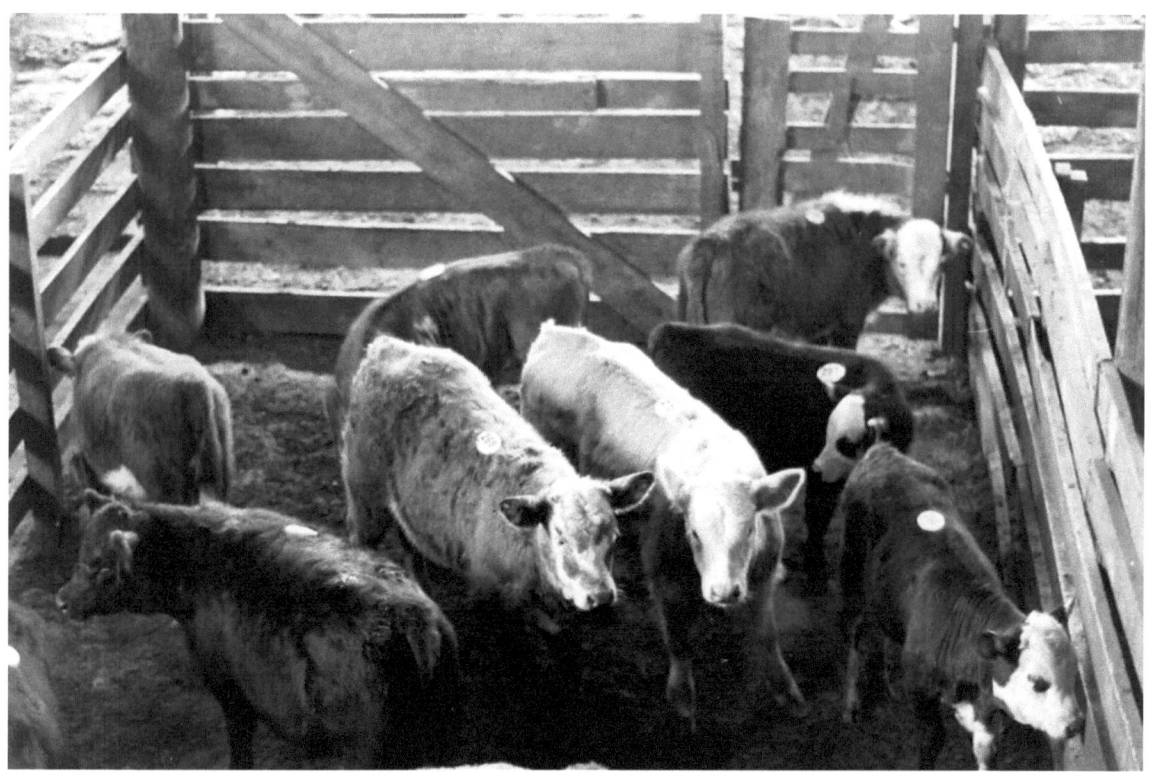

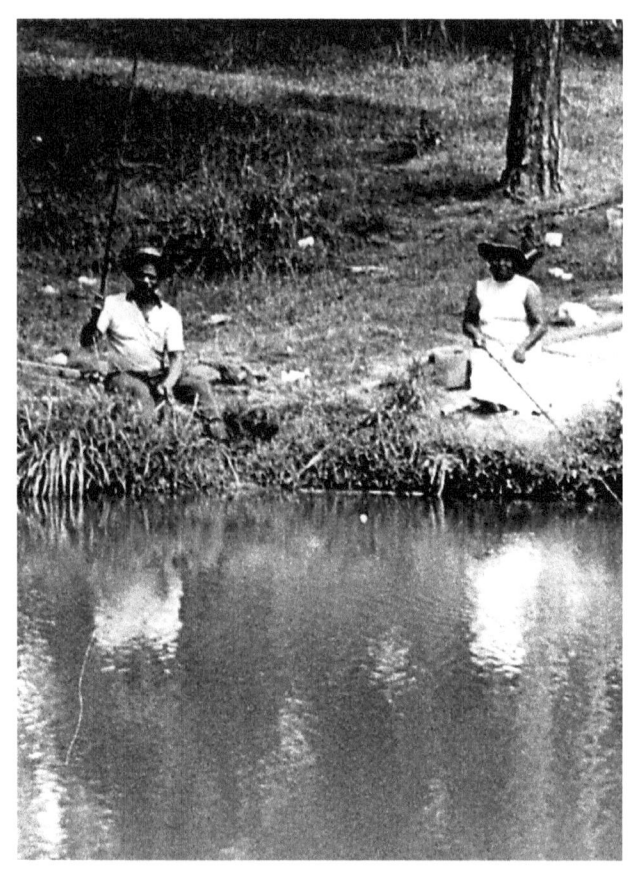

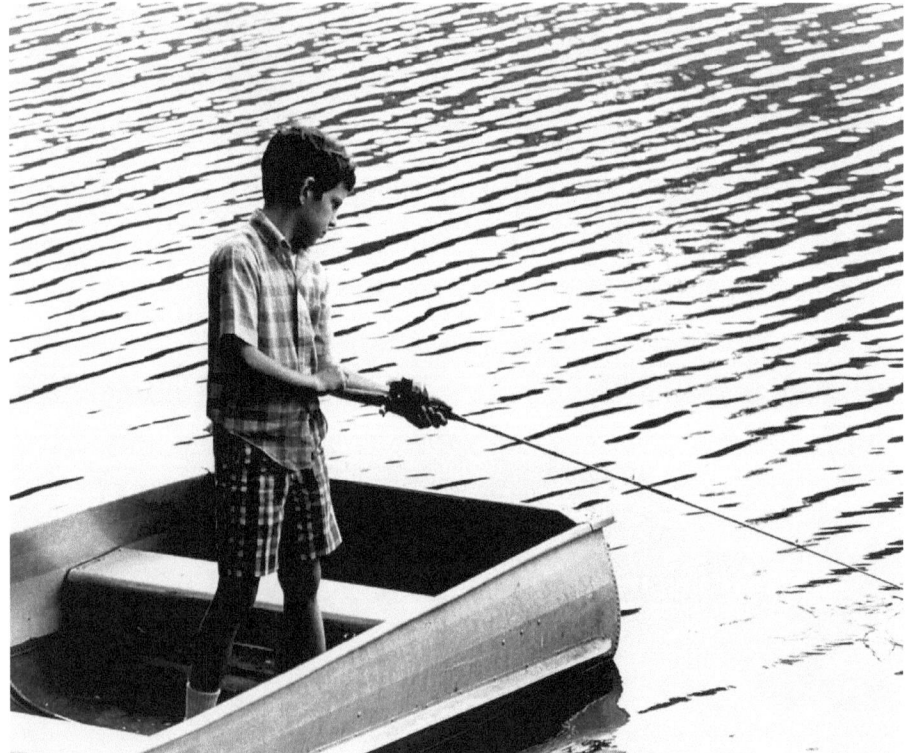

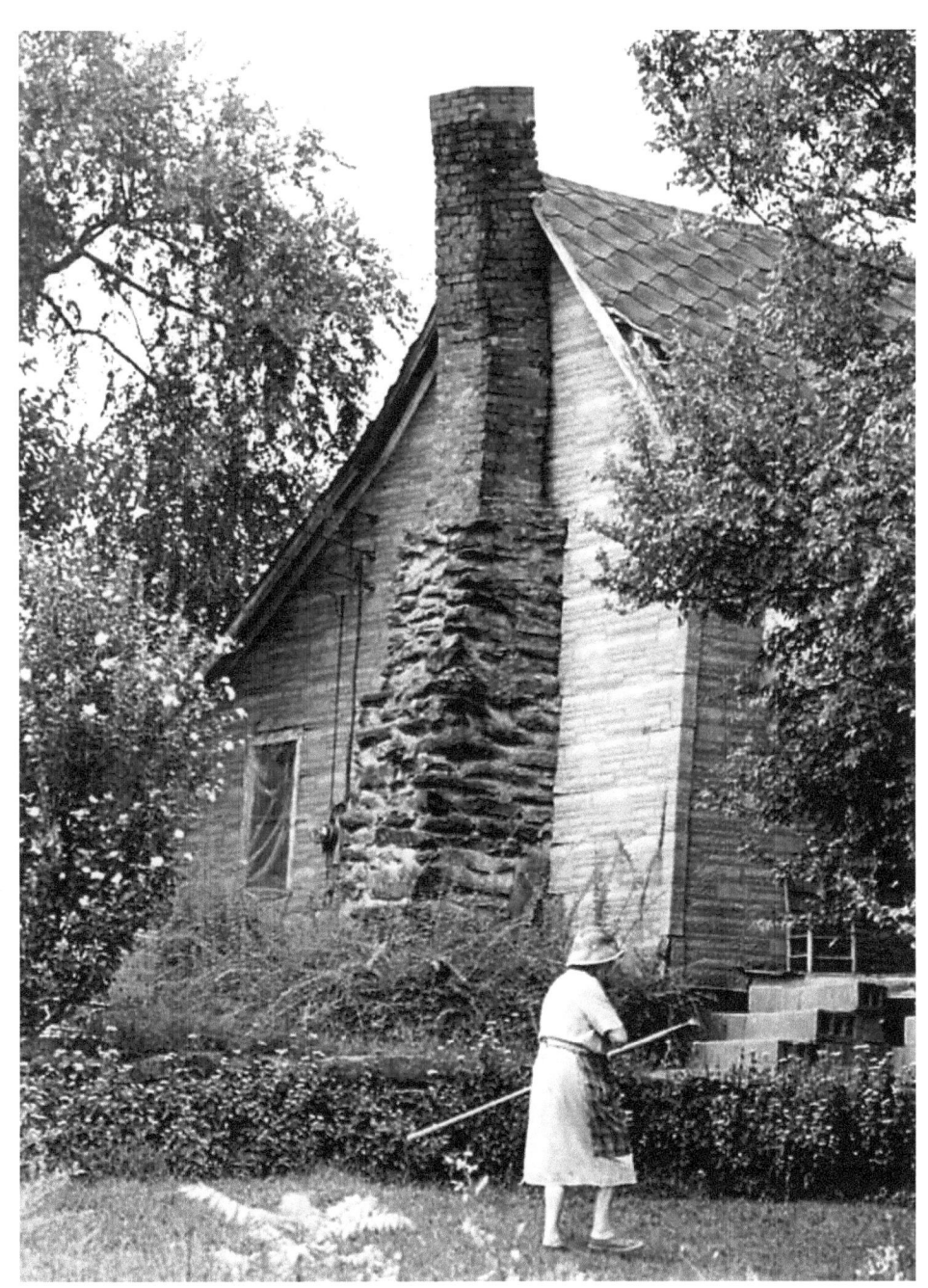

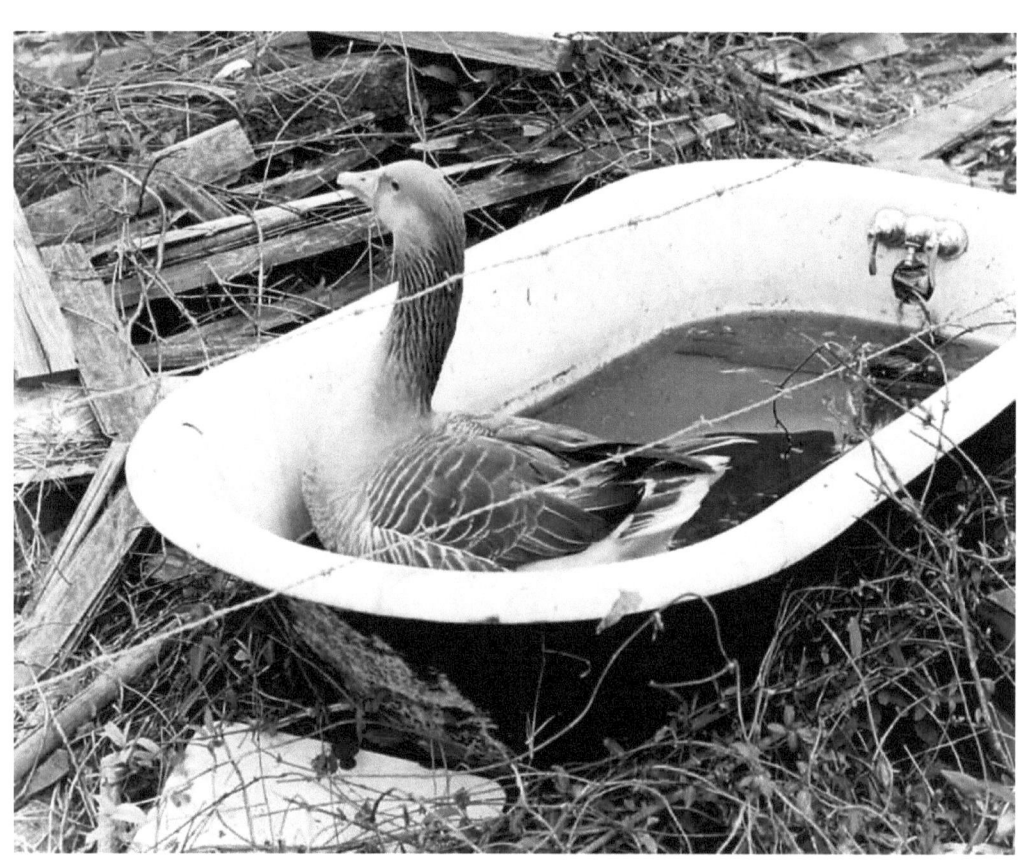

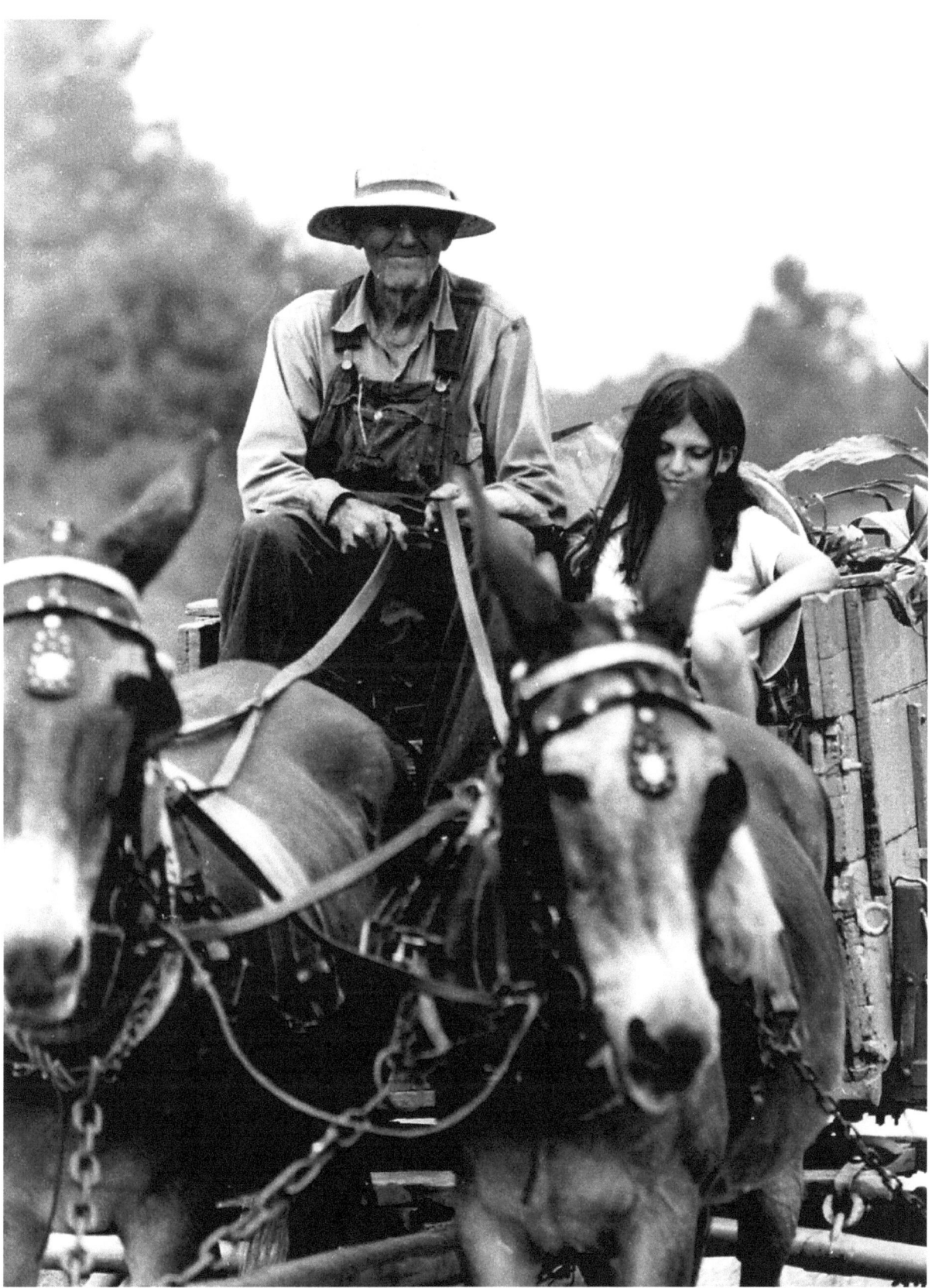

X

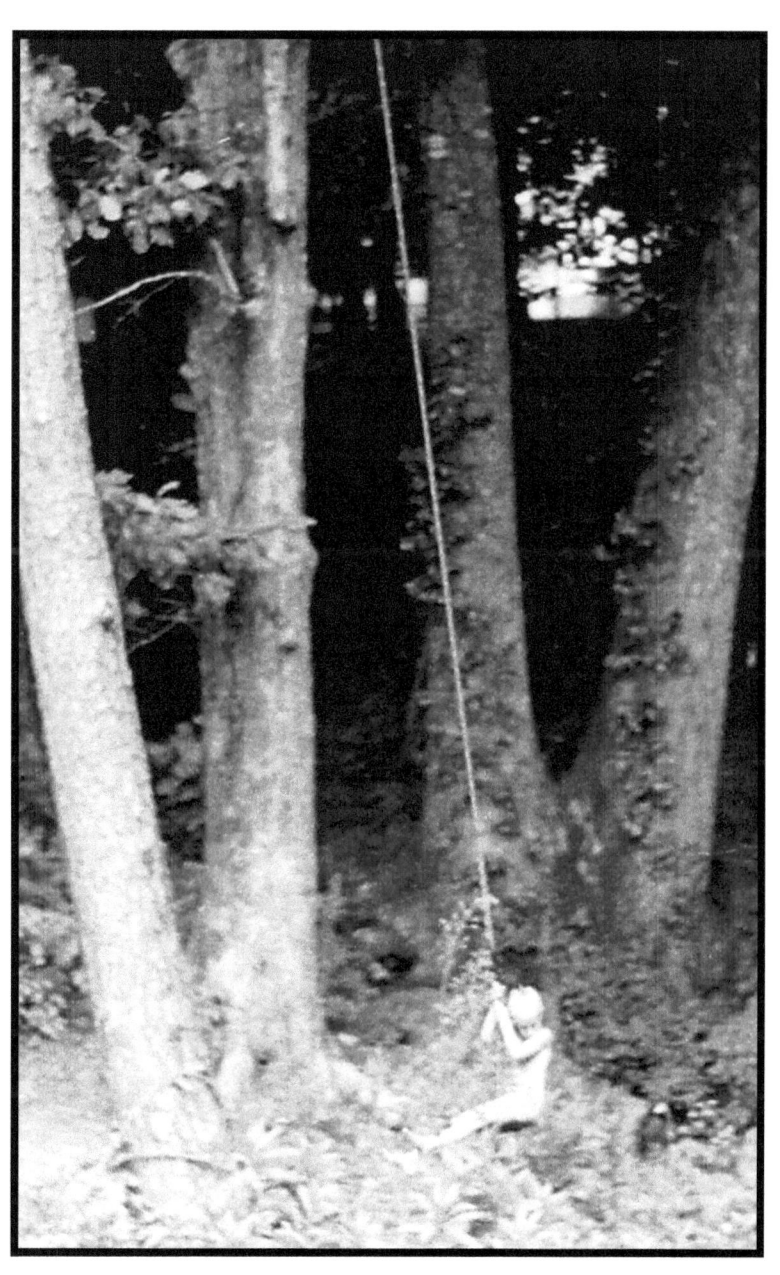

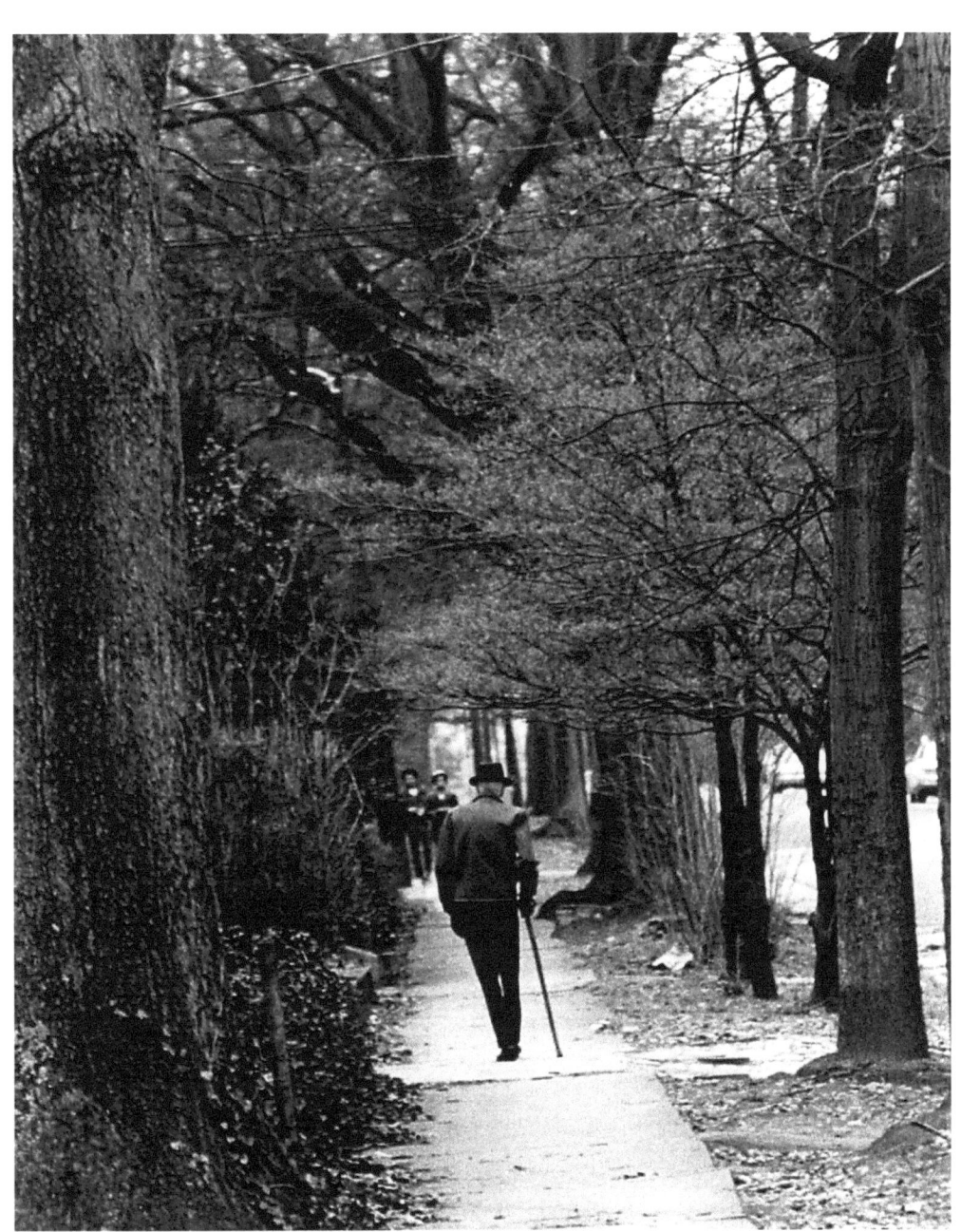

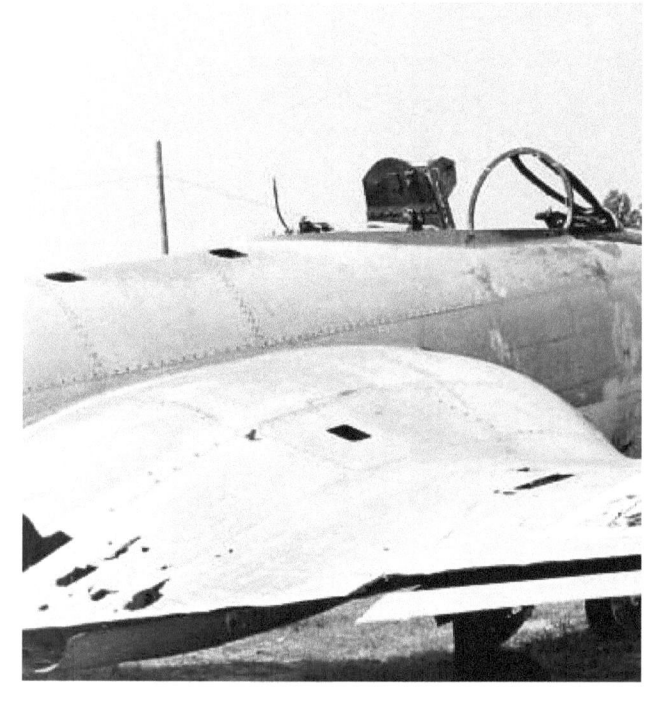

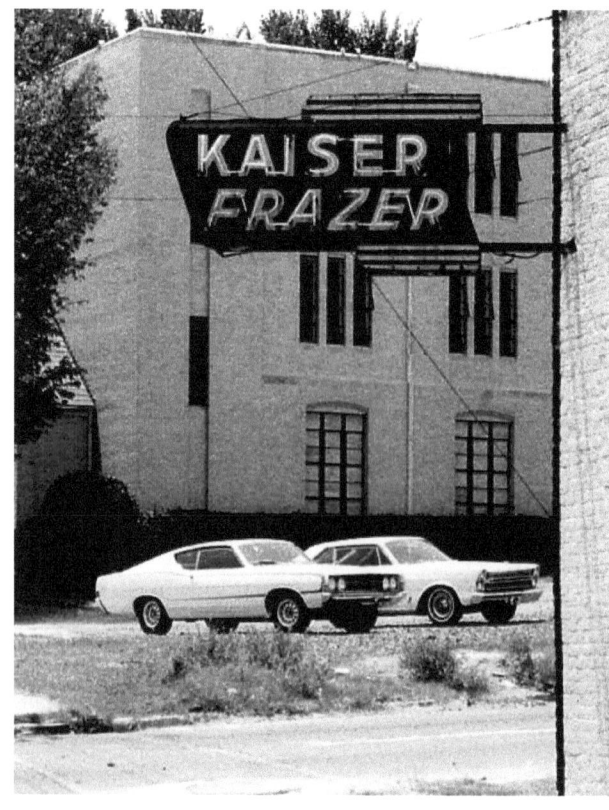

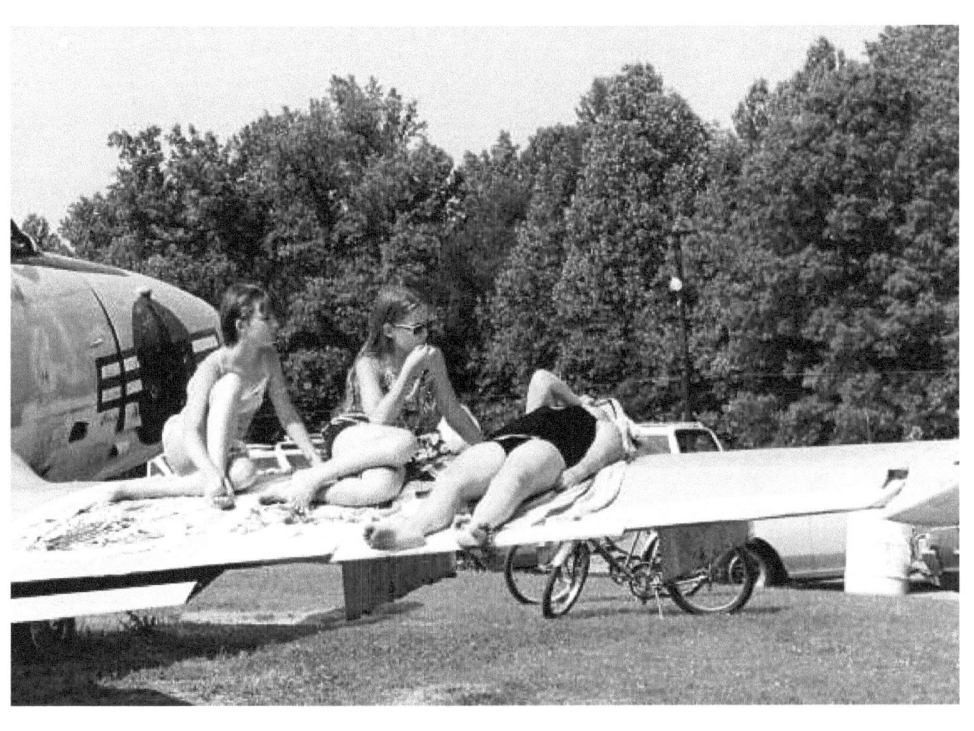

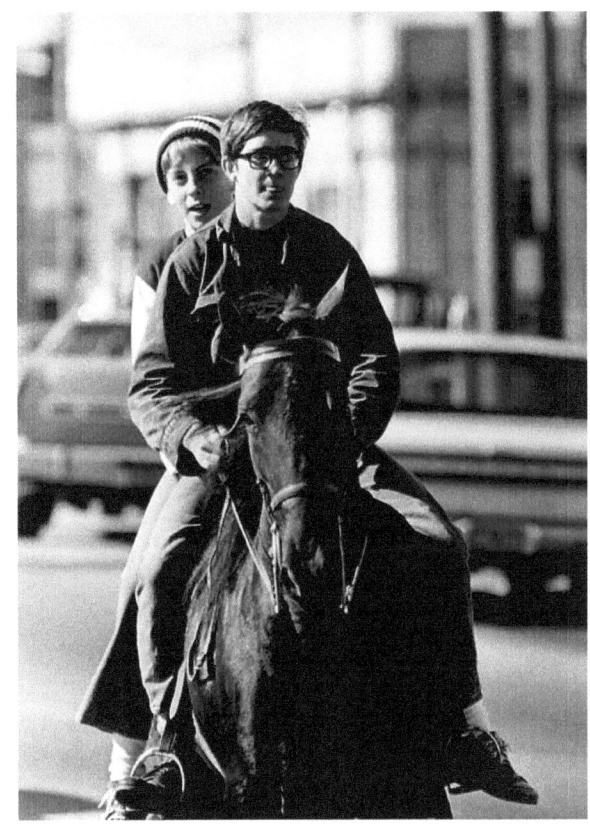

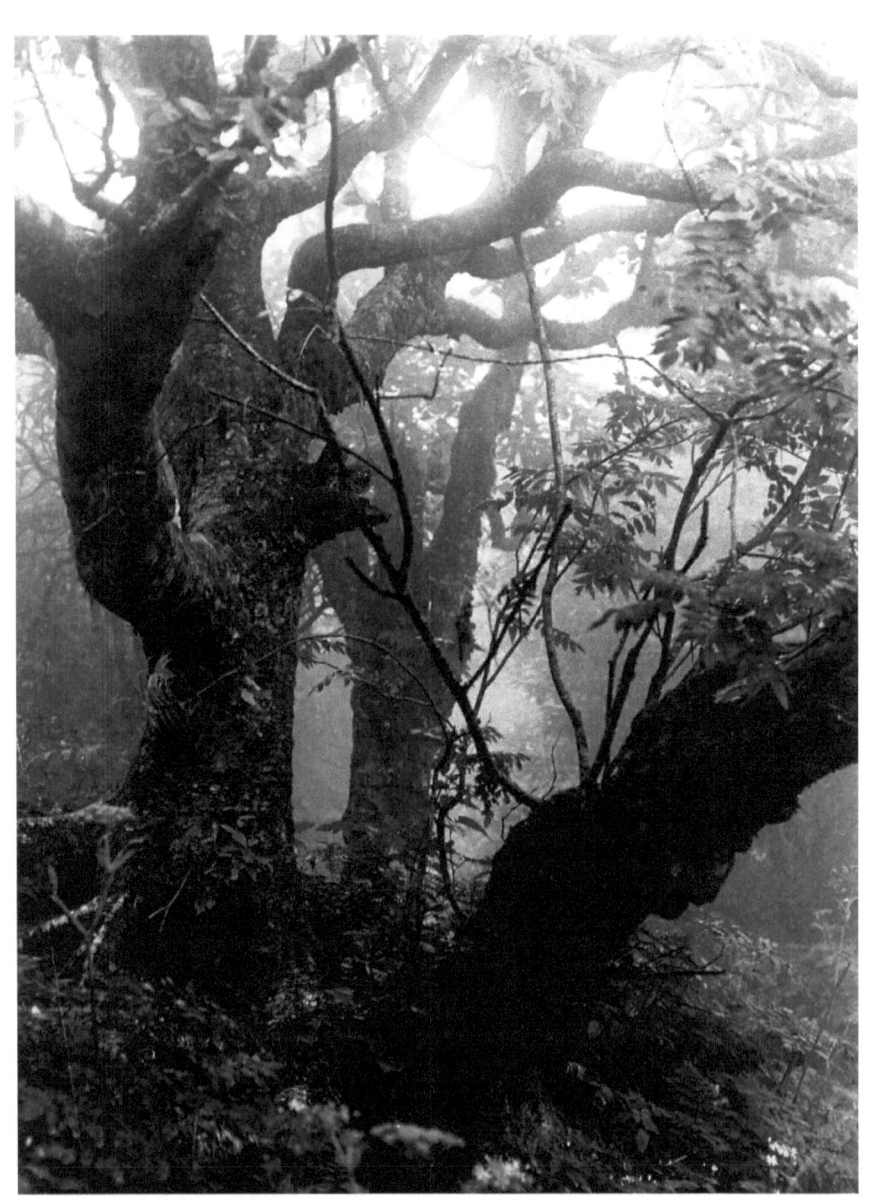

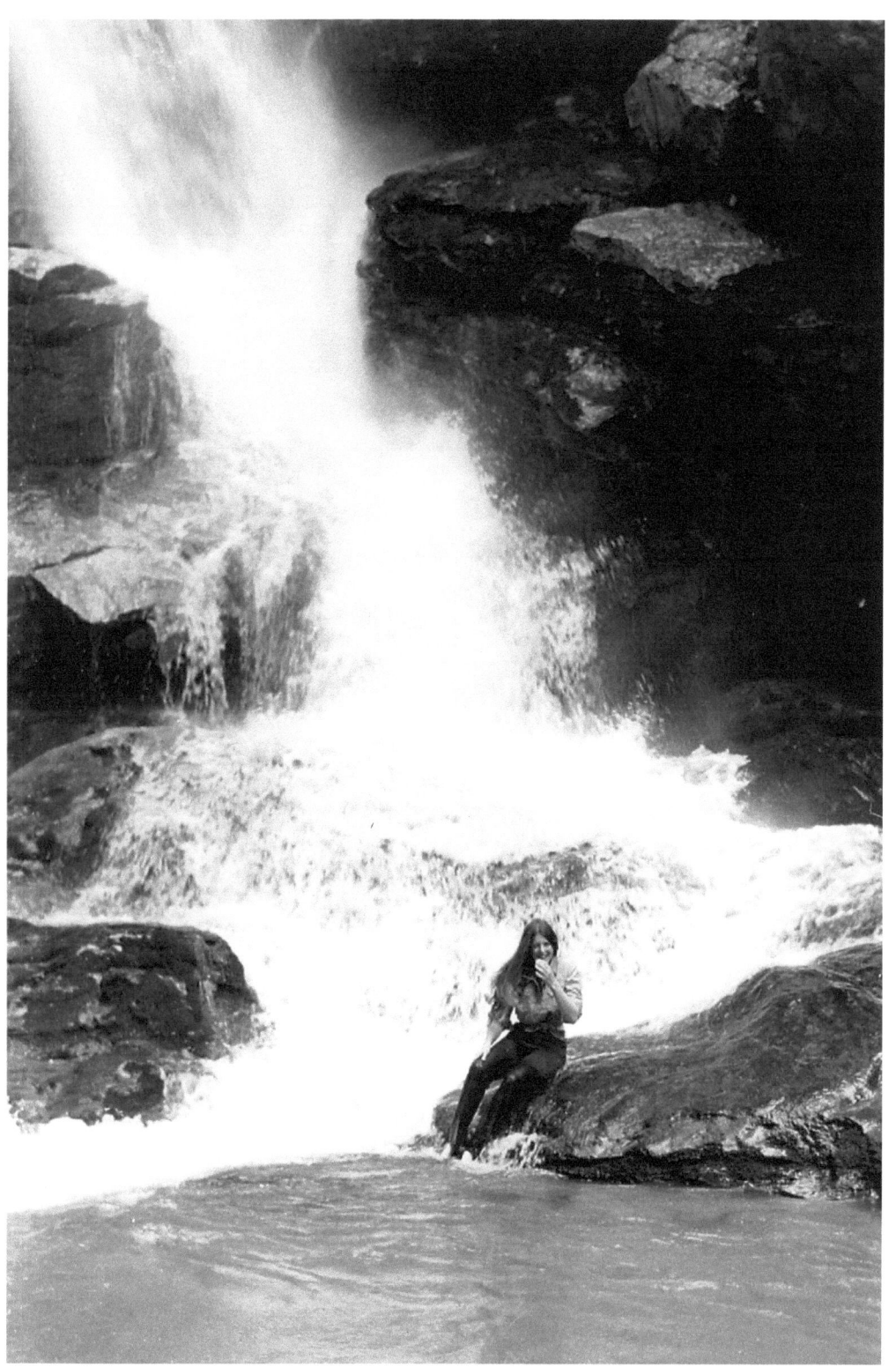

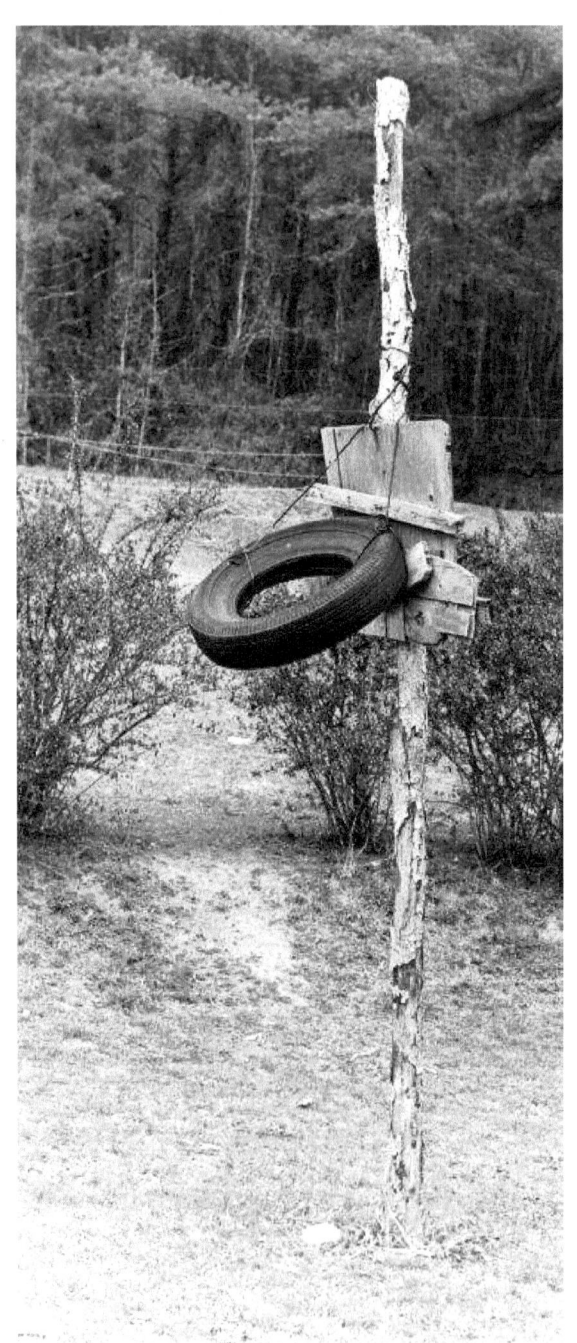

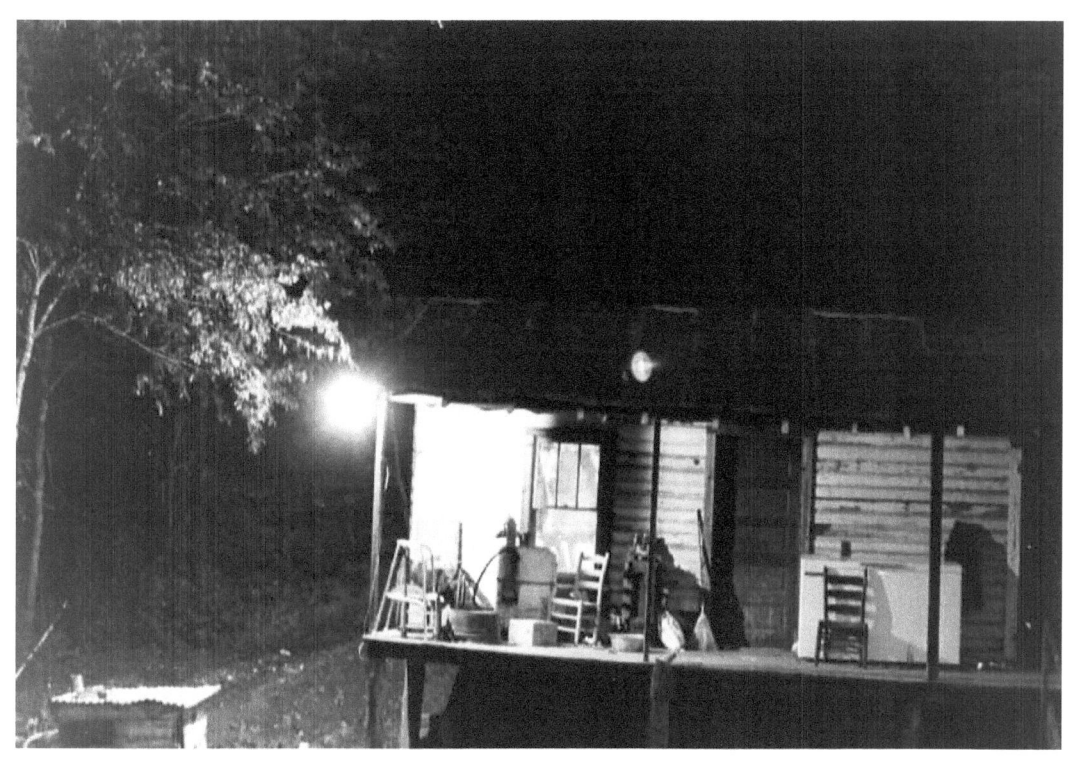

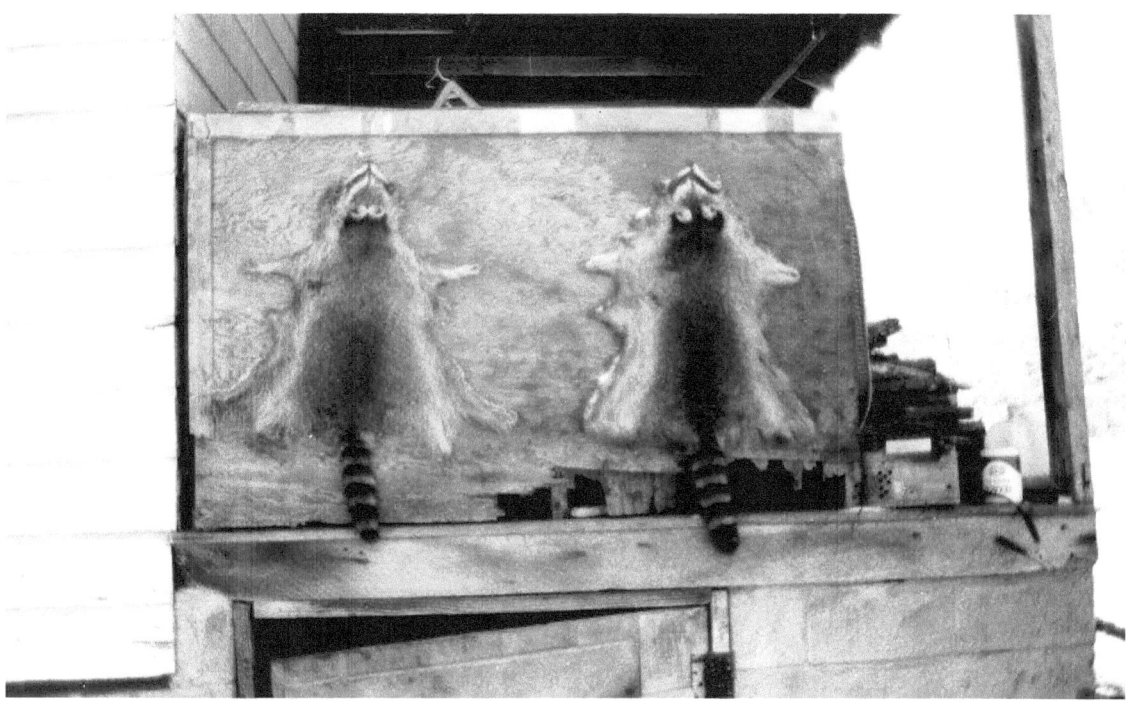

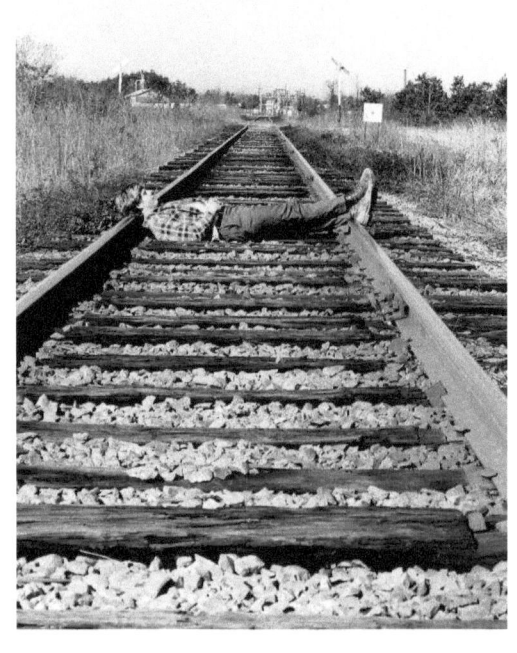

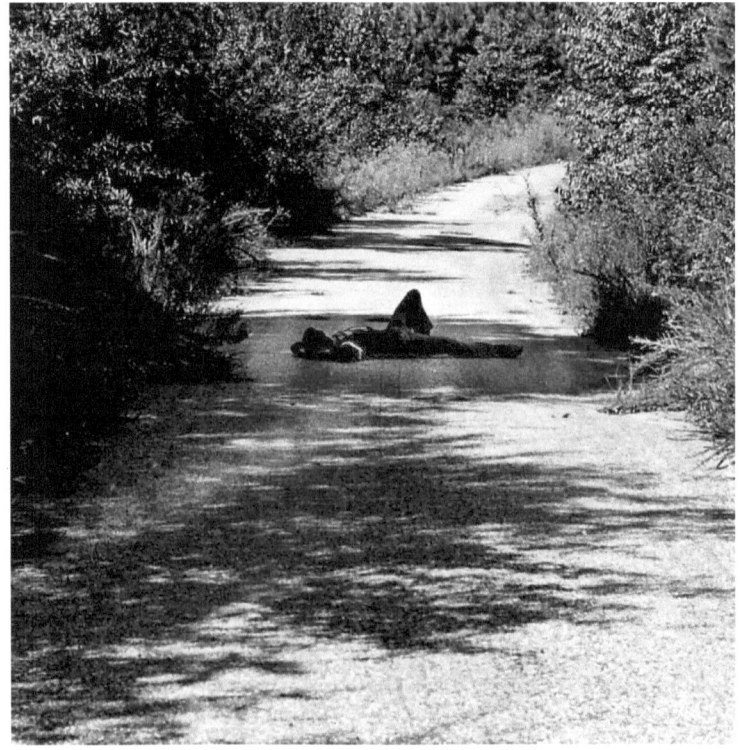

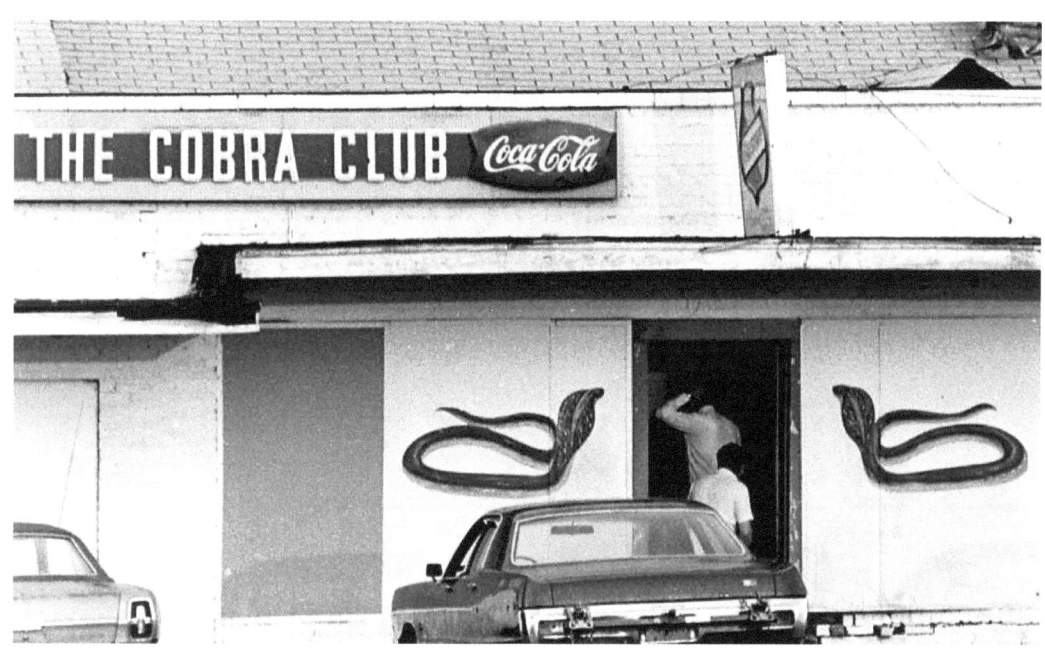

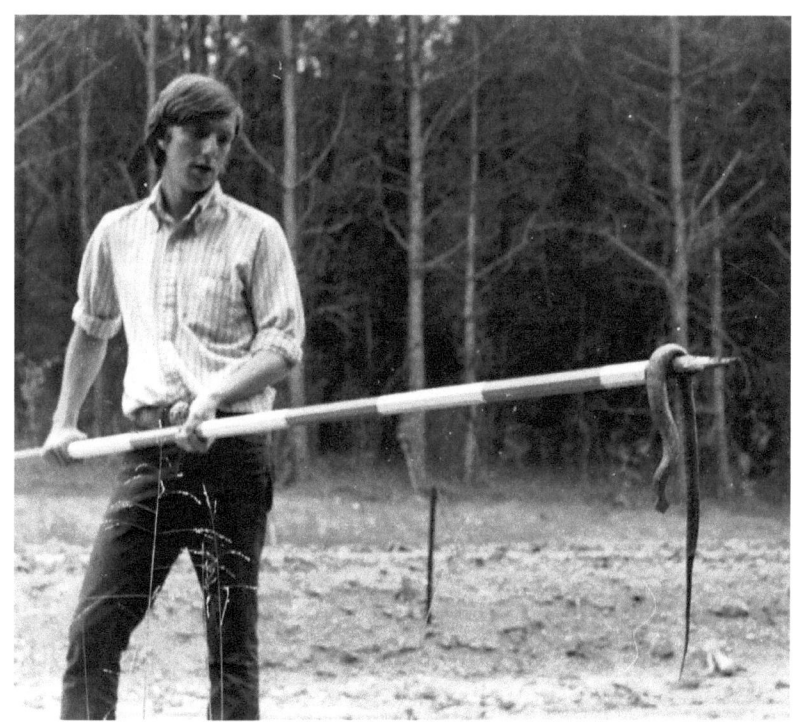

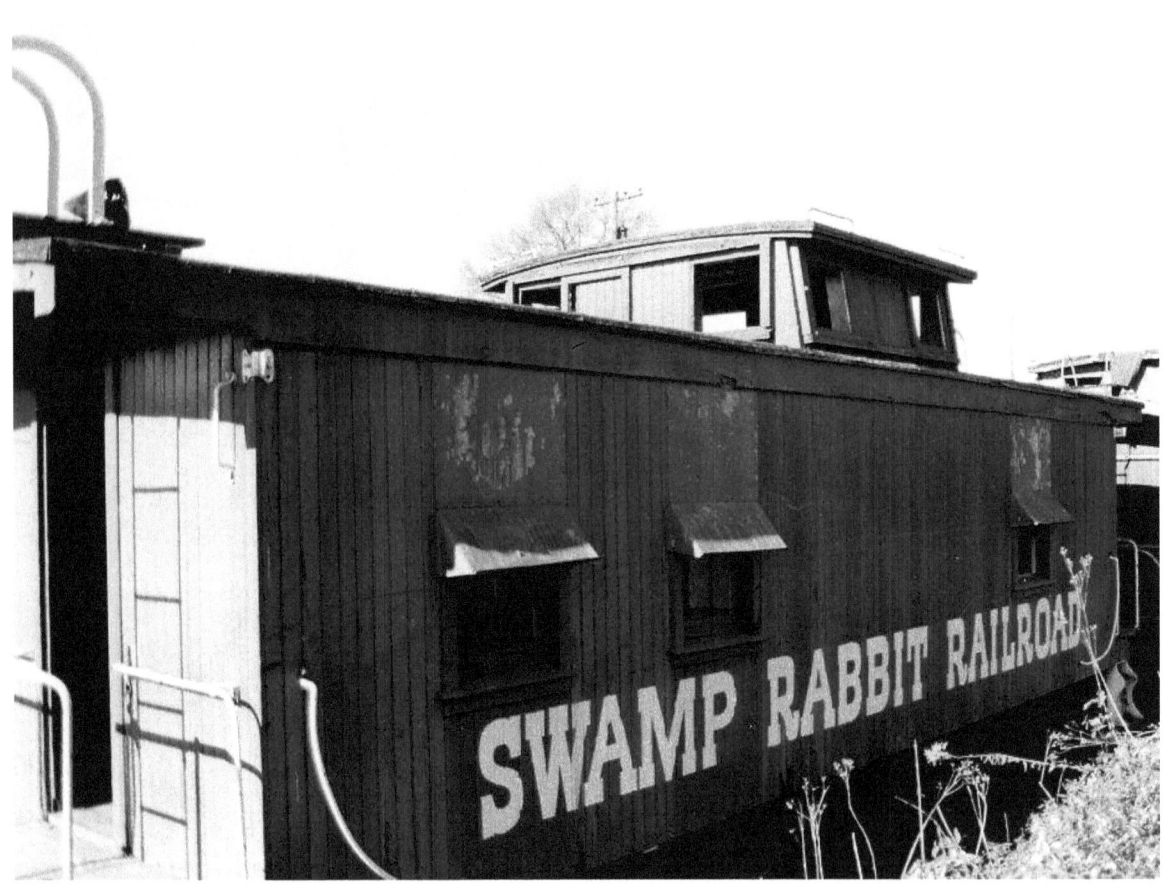

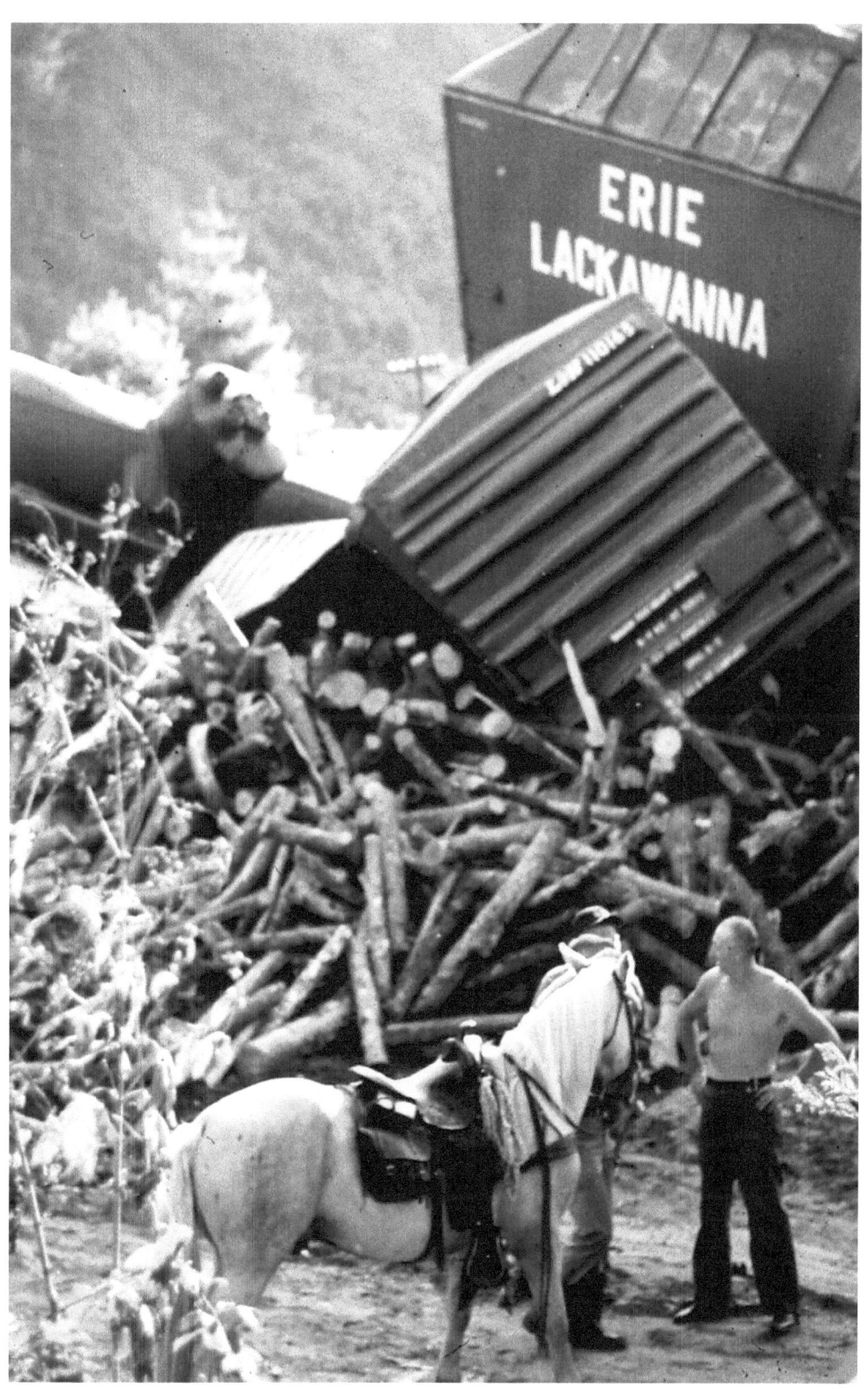

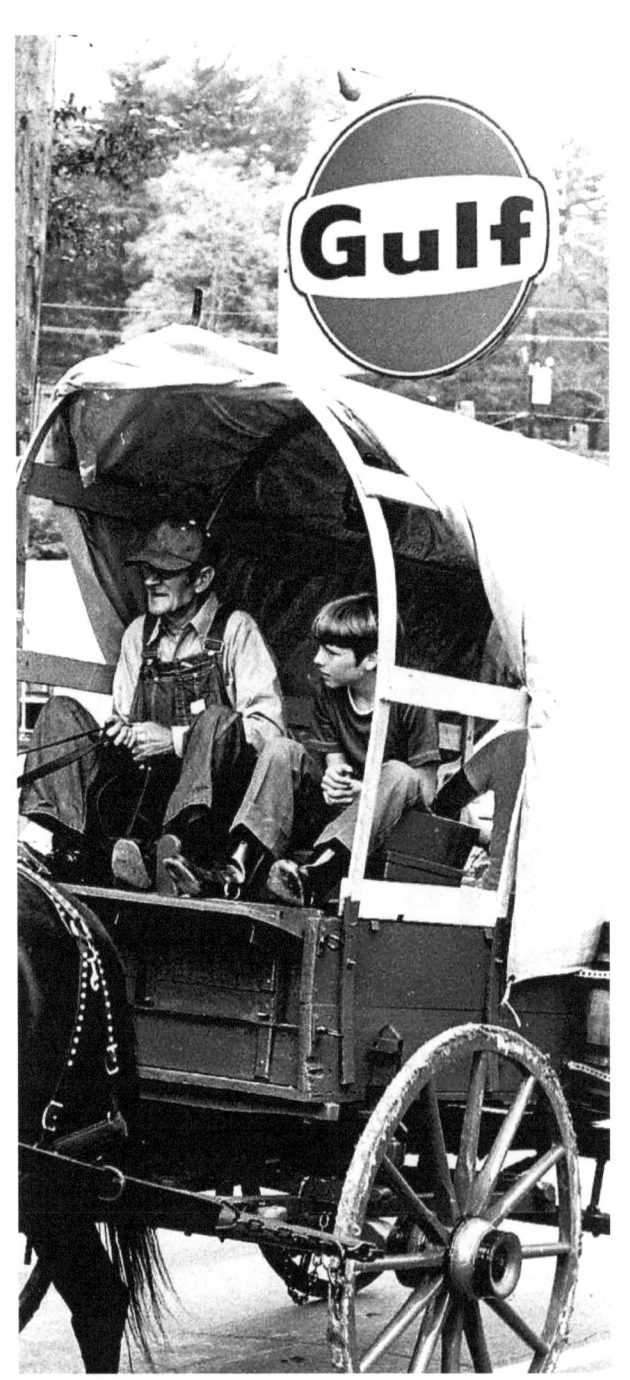

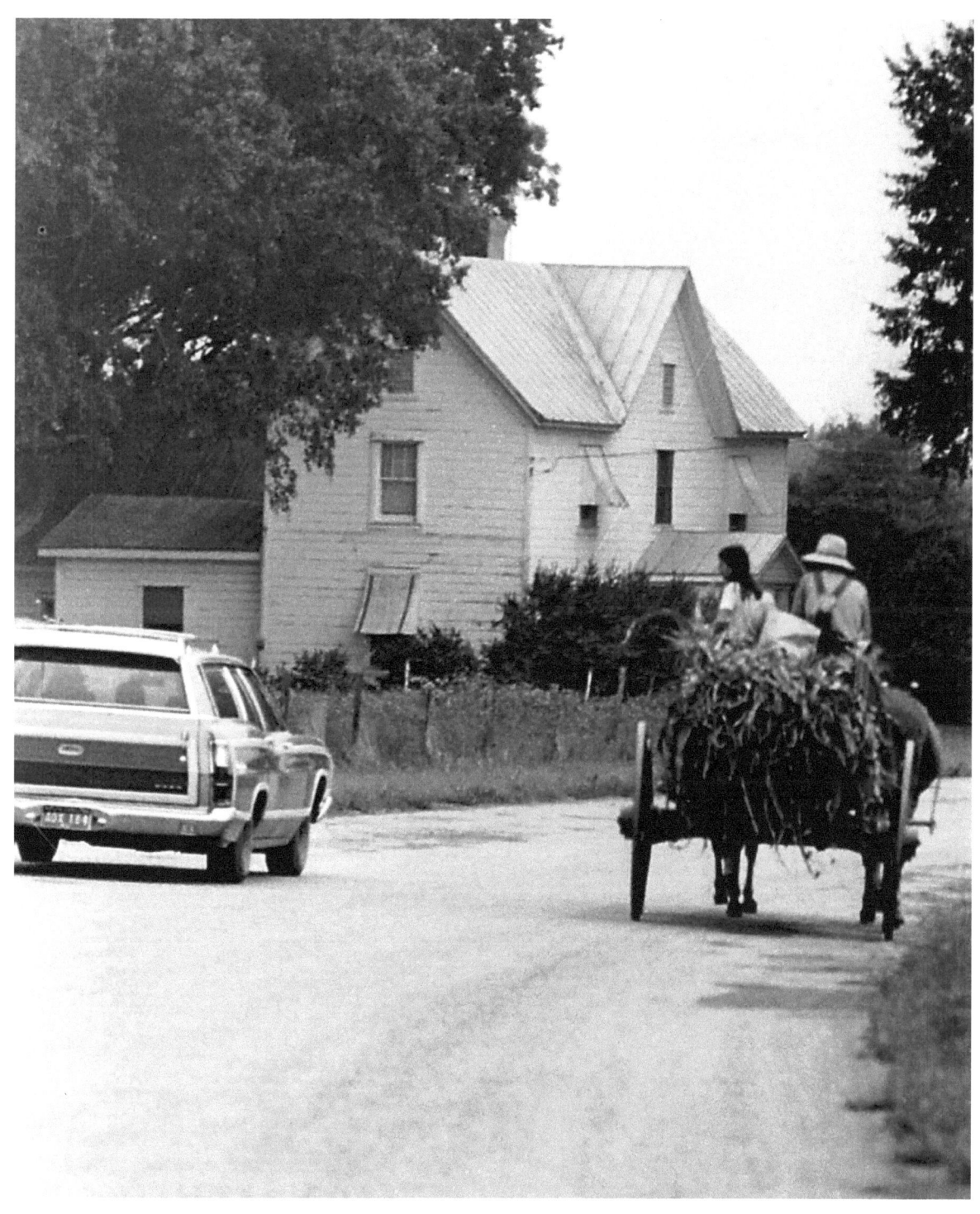

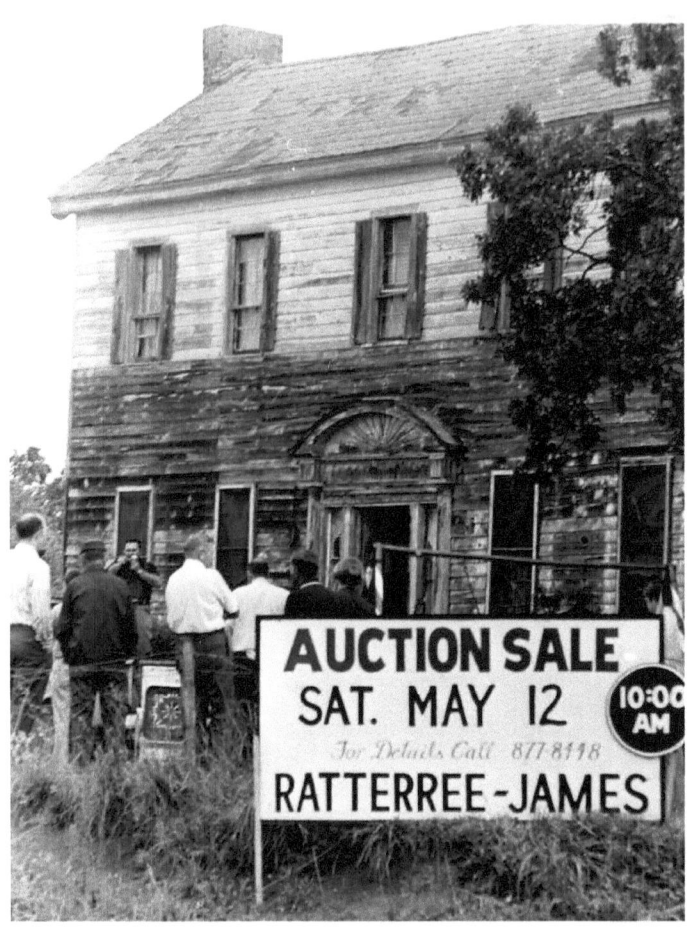

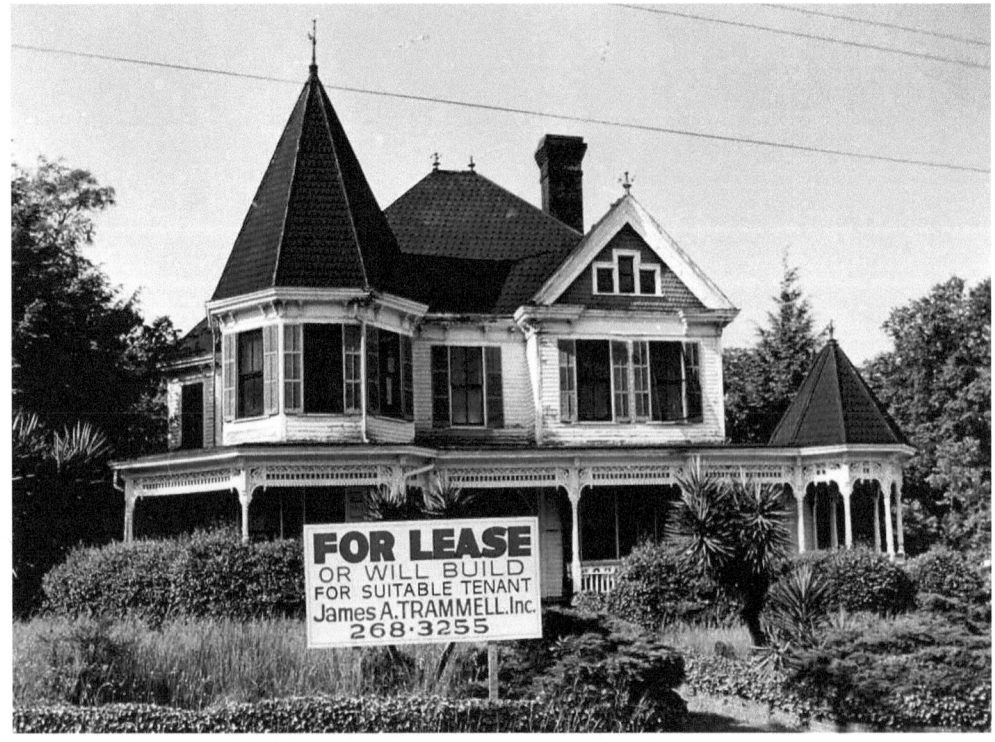

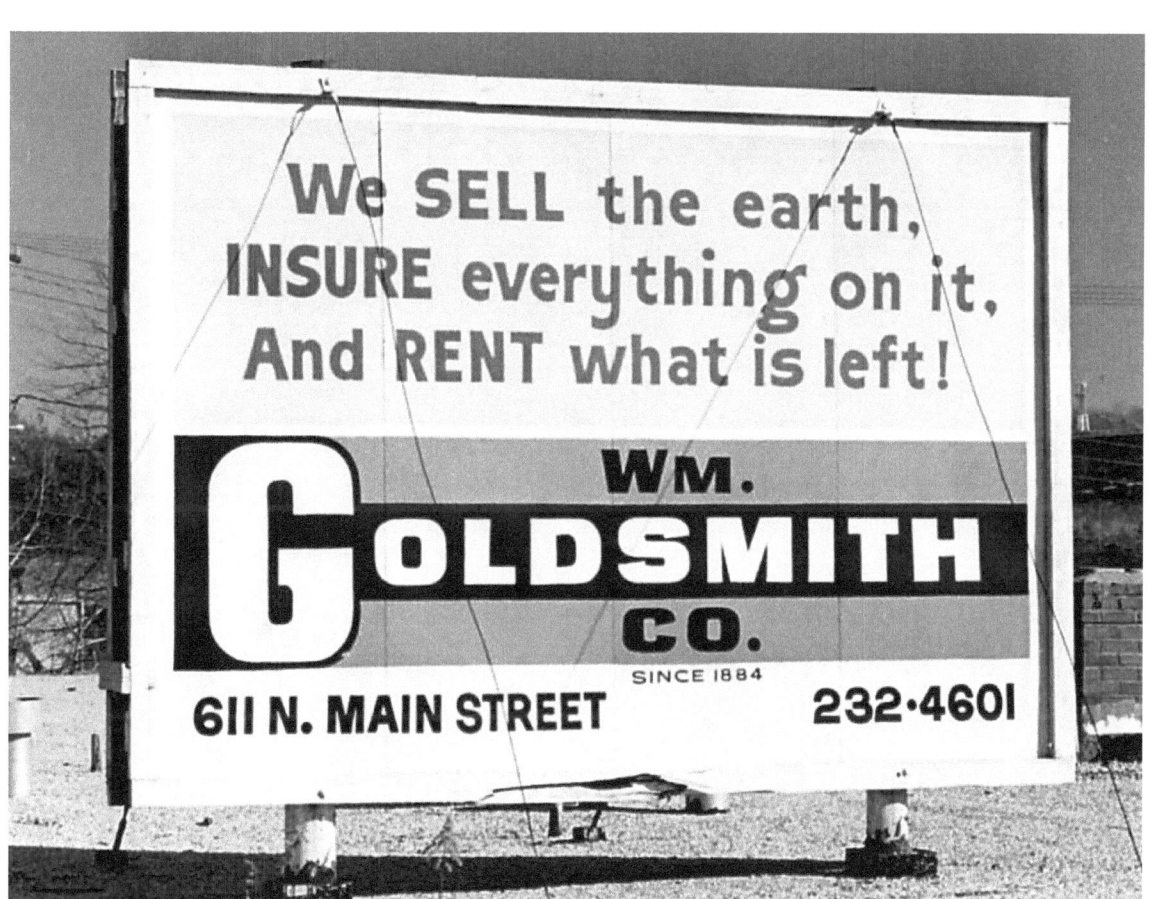

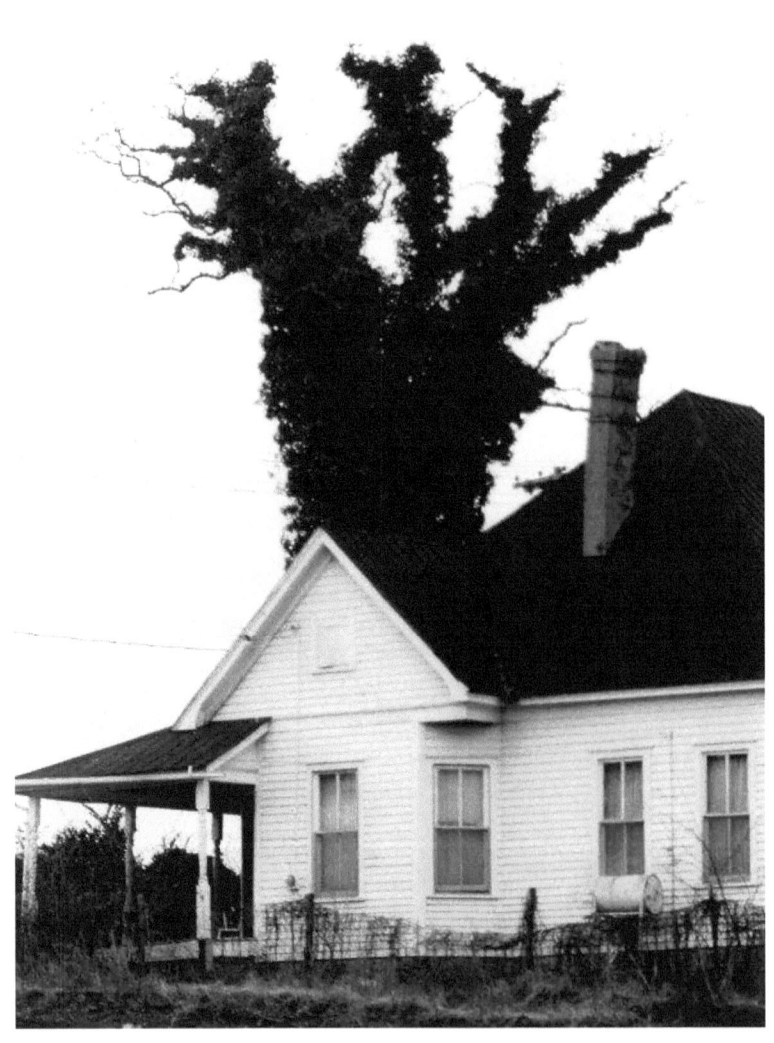

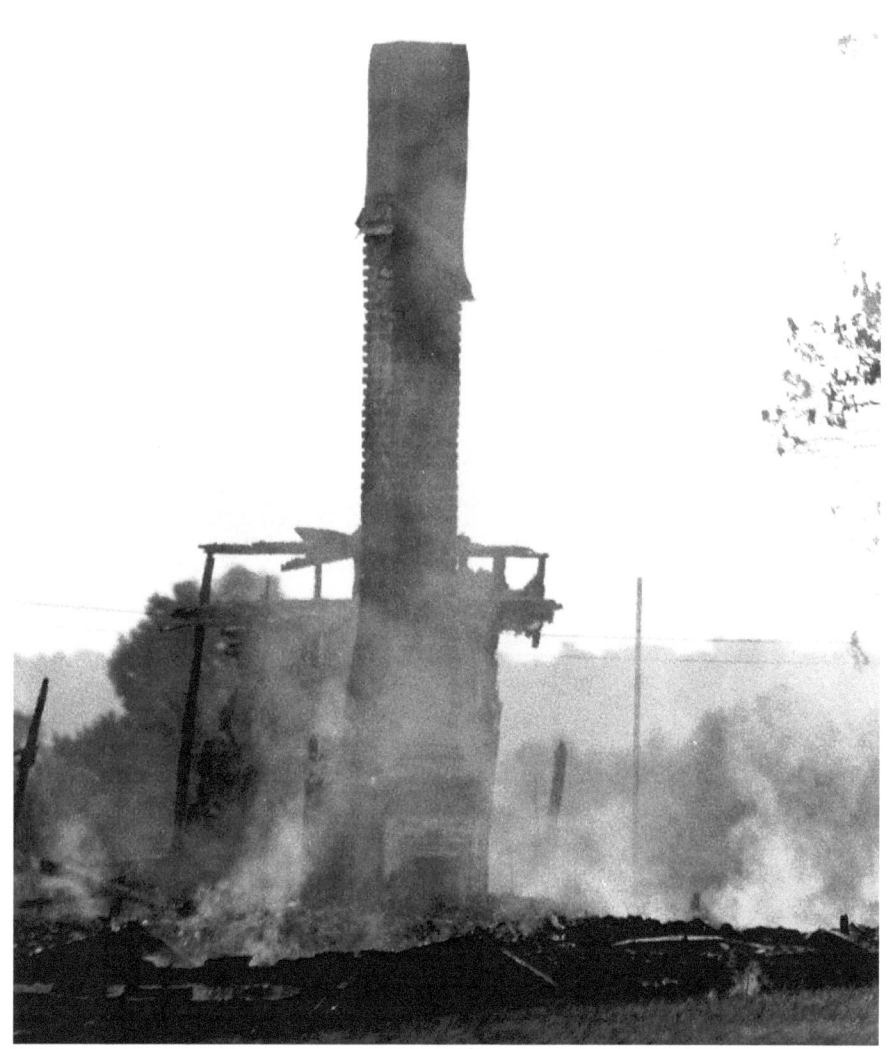

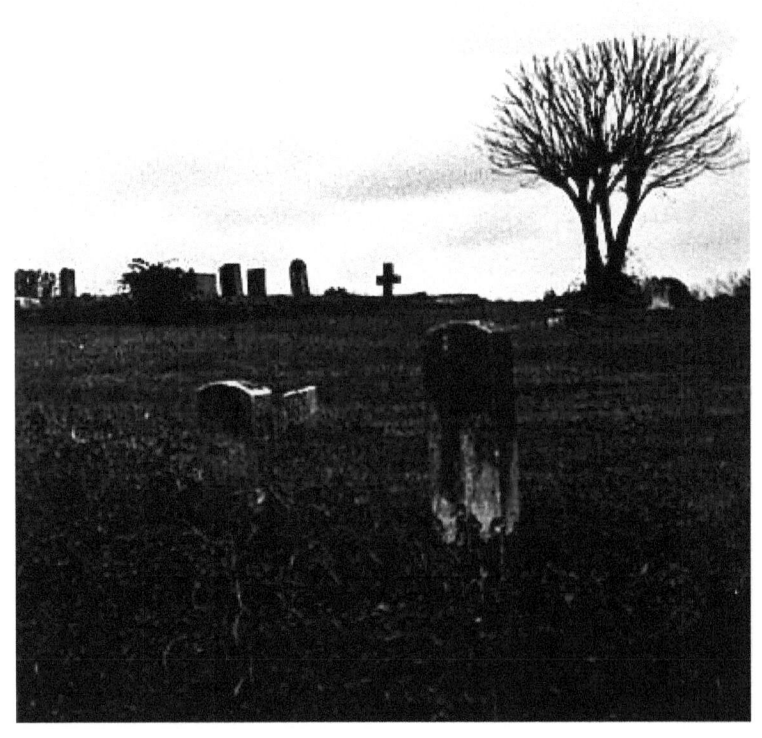

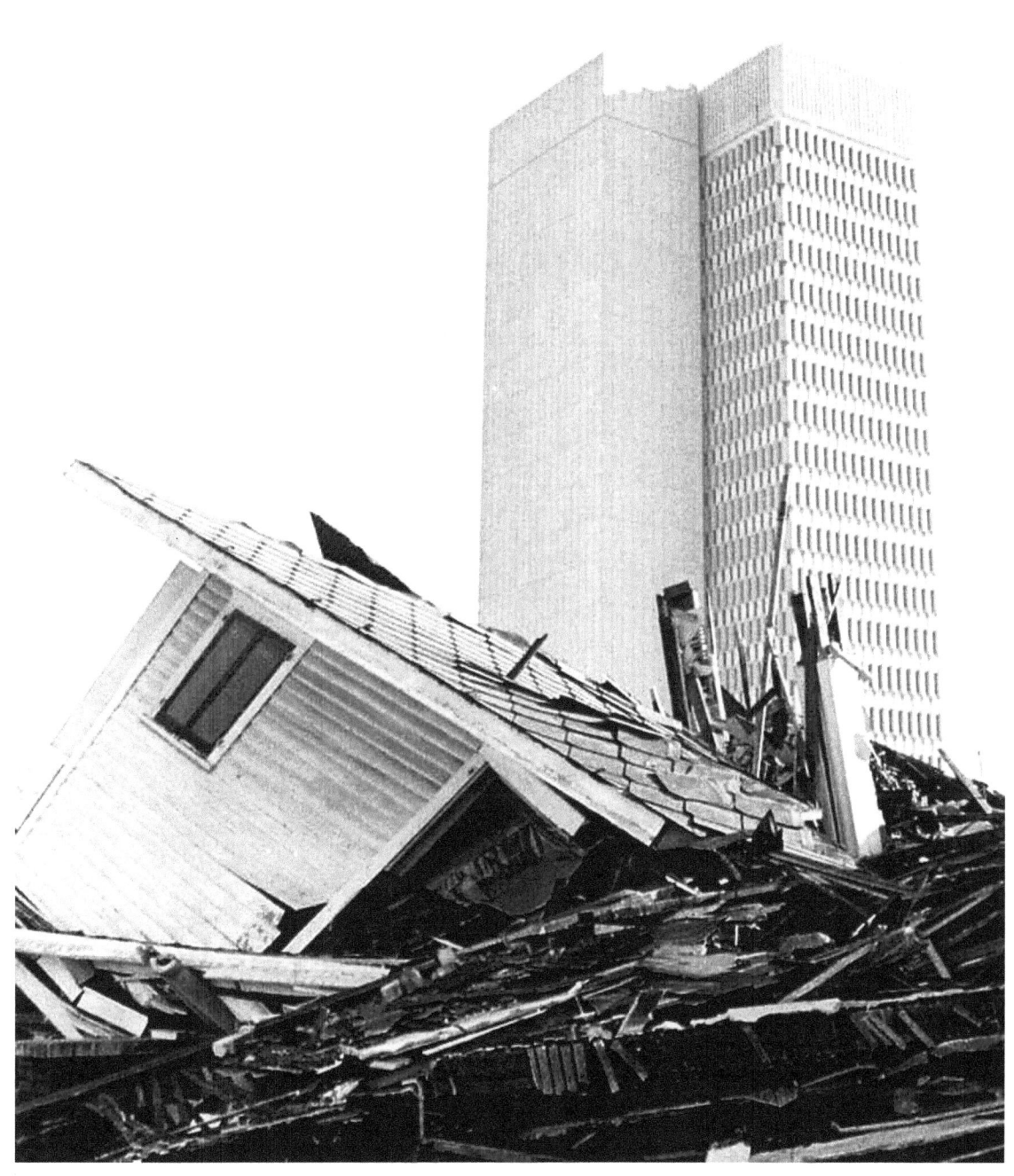

Location of Photographs
All photos taken between 1969 - 1974

I

1 – Helms' Barber Shop	Saluda, NC
2 – Girl in striped shirt	Fountain Inn, SC
3 – Woman with tall hairdo	Greenville, SC
4 – Pretty Parlor	Greenville County, SC
5 – Woman with balloons	Salley, SC
6 – Woman with "Mother" necklace	Henderson County, NC
7 – Salvation Army woman	Fountain Inn, SC
8 – Two athletes	Saluda, NC
9 – Boy sitting in tires	Greenville County, SC
10 – Man blowing smoke	Greenville, SC
11 – Three men in front of barber shop	Saluda, NC
12 – Man with Dali-style moustache	Salley, SC
13 – Man with hat	Salley, SC
14 – Man in tunnel with icicles	Asheville, NC
15 – Man with wrapped feet in snowstorm	Greenville, SC
16 – Man with beer	Spartanburg County, SC
17 – Man with hat and magazine	Salley, SC
18 – Profile of man with colorful hat	Greenville, SC
19 – Man with baseball cap	Salley, SC
20 – Man with hat and sunglasses	Greenville County, SC
21 – Man with sombrero	Fountain Inn, SC
22 – Girl with raccoon	Simpsonville, SC
23 – Woman with crocheted hat	Piedmont, SC

II

1 – We is open	Greenville County, SC
2 – Swedish massage	Greenville, SC
3 – Greenville Frame Center	Greenville, SC
4 – Kentucky Fried Chicken	Greenville, SC
5 – Kentucky Fried Chicken	Greenville, SC
6 – Hot foods vary tasty	Greenville, SC
7 – Store paraking	Greenville, SC
8 – To enjoy life, drink	Greenwood, SC
9 – Humpin to please	Spartanburg, SC
10 – Bueaty pageant	Simpsonville, SC
11 – Is-a-bell	Aiken County, SC
12 – Absolutely no dumping	Laurens County, SC
13 – Stop painting on tower	Greenville County, SC
14 – Prices are born here	Greenville, SC

8 – American Pie	Spartanburg County, SC
9 – Superfly	Greenwood, SC
10 – Whuppett	Greenwood, SC
11 – Two men working under car	Greenville County, SC
12 – Wrecked pickup truck	Easley, SC
13 – Wrecked motorcycle	Greenville, SC
14 – Wrecked semi on bridge	Spartanburg County, SC
15 – Abandoned gas station	Rutherford County, NC

V

1 – Man hauling firewood up driveway	Greenville, SC
2 – Two men working in dye house	Piedmont, SC
3 – Man working on loom	Piedmont, SC
4 – Man with folded hands	Piedmont, SC
5 – Man working in laundry	Greenville, SC
6 – Woman working in laundry	Greenville, SC
7 – Man working with jackhammer	Enka, NC
8 – Cook making hamburgers	Greenville, SC
9 – Curb boys	Greenville, SC
10 – Curb boy	Greenville, SC
11 – Railroad workers carrying tie	Greenville County, SC
12 – Railroad workers swinging hammers	Greenville County, SC
13 – Railroad workers carrying tie	Greenville County, SC
14 – Highway construction workers	Greenville County, SC
15 – Construction worker with hook	Enka, NC
16 – Worker with watermelon	Greenville County, SC
17 – Worker with watermelon	Greenville County, SC
18 – Man splitting firewood	Greenville, SC
19 – Man with ax cutting tar	Enka, NC
20 – Appliance salesman	Greenville, SC
21 – Woman carrying sack	Simpsonville, SC
22 – Man carrying sack full of cotton	Eutawville, SC
23 – Man with sack and dog	Greenville, SC
24 – Man in middle of machinery	Piedmont, SC

VI

1 – Brace of black powder revolvers	Travelers Rest, SC
2 – Man with pearl handled revolver	Travelers Rest, SC
3 – Man with deer in jeep	Belton, SC
4 – Man with deer on jeep	Belton, SC
5 – Man with shotgun on shoulder	Belton, SC

6 – Men with shotguns in pickup truck	Belton, SC
7 – Man shooting Kentucky musket	Travelers Rest, SC
8 – Men shooting rifles	Travelers Rest, SC
9 – Barrel full of bullet holes	Travelers Rest, SC
10 – Freezer full of bullet holes	Travelers Rest, SC
11 – Man holding rabbit-eared shotgun	Fountain Inn, SC
12 – Man holding long barreled Colt 45	Fountain Inn, SC
13 – Fireworks	Greenville County, SC
14 – Girl asleep at gun show	Greenville, SC

VII

1 – Man with rebel flag jacket	Greenville County, SC
2 – White is beautiful	Greenville, SC
3 – Truck with rebel flag	Greenville County, SC
4 – Charlie's machine shop	Greenville, SC
5 – Privately owned, whites only	Greenville County, SC
6 – KKK Grand Dragon and wife	Greenville County, SC
7 – KKK woman in curlers	Greenville County, SC
8 – KKK speaker at podium	Greenville County, SC
9 – KKK man and boy with flag	Greenville County, SC
10 – KKK man with people by truck	Greenville County, SC
11 – KKK pledge of allegiance	Greenville County, SC
12 – Softball players	Greenville County, SC
13 – Two girls carrying laundry basket	Simpsonville, SC
14 – Two children on swings	Greenville, SC
15 – Three children at play	Greenville, SC
16 – Children dancing in circle	Greenville, SC
17 – Two girls on swing	Greenville, SC

VIII

1 – Three people by Ferris wheel	Greenville County, SC
2 – People at gaming table	Greenville County, SC
3 – Barker and man at fair	Greenville County, SC
4 – Family winning jackpot at fair	Greenville County, SC
5 – Country band at fair	Greenville County, SC
6 – Bluegrass band	Asheville, NC
7 – Bluegrass band	Salley, SC
8 – Man with musical toilet seat	Salley, SC
9 – Boy playing drums	Saluda, NC
10 – Boy playing tuba	Greenville, SC
11 – Coon Dog Day sign	Saluda, NC

12 – Two men in Model A Ford	Greenville, SC
13 – Coon Dog King	Saluda, NC
14 – Coon in tree with snarling dogs	Saluda, NC
15 – Coon in tree, man blowing horn	Saluda, NC
16 – Edsel Club car	Saluda, NC
17 – Saluda Women's Club float	Saluda, NC
18 – Miss Camp Palmetto	Saluda, NC
19 – People on washtub float	Saluda, NC

IX

1 – Two billy goats butting heads	Fountain Inn, SC
2 – Woman selling beets	Greenville, SC
3 – Man selling scuppernong grapes	Greenville, SC
4 – Farmer holding cultivator	Travelers Rest, SC
5 – Farmer and girl in wagon	Simpsonville, SC
6 – Farmer with mule and plow	Simpsonville, SC
7 – Farmer with tractor and plow	Unknown
8 – Cracked earth	Cleveland County, NC
9 – Man selling candied apples	Greenville, SC
10 – Hi Lo House	Greenville, SC
11 – Gas station selling pumpkins	Greenville, SC
12 – Men at cattle auction	Spartanburg County, SC
13 – Auctioneers	Spartanburg County, SC
14 – Cattle at auction	Spartanburg County, SC
15 – Couple fishing	Greenville County, SC
16 – Boy fishing from boat	Asheville, NC
17 – Woman with hoe in front of old house	Simpsonville, SC
18 – Goose in bathtub	Fountain Inn, SC
19 – Farmer and girl in mule wagon	Simpsonville, SC

X

1 – Boy on swing	Greenville County, SC
2 – Man with cane under trees	Greenville, SC
3 – Girls sunbathing on fighter wing	Unknown
4 – Kaiser Frazer sign	Shelby, NC
5 – Two boys on horse	Greenville, SC
6 – Trees in morning fog	Clingmans Dome, NC
7 – Woman sitting by Big Bradley Falls	Saluda, NC
8 – Rubber tire basketball hoop	Unknown
9 – Small house at night	Buncombe County, NC
10 – Raccoon skins	Pickens County, SC

11 – Man lying on railroad tracks	Greenville County, SC
12 – Man lying in road	Greenville County, SC
13 – Cobra Club	Greenville County, SC
14 – Man with snake	Greenville County, SC
15 – Swamp Rabbit Railroad	Greenville County, SC
16 – Train wreck	Haywood County, NC
17 – Gulf sign and old wagon	Saluda, NC
18 – Mule wagon alongside station wagon	Simpsonville, SC
19 – Auction sale	Greenville County, SC
20 – For lease	Greenville, SC
21 – We Sell the Earth	Greenville, SC
22 – Tree with kudzu and house	Greenville County, SC
23 – Burned out house	Greenville County, SC
24 – Cemetery	Greenville, SC
25 – Daniel Building and demolished house	Greenville, SC

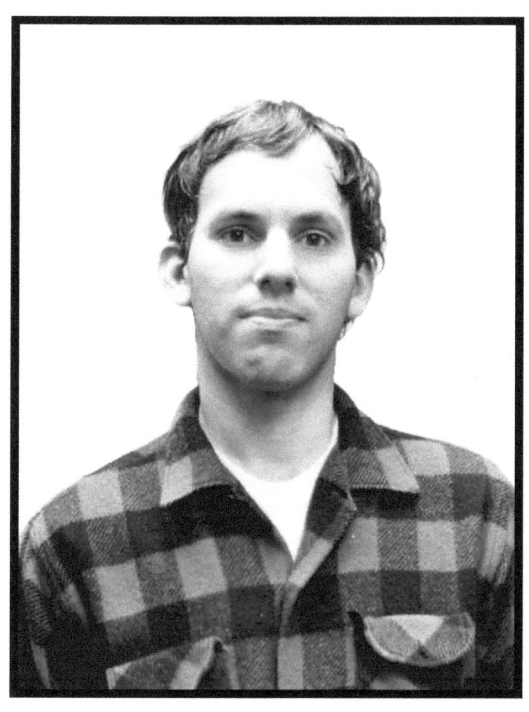 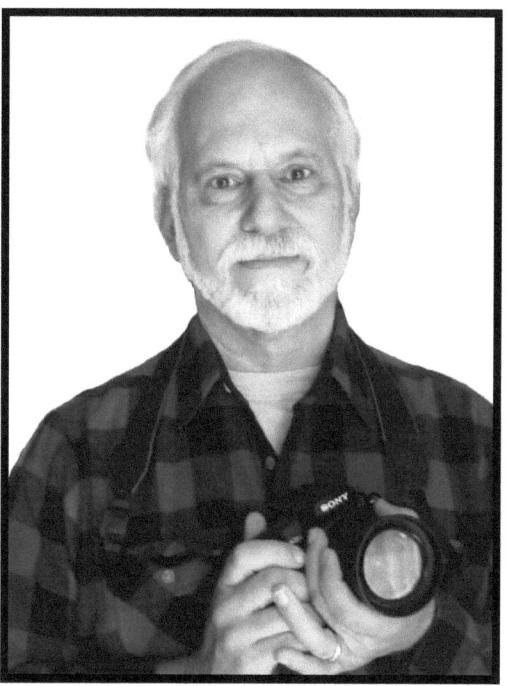

1974   2009

Joe Randazzo has traveled extensively and writes about what he sees. He believes in the heroism of the ordinary working person, the transformative power of love, and the rejuvenating effects of a truly fine pizza. He is the author of five previous books. His artwork has been exhibited at many venues throughout New England including Castleton State College, T. W. Wood Art Gallery, and the Helen Day Art Center.

He was a contributing editor to *South Carolina Magazine*, and his photos have appeared in the *National Humane Review*, *National Wildlife, Environmental Quality, Greenville News*, *Asheville News, Shelby Daily Star*, and *The Burlington Free Press*. Mr. Randazzo lives in South Burlington, Vermont with his wife Rita.

www.ingramcontent.com/pod-product-compliance
Lightning Source LLC
Chambersburg PA
CBHW050712180526
45159CB00003B/1005